The Art of Contentment

The Art of Contentment

Edited by EDGAR ANDREW COLLARD

Doubleday Canada Ltd., Toronto, Ontario
Doubleday & Company, Inc., Garden City, New York
1974

ISBN: 0-385-06342-3
Library of Congress Catalog Card Number 73-75380
Copyright © 1974 by Edgar Andrew Collard
All Rights Reserved
Printed in the United States of America
First Edition

The editor gratefully acknowledges permission to use in this book material held in copyright by the following:

Agenzia Letteraria Internazionale and Baron Cecil Anrep as proprietor of the copyright in Bernard Berenson's literary work for excerpts from *Sunset and Twilight* by Bernard Berenson.

George Allen & Unwin Ltd. for selections from *Visits to Walt Whitman in 1890–1891* by J. W. Wallace.

The Bobbs-Merrill Company, Inc., for excerpts from *On the Green Carpet* by Robert P. Tristram Coffin, copyright, 1951, by The Bobbs-Merrill Company, Inc.; reprinted by permission of the publisher.

The Bodley Head, London, and Macmillan Publishing Co., Inc., for excerpts from *A Son of the Middle Border* by Hamlin Garland. Copyright 1917 by Hamlin Garland. Renewed 1945 by Mary I. Lord and Constance G. Williams.

Sir Arthur Bryant for an excerpt from his book *Historian's Holiday*. The material also appears in his *The Lion and the Unicorn*.

Jonathan Cape Ltd. for materials from *Poems and the Spring of Joy* by Mary Webb. Used by permission of the Executors of the Mary Webb Estate, and from *Travels in Arabia Deserta* by Charles Montagu Doughty, used by permission of Jonathan Cape Ltd. and the Executors of the Charles Montagu Doughty Estate. Jonathan Cape Ltd. and Macmillan Publishing Co., Inc., for extracts from *Kilvert's Diary*, edited by William Plomer, copyright 1947 by Macmillan Publishing Co., Inc.

Cassell & Co. Ltd. for an excerpt from *Traveller's Rest* by Philip Gosse.

Geoffrey Chapman Publishers, London, and McGraw-Hill Book Company for excerpts from *Journal of a Soul* by Pope John XXIII. Copyright 1965 by Geoffrey Chapman Ltd. Used with permission of McGraw-Hill Book Company and Geoffrey Chapman Ltd.

Chatto and Windus Ltd. for excerpts from *Echoes* by Sir Compton Mackenzie, and used by permission of the Executors of the Estate of Sir Compton Mackenzie.

Collins Publishers, London, for a passage from *Autobiography* by Neville Cardus.

Peter Davies Ltd. for material from *Advice to Young Men and (Incidentally) to Young Women* by William Cobbett, published by Peter Davies Ltd. and used by permission.

Doubleday & Company, Inc., for materials from *Footnotes on Nature* by John Kieran, copyright 1947 by John Kieran, and from *Conjectures of a Guilty Bystander* by Thomas Merton, copyright © 1965, 1966 by The Abbey of Gethsemani, all selections being reprinted by permission of Doubleday & Company, Inc.

Dover Publications, Inc., and George Allen & Unwin Ltd. for extracts from *The Gardener's Year* by Karel Capek.

E. P. Dutton & Co., Inc., for extracts from the book *Myself and My Friends* by Lillah McCarthy. Published by E. P. Dutton & Co., Inc., and used with their permission; for material from the book *Far Away and Long Ago* by W. H. Hudson. Copyright 1918 by E. P. Dutton & Co., Inc. Renewal, 1946, by Royal Society for the Protection of Birds. Published by E. P. Dutton & Co., Inc., and used with their permission.

Mrs. Christine Eade for a passage from *Churchill by His Contemporaries*, edited by Charles Eade.

Faber and Faber Ltd. and Sir John Rothenstein for material from *Men and Memories* by William Rothenstein.

Dr. Frederick Franck for an extract from *Days with Albert Schweitzer* by Frederick Franck.

The Hamlyn Publishing Group Limited, London, for selections from *Thoughts and Adventures* by Sir Winston Churchill. Reproduced by permission of The Hamlyn Publishing Group Limited from *Thoughts and Adventures*.

Harcourt Brace Jovanovich, Inc., Constable Publishers and John Russell for selections from "Interruption," "Joy," and "Afterthoughts" from *All Trivia* by Logan Pearsall Smith, copyright, 1933, 1934, by Harcourt Brace Jovanovich, Inc.; copyright, 1961, 1962, by John Russell. Reprinted by permission of Harcourt Brace Jovanovich, Inc., Constable Publishers, and John Russell. Harcourt Brace Jovanovich, Inc., and William Heinemann Ltd. for material from *Flight to Arras* by Antoine de Saint-Exupéry, translated by Lewis Galantière, copyright, 1942, by Harcourt Brace Jovanovich, Inc.; reprinted by permission of Harcourt Brace Jovanovich, Inc., and William Heinemann Ltd. Harcourt Brace Jovanovich, Inc., for a selection from *The Woman Within* by Ellen Glasgow, copyright, 1954, by Harcourt Brace Jovanovich, Inc., and reprinted with their permission. Harcourt Brace Jovanovich, Inc., and The Hogarth Press Ltd. for selections from *A Room of One's Own* by Virginia Woolf, copyright, 1929, by Harcourt Brace Jovanovich, Inc.; copyright, 1957, by Leonard Woolf. Reprinted by permission of the publishers.

Harper & Row, Publishers, Inc., for materials from *Charles W. Eliot: The Man and His Beliefs* by William Allan Neilson. Copyright 1926 by William Allan Neilson; and from *Mark Twain's Autobiography*. Copyright 1924 by Clara Gabrilowitsch; renewed, 1952 by Clara Clemens Samossoud. Both by permission of Harper & Row, Publishers, Inc.

David Higham Associates, Ltd., for an extract from *Museum Piece* by James Laver.

Hodder and Stoughton Limited and Mr. Cecil Roberts for material from *Gone Rambling* by Cecil Roberts and used by permission of the publishers, Hodder and Stoughton Limited.

Houghton Mifflin Company for selections from *Yosemite* and *The Sierra Nevada* by Ansel Adams and edited by Charlotte E. Mauk; *Travels in Alaska* by John Muir; *Under the Maples* and *Winter Sunshine*, both by John Burroughs; *Walden or Life in the Woods* by Henry David Thoreau; *The Heart of Emerson's Journals*, edited by Bliss Perry. Also to Houghton Mifflin Company and A. P. Watt for extracts from *Memory Hold-the-Door* by John Buchan, published in the United States under the title *Pilgrim's Way*, and used with the permission of The Tweedsmuir Estate, Houghton Mifflin Company, and Hodder and Stoughton Limited. Houghton Mifflin Company and Hodder and Stoughton Limited for material from *The Eye of the Wind* by Peter Scott. Used by permission of the publishers.

Miss Nannine Joseph and the Estate of Mark Van Doren for an extract from *The Autobiography of Mark Van Doren*.

Mrs. Henry R. Labouisse for the excerpt from *Pierre Curie* by Marie Curie.

Mr. Frank Swinnerton for permission to include the selections from his *Tokefield Papers*.

The Viking Press for an excerpt from "Remote from Where?" from *Under Whatever Sky* by Irwin Edman. Copyright 1945–51 by Irwin Edman; reprinted by permission of The Viking Press, Inc.

Frederick Warne & Co., Ltd., for extracts from *Leigh Hunt As Poet and Essayist*, edited by Charles Kent, published by Frederick Warne & Co., Ltd.

A. Watkins, Inc., and David Higham Associates, Ltd., for a selection from *The Scarlett Tree* by Osbert Sitwell, copyright 1946 by Sir Osbert Sitwell.

A. P. Watt & Son for selections from *A Summer in Italy* by Sean O'Faolain, used by permission of Sean O'Faolain, and for selections from *Fly Fishing* by Edward Grey, by permission of The Estate of Viscount Grey of Falloden.

Yale University Press for material from *The Self: Its Body and Freedom* by William Ernest Hocking.

To Elizabeth, my wife

"How delightful it is when the mind of the female is
so happily disposed, and so richly cultivated, as to participate
in the literary avocations of her husband!"

Isaac D'Israeli, *Curiosities of Literature*, 1st series, 1791.

Contents

PREFACE   xiii

Part One: CONTENTED ATTITUDES

LIVING IN THE PRESENT   3
WHERE YOU ARE   8
PLAIN THINGS   11
LITTLE THINGS   16
WITH A CERTAIN EASE   20
HOME   24
RITUAL   29
WORK   31

Part Two: RECREATIONS

EAGER LEISURE   41
EATING   45
BOOKS   49
MUSIC   58
GARDENS   65
FIRESIDE   70
WALKING   74
FISHING   78

Part Three: ONESELF AND OTHERS

TOLERANCE   87
GOOD HUMOR   93
GOOD COMPANY   97
COMPANIONABLE SILENCE   101
ALONE   106

Part Four: UNEXPECTED CONTENTMENT

IN SICKNESS   115
IN SADNESS   122
BY SURPRISE   129

Part Five: CONTENTMENT OUT-OF-DOORS

NATURE   137
SUN   143
RAIN   150
SEA   154
FLOWING WATERS   159
WIND   164
TREES   167
SOUNDS   173
CAMPING   178

Part Six: THE END OF THE DAY

SUNSET   185
NIGHT   189
AGE   194
MEMORY   202
SLEEP   209

INDEX   217

Preface

When Robert Gibbings made himself a wooden bench for his garden, he wrote: "And then I sat back and the scent of new-sawn timber mingled with the scent of new-mown lawn. A thrush was singing from the pear-tree, two goldfinches were searching among the tulips, a sulphur yellow butterfly flittered past, and behold it was very good."

When Henry David Thoreau sat in his hut by Walden Pond and listened to the falling rain, he wrote: "The gentle rain which waters my beans and keeps me in the house to-day is not drear and melancholy, but good for me too . . . Some of my pleasantest hours were during the long rain-storms in the spring or fall, which confined me to the house for the afternoon as well as the forenoon, soothed by their ceaseless roar and pelting; when an early twilight ushered in a long evening in which many thoughts had time to take root and unfold themselves."

The art of contentment is the art of feeling that life is good—at least for the day, or the hour. The sources of this feeling are usually the simplest. Of all the experiences of contentment gathered together in this anthology very few do not relate to things available to everyone. It is true that not everyone can live in sight of the sea, but there are sources of contentment in field and stream. Those who must live in cities, and never know sea or countryside, have open to them the satisfactions of city life, including such things as Axel Munthe noted with pleasure: "a cat vanishing round the corner of a house, a geranium in a high window, a piece of stick floating like a galleon in a gutter or even the specks of sunlight sparkling through the leaves of a tree in the depths of a gloomy courtyard."

The art of contentment is the recognition that the most satisfying and the most dependably refreshing experiences of life lie not in great things but in little. The rarity of happiness among those who achieved much is evidence that achievement is not in itself the assurance of a happy life. The great, like the humble, may have to find their satisfaction in the same plain things.

This fact impressed the historian William Edward Hartpole Lecky when he wrote his book *The Map of Life*: "It would probably be found upon examination that most men who have devoted their lives successfully to great labours and ambitions and who have received the most splendid gifts from Fortune have nevertheless found their chief pleasure in things unconnected with their main pursuits and generally within the reach of common men. Domestic pleasures, pleasures of scenery, pleasures of reading, pleasures of travel or sport have been the highest enjoyment of men of great ambition, intellect, wealth and position."

Lecky had met an old member of Parliament who had known the House of Commons for nearly fifty years in one of the most stirring periods of English history. But it was curious to observe how speedily and inevitably he passed from such matters of history to the trees about his house, which he had planted and watched at every stage of their growth. Lecky also knew a writer who had devoted almost his whole life to one gigantic work, and, to his own surprise, brought it at last to a successful end. He observed that "amid the congratulations that poured in to him from every side he could not help feeling when he analyzed his own emotions how tepid was the satisfaction which such a triumph could give him, and what much more vivid gratification he had come to take in hearing the approaching steps of some little children he had taught to love him."

This turning to plain things for satisfaction does not mean that contentment is an insidious influence, enervating and undermining the will to achieve. Though the indolent may be contented after their own fashion, they probably never experience the contentment that lies in concentrating on work. But a person must have the enthusiasm for his work that (in Bernard Berenson's words) means he "enjoys his task so much that he puts payments, compensations, rewards, honours, last." Such a worker, even if he has too much to do, is likely to be happier than the one who has too little.

Moreover, no one can savour contentment so keenly as in the "eager leisure" that comes in the intervals between hard work. That "eager leisure" may mean only a return to plain satisfactions, but the intervals are looked forward to with keenness and remembered with delight.

In fact, such intervals of contented leisure may give the relief and renewal that the ambitious need most of all. This is seen in the life of Sir Winston Churchill. No man could have been more fired by ambition or more ready for the struggle. Yet he was refreshed by the brief intervals he could devote to his painting. Here he found his deep contentment. It opened his eyes, as contentment always does, to the wonder that is at hand.

Not until he was in his forties did Churchill take up painting and feel himself entering into a contentment he had not known before. What he discovered is that contentment opens the eyes to the things that are round about—ordinary things, long seen but not known. "One is quite astonished," he wrote, "to find how many things there are in the land-scape, and in every object in it, one never noticed before. . . . I found myself instinctively as I walked noting the tint and character of a leaf, the dreamy purple shades of mountains, the exquisite lacery of winter branches, the dim pale silhouettes of far horizons. And I had lived for over forty years without ever noticing any of them except in a general way, as one might look at a crowd and say, 'What a lot of people!' "

This discovery of contentment through painting was the discovery of the wonder of plain things. Sir William Orpen advised him to visit Avignon on account of its wonderful light. But Churchill, though at times he painted abroad, felt no need to go beyond his own country. At the beginning and close of almost every day the Thames displayed to him "glories and delights which one must travel far to rival."

He also, in his contentment, became aware of how much of loveliness and interest may lie not only in plain things but in the very plainest of them. He had been shown a picture by Cézanne of the blank wall of a house, in which Cézanne had discovered the most delicate lights and shades. "Now I often amuse myself," said Churchill, "when I am looking at a wall or a flat surface of any kind by trying to distinguish all the different colours and tints which can be discerned upon it, and consider-ing whether these arise from reflections or from natural hue. You would be astonished the first time you tried this to see how many and what beautiful colours there are even in the most commonplace objects and the more carefully and frequently you look the more variations do you perceive."

"Even in the most commonplace objects"—this phrase comes close to the heart of contentment. Contentment is concerned with the mo-ment, and with the here and the now. Though the Constitution of the United States speaks of the right to "the pursuit of happiness," con-tentment is a form of happiness but it is not a pursuit. Nothing can be pursued unless it is distant in time or place. And any sort of pursuit, though having the excitements of the chase, has its hazards also: un-certainty, strain, frustration, disappointment, and the possibility that what may be overtaken may then escape and may have to be pursued again.

Contentment, however, cannot be concerned with what is not at hand. It is not a pursuit, but an awareness. It is a realization that the most precious possessions may be the most readily available. The con-tented may be the inheritors of the earth and the true fullness thereof. They may be filled with good things, while the pursuers of other kinds of happiness may go empty away. Contentment is discovery without jour-neying.

The contented, with their awareness of the available goodness of life, may doubt whether the disillusioned have ever really known what life is. This doubt is in the questioning by W. H. Hudson: "When I hear people say they have not found the world and life so agreeable or interesting as to be in love with it, or that they look with equanimity to its end, I am apt to think they have never been properly alive nor seen with clear vision the world they think so meanly of, or anything in it— not a blade of grass."

There is no one who has not experienced some contentment in his life. It enters into lives even when they are restless and bitter, or have tragic endings. This anthology has passages of contentment from such unlikely books as Barbellion's *The Journal of a Disappointed Man.* William Cowper, though he died in absolute despair, had once known the peace of garden and riverbank. John Ruskin had known the satisfaction of sketching a blade of grass or the bough of a tree, though he died confused by fitful angers. Antoine de Saint-Exupéry went to a strange death, but he had savoured the supreme contentment of an aviator mounting into the night.

In the same way that those who suffer from sleeplessness may still sleep more than they realize or acknowledge, so is there no man, whatever his fate or temperament, who has never enjoyed his food or drink, or has never sunk to rest without a sense of blessing, or has never sat in the sunshine of an October noon without feeling peace in his bones. No man's life is a total winter of his discontent.

Just because contentment has its sources in such plain things, in the soil of the ordinary day, it can never become obsolete. If it were a doctrine, it might wither as old faiths fade. If it were a theory, it might be disproved by new knowledge. If it were merely part of a social structure, it might fall victim to social change. But contentment is none of these things.

It is true that misuses or fashions in contentment may change. Those today who preach contentment to the poor find in the poor a less receptive audience. Those who have used contentment as a mere resignation before inevitable evils may find themselves in an age disposed to regard fewer and fewer evils as inevitable. If contentment were nothing more than submission or resignation it would be dying, without hope.

But contentment is far more. It is not a narrowing of life; it is life-expanding. It is not a bowing of the head; it is the removal of scales from the eyes. It is a hardy, practical working peace, not in battle with conflicting theories of life, but living its own experience, justifying itself to itself, satisfying its own needs.

The experiences of contentment are timeless, because, being so simple, they are deeply part of renewed experience. It is still possible to enjoy an "epicurism of sleep," such as Samuel Pepys enjoyed at the inn

at Welling in 1661: "there being now and then a noise of people stirring that waked me, and then it was a very rainy night, and then I was a
little weary, that what between waking and then sleeping again, one after another, I never had so much content in all my life . . ."

It is still possible, like Izaak Walton, to "sit on cowslip banks, hear
the birds sing, and possess ourselves in as much quietness as these silent
silver streams, which we do now see glide so quietly by us."

The character of unchanging contentment is in the picture of Alphonse Daudet listening to music "seated in his big armchair," with
closed eyes and "half-opened lips," seeming "to drink in the sound"; or
in Francis Kilvert's description of his contentment in walking through
the fields at harvest time and listening "to the rustle and solemn night
whisper of the wheat."

The enduring contentment of plain things is in Walt Whitman's exclamation, "How delicious the air is!" It was a warm summer twilight,
and he had been taken in his wheelchair to the wharf. The old feeling for
home is in the words of Sir Walter Scott at his last homecoming: " 'I
have seen much,' he kept saying, 'but nothing like my ain house.' "

As contentment is closely interwoven with the texture of every day, it
is as many-sided and as varied as the discovered wonder of plain things.
This anthology is an attempt to assemble experiences of contentment's
range, though no such exploration could ever be more than a sampling.

There may never have been a time when contentment was so rare in
the world. Yet it is not rare because it is little needed, or because the
need is little felt. The search for relief from pressure and tension is
often desperate, and takes strange forms.

But the sources of true contentment do not run dry. They are to be
found where they have always been. The experiences of contentment
gathered in this anthology are experiences still available to all. The art of
contentment is the art of becoming aware that what is sought is already
at hand. It is the art of entering into the spaciousness of the here and
now. It is an art as new as it is old—the art of discovering the world in a
grain of sand, and eternity in an hour.

Edgar Andrew Collard

PART ONE

Contented Attitudes

LIVING IN THE PRESENT

———◆———

In any case I must say this: If I have ever seemed to chime in with those who, though they are fortunate themselves, merely whine that the world they find is not good enough to live in, I much regret the fact. All postponements are potentially dangerous and to postpone life itself is the most stupendous of follies. One can no more live in the future than one can live in some good old day of the past. One must live now or not at all; and not to live at all is the greatest of mistakes. At the very worst one can say with Johnson: "He who sees before him to his third dinner, has a long prospect." I find that kind of courage admirable, and I think it wiser to eat one's three dinners than to refuse them on the ground that the times are out of joint and one's appetite taken away.

Joseph Wood Krutch, *More Lives Than One* (New York: Sloane, 1962), p. 370.

———◆———

"My experience," said an old gentleman to me, "has been that I never could succeed in getting the special kind of happiness I had wanted or hoped for, but that other kinds of happiness which I did not want and had never hoped for were supplied to me, in the course of life, most lavishly and abundantly. I therefore ended by discovering, though it took me a long time to make the discovery, that the right way to enjoy the happiness within my reach was not to form an ideal of my own and be disappointed when it was not realized—for that it never was— but to accept the opportunities for enjoying life which were offered by life itself from year to year and from day to day. Since I took things in this temper, I have enjoyed really a great amount of happiness, though it has been of a kind entirely different from anything I ever anticipated or laid plans for when I was young."

Philip Gilbert Hamerton, *The Quest of Happiness* (Boston: Roberts Brothers, 1897), pp. 175–76.

. . . I can think of nothing sadder than to live a happy life without recognising it.

Peter Scott, *The Eye of the Wind* (London: Hodder, 1961), p. 662.

———◆———

Another consideration in the cultivation of happiness is the importance of acquiring the habit of realising our blessings while they last. It is one of the saddest facts of human nature that we commonly only learn their value by their loss. This . . . is very evidently the case with health. By the laws of our being we are almost unconscious of the action of our bodily organs as long as they are working well. It is only when they are deranged, obstructed or impaired that our attention becomes concentrated upon them. In consequence of this a state of perfect health is rarely fully appreciated until it is lost and during a short period after it has been regained. . . .

And what is true of health is true of other things. It is only when some calamity breaks the calm tenor of our ways and deprives us of some gift of fortune we have long enjoyed that we feel how great was the value of what we have lost. There are times in the lives of most of us when we would have given all the world to be as we were but yesterday, though that yesterday had passed over us unappreciated and unenjoyed.

William Edward Hartpole Lecky, *The Map of Life* (London: Longmans, 1899), pp. 24–25.

———◆———

In September I picked about two hundred barrels of apples . . . and shipped them off to market. What finer occupation is there in the wide world than that of picking apples of a bright Autumn day with a light west wind blowing and scattered white clouds floating fleecily across a deep blue sky? This is not just a reminiscent dream with me. I knew at the time and so said to myself that it was simply wonderful to be twenty or thirty feet up an extension ladder (our old trees had been allowed to grow too high) picking deep red Baldwin apples in the sparkling sunlit atmosphere, with the landscape all around set in gorgeous Autumn colors. It is no wonder that I sang at my work as the ladder swayed and the apple tree branches and leaves rustled in the cool breeze of the northwest. . . .

On bright September days I rode across the harvest fields and down the colored archways of the country lanes, knowing that it was good for me to be there. At twilight there were Sugar Maples that seemed to be lighted from within by some mysterious rose-purple glow that came through their red-and-yellow leaves. I felt the beauty of such surroundings to whatever depths were in me, and I still recall the very spot on the wood road where, in the thrill of one of those Autumn rides, I said to myself: "This is surpassingly beautiful and I love it. Never in the future can I be any happier than I am now."

John Kieran, *Footnotes on Nature* (New York: Doubleday, 1947), pp. 10–11.

———◆———

Enjoy the present, whatsoever it be, and be not solicitous for the future; for if you take your foot from the present standing, and thrust it forward towards to-morrow's event, you are in a restless condition: it is like refusing to quench your present thirst by fearing you shall want drink the next day. If it be well to-day, it is madness to make the present miserable by fearing it may be ill to-morrow—when your belly is full of to-day's dinner, to fear you shall want the next day's supper; for it may be you shall not, and then to what purpose was this day's affliction? But if to-morrow you shall want, your sorrow will come time enough, though you do not hasten it: let your trouble tarry till its own day comes. But if it chance to be ill to-day, do not increase it by the care of to-morrow. Enjoy the blessings of this day, if God sends them, and the evils of it bear patiently and sweetly; for this day is only ours: we are not yet born to the morrow. He, therefore, that enjoys the present if it be good, enjoys as much as is possible; and if only that day's trouble leans upon him, it is singular and finite. "Sufficient to the day ✶(said Christ) is the evil thereof:" sufficient, but not intolerable. But if we look abroad, and bring into one day's thoughts the evil of many, certain and uncertain, what will be, and what will never be, our load will be as intolerable as it is unreasonable.

Jeremy Taylor, *The Rule and Exercises of Holy Living,* 1650 (London: Rivington, 1870), chap. II, p. 106.

As to your method of work, I have a single bit of advice, which I give with the earnest conviction of its paramount influence in any success which may have attended my efforts in life—*Take no thought for the morrow*. Live neither in the past nor in the future, but let each day's work absorb your entire energies, and satisfy your widest ambition. That was a singular but very wise answer which Cromwell gave to Bellevire— "No one rises so high as he who knows not whither he is going," and there is much truth in it. The student who is worrying about his future, anxious over the examinations, doubting his fitness for the profession, is certain not to do so well as the man who cares for nothing but the matter in hand, and who knows not whither he is going!

Sir William Osler, "Aequanimitas," *Aequanimitas, With other Addresses*, 2d ed. (London: H. K. Lewis, 1930), p. 213.

◆

I am aware of two mental or moral conditions which have contributed to my safe endurance of physical and mental strains. The first is a natural gift, namely, a calm temperament; the second is the result of a combination of this temperament with a deliberate practice of avoiding alike anticipations of disappointment and vain regrets. When necessarily involved in contests or critical undertakings, I tried first to do my best in the actual struggle, and then not to concern myself too much about the issue. That was not my responsibility. When blocked or defeated in an enterprise I had much at heart, I always turned immediately to another field of work where progress looked possible, biding my time for a chance to resume the obstructed road. An administrator can thus avoid waste of energy and a chronic state of disappointment and worry.

Charles W. Eliot, "How I Have Kept My Health," *A Late Harvest* (Boston: Atlantic Monthly, 1924), p. 12.

◆

The "veritable life" of our emotions and our relationships also is intermittent. When you love someone you do not love them all the time, in exactly the same way, from moment to moment. It is an impossibility. It is even a lie to pretend to. And yet this is exactly what most of us demand. We have so little faith in the ebb and flow of life, of love, of relationships. We leap at the flow of the tide and resist in terror its ebb. We are afraid it will never return. We insist on permanency, on duration, on continuity; when the only continuity possible, in life as in love, is in growth, in fluidity—in freedom, in the sense that the dancers are free, barely touching as they pass, but partners in the same pattern. The only real security is not in owning or possessing, not in demanding or expecting, not in hoping, even. Security in a relationship lies neither in looking back to what it was in nostalgia, nor forward to what it might be in dread or anticipation, but living in the present relationship and accepting it as it is now. For relationships, too, must be like islands. One must accept them for what they are here and now, within their limits— islands, surrounded and interrupted by the sea, continually visited and abandoned by the tides. One must accept the security of the wingèd life, of ebb and flow, of intermittency.

Anne Morrow Lindbergh, *Gift From the Sea* (New York: Pantheon Bks., 1955), pp. 108–9.

———◆———

Above all, we cannot afford not to live in the present. He is blessed over all mortals who loses no moment of the passing life in remembering the past. Unless our philosophy hears the cock crow in every barn-yard within our horizon, it is belated. That sound commonly reminds us that we are growing rusty and antique in our employments and habits of thought. His philosophy comes down to a more recent time than ours. There is something suggested by it that is a newer testament, —the gospel according to this moment. He has not fallen astern; he has got up early, and kept up early, and to be where he is is to be in season, in the foremost rank of time. It is an expression of the health and soundness of Nature, a brag for all the world,—healthiness as of a spring burst forth, a new fountain of the Muses, to celebrate this last instant of time. . . .

The merit of this bird's strain is in its freedom from all plaintiveness. The singer can easily move us to tears or to laughter, but where is he who can excite in us a pure morning joy? When, in doleful dumps, breaking the awful stillness of our wooden sidewalk on a Sunday, or, perchance, a watcher in the house of mourning, I hear a cockerel crow far or near, I think to myself, "There is one of us well, at any rate,"—and with a sudden gush return to my senses.

Henry David Thoreau, "Walking," *Excursions,* 1863 (Boston: Houghton, 1899), chap. VI, pp. 301–2.

WHERE YOU ARE

———◆———

. . . I know that nothing which truly concerns man is calculable, weighable, measurable. True distance is not the concern of the eye; it is granted only to the spirit. . . .

There is a cheap literature that speaks to us of the need of escape. It is true that when we travel we are in search of distance. But distance is not to be found. It melts away. And escape has never led anywhere. The moment a man finds that he must play the races, go to the Arctic, or make war in order to feel himself alive, that man has begun to spin the strands that bind him to other men and to the world. But what wretched strands! A civilization that is really strong fills man to the brim, though he never stir. What are we worth when motionless, is the question.

Antoine de Saint-Exupéry, *Flight to Arras*, tr. by Lewis Galantière (New York: Reynal, 1942), pp. 112–13.

———◆———

The soul is no traveller; the wise man stays at home, and when his necessities, his duties, on any occasion call him from his house, or into foreign lands, he is at home still and shall make men sensible by the expression of his countenance that he goes, the missionary of wisdom and virtue, and visits cities and men like a sovereign and not like an interloper or a valet.

I have no churlish objection to the circumnavigation of the globe for the purposes of art, of study, and benevolence, so that the man is first domesticated, or does not go abroad with the hope of finding somewhat greater than he knows. He who travels to be amused, or to get somewhat which he does not carry, travels away from himself, and grows old even in youth among old things. In Thebes, in Palmyra, his will and mind have become old and dilapidated as they. He carries ruins to ruins.

Travelling is a fool's paradise.

Ralph Waldo Emerson, "Self-Reliance," *Essays*, 1st series, 1841 (Boston: Houghton, 1898), chap. II, pp. 79–80.

Sir William Orpen advised me to visit Avignon on account of its wonderful light, and certainly there is no more delightful centre for a would-be painter's activities: then Egypt, fierce and brilliant, presenting in infinite variety the single triplex theme of the Nile, the desert, and the sun; or Palestine, a land of rare beauty—the beauty of the turquoise and the opal—which well deserves the attention of some real artist, and has never been portrayed to the extent that is its due. And what of India? Who has ever interpreted its lurid splendours? But after all, if only the sun will shine, one does not need to go beyond one's own country. There is nothing more intense than the burnished steel and gold of a Highland stream; and at the beginning and close of almost every day the Thames displays to the citizens of London glories and delights which one must travel far to rival.

Sir Winston Churchill, "Painting as a Pastime," *Thoughts and Adventures* (London: Thornton Butterworth, 1942), p. 320.

———◆———

Everyone, I suppose, knows the story of the Boston boy who, over lunch in Harvard Square, remarked to the Kansas boy that Kansas was far away. "Far from where?" was the sturdy Midwestern reply. I thought of the story one summer when I was living on a small ranch in Wyoming. We were forty miles from the nearest telegraph office, ten miles from the nearest telephone, two hundred miles from the nearest railroad to the East, the center of my universe. Mails seemed oddly slow. They came every day on an R.F.D. route but, because of difficult connections, even airmail from New York took anywhere from three to four days.

"Well, you have made yourself inaccessible," one friend wrote, though whether he was merely noting the fact or complaining about it I could not determine. It was out of the world, I wrote to my friend, delightfully remote. But within a few days I found myself wondering—remote from where, remote from what? The papers arriving late did, it seemed, carry news that was remote from me. In vast metropolitan centers, one is no nearer great events than when one is in Wyoming. Actually, if, as some think, the decisive events of the future are being shaped in China, here I was two thousand miles nearer Shanghai than I would have been in New York. Remote from the world of society, fashion, and power? Most of us are remote from those in New York. Removed from one's immediate obligations and responsibilities? In a way, yes—from friends, yes. But how much more clear and near some of these seemed, seen in the perspective of imagination in this lucid altitudinous light. And as for oneself, how much closer one seemed to oneself, one's private and authentic being, without the distractions of the telephone and telegram and frequent mail. By the end of the summer, I decided that remote meant remote from these pines, from those cleanly lined mountain peaks, from this transparent air. Here, one was distant simply from the circumference of life, and a little nearer oneself. What was it Shelley said about poetry, the center and circumference of knowledge? Here in this silence, among the pines and aspen, one felt one was at the center chiefly.

Irwin Edman, "Remote from Where?" *Under Whatever Sky* (New York: Viking, 1951), pp. 171–72.

———◆———

I cannot leave the country for the city now: too much going on up here—grass growing, birds nesting, toads singing, *arbutus blooming,* and crimson plush all over the soft maples. Come up on Sunday and see and hear for yourself.

John Burroughs, letter to Robert Underwood Johnson, April 23, 1901, in Robert Underwood Johnson, *Remembered Yesterdays* (Boston: Little, Brown, 1923), p. 340.

———◆———

. . . Not long ago I was urging a young naturalist of twenty-six to spend the next summer in Europe. He thought it was hardly right for him to allow himself that indulgence; and when I urged that the journey would be very enjoyable as well as profitable, he replied, "Yes, but you know I can be happy anywhere in the months when things are growing." He meant that the pleasures of observation were enough for him, when he could be out of doors. That young man was poor, delicate in health, and of a retiring and diffident disposition, yet life was full of keenest interest to him.

Charles W. Eliot, "The Happy Life," *Charles W. Eliot: The Man and His Beliefs,* ed. William Allan Nielson (New York: Harper, 1926), vol. II, pp. 421–22.

For in truth I don't enjoy the physical act of walking so much as I used to do; in fact, I enjoy it very little. I remind myself that when my pleasure in the physical act was greatest, my pleasure in nature was smallest; was, indeed, so small that as I rushed through the countryside I thought only of gamekeepers, the route and the map and reached the age of forty-five knowing very little of the habits of beasts and birds and the names of only a few wild flowers. Now that I move slowly, I enjoy looking at things more. Perhaps it is not until I am completely stationary that I shall derive from natural surroundings, the full measure, the benison that they have to bestow. After all, Epicurus sat under a fig tree and Diogenes in a tub. I haven't quite got to that stage yet, but I alter the position of my body in space less frequently than I did, and can say truthfully with Henry James that the older I grow, the more I enjoy the pleasures of not travelling.

C. E. M. Joad, *A Year More or Less* (London: Gollancz, 1948), p. 200.

PLAIN THINGS

———◆———

Just as in his scientific work he [Albert Einstein] felt increasingly impelled towards the simple and fundamental, so did he behave in private life. He shaved himself with the same soap as that which he used for washing. "Two cakes of soap are far too complicated for me", he maintained. And the same man on whom for many years the curious eyes of the world were so often focused, at the age of 75 still went to his place of work bare-headed and on foot, without socks, in an old, unobtrusive overcoat and pullover, a pair of creaseless 'corkscrew' trousers and frayed sandals.

Carl Seelig, *Albert Einstein* (London: Staples Press, 1956), p. 173.

. . . I was commissioned to execute a memorial tablet to the Rev. Dr. McCosh of Princeton . . . Father, then an invalid, was in the habit of coming to the studio and lying upon a couch . . . He was in the studio at the time Dr. McCosh first entered. . . .

Then after a moment, Dr. McCosh questioned father about his native place. Father delightedly and effusively told of the charm of the South, the blue sky, the oranges, the figs, the sea, the gentle weather, and all that was luscious in southern life. Dr. McCosh listened quietly, and after a pause, as if to show that he fully grasped father's colored description, added softly:

"Ah, well, well, well, that's all verrry well, verrry well, yourrr figs and yourrr grapes, and yourrr blue sky, yourrr mountains, and all that. It's no doubt verrry delightful, verrry delightful. But I prefer the gooseberry."

Augustus Saint-Gaudens, *The Reminiscences of Augustus Saint-Gaudens*, ed. Homer Saint-Gaudens (New York: Century, 1913), vol. I, pp. 368–71.

◆

. . . I have ultimately become a sort of hermit, not from fear or horror of mankind, but by sheer preference for peace and obscurity. Fortune has become indifferent to me, except as fortune might allow me to despise fortune and to live simply in some beautiful place. I have cut off all artificial society, reducing it to the limits of sincere friendship or intellectual sympathy. Instead of collecting pictures and books, as I had a tendency to do in the early 1890's, I have distributed my few possessions, eschewed chattels of every kind, a fixed residence, servants, carriages, or anything that would pin me down materially or engulf me in engagements. I have indulged rather freely at certain times in good food and good drink; but I think the glamour of those pleasures was due almost entirely to conviviality, that is to say, to a momentary imitation of friendship. In themselves, when I was alone, food and drink were never important to me. I was almost happier when I could be frugal, as at my father's at Avila, in the Duval restaurants in Paris, in the teashops in London, or now, where I write these words, under the drastic restrictions of war, in the clinic of the Blue Sisters upon the Caelius. I am happy in solitude and confinement . . .

George Santayana, *My Host the World* (New York: Scribner, 1953), vol. III, p. 7.

———◆———

One learns first of all in beach living the art of shedding; how little one can get along with, not how much. Physical shedding to begin with, which then mysteriously spreads into other fields. Clothes, first. Of course, one needs less in the sun. But one needs less anyway, one finds suddenly. One does not need a closet-full, only a small suit-case-full. And what a relief it is! Less taking up and down of hems, less mending, and—best of all—less worry about what to wear. One finds one is shedding not only clothes—but vanity.

Next, shelter. One does not need the airtight shelter one has in winter in the North. Here I live in a bare sea-shell of a cottage. No heat, no telephone, no plumbing to speak of, no hot water, a two-burner oil stove, no gadgets to go wrong. No rugs. There were some, but I rolled them up the first day; it is easier to sweep the sand off a bare floor. But I find I don't bustle about with unnecessary sweeping and cleaning here. I am no longer aware of the dust. I have shed my Puritan conscience about absolute tidiness and cleanliness. Is it possible that, too, is a material burden? No curtains. I do not need them for privacy; the pines around my house are enough protection. I want the windows open all the time, and I don't want to worry about rain. I begin to shed my Martha-like anxiety about many things. Washable slipcovers, faded and old—I hardly see them; I don't worry about the impression they make on other people. I am shedding pride. As little furniture as possible; I shall not need much. I shall ask into my shell only those friends with whom I can be completely honest. I find I am shedding hypocrisy in human relationships. What a rest that will be! The most exhausting thing in life, I have discovered, is being insincere. That is why so much of social life is exhausting; one is wearing a mask. I have shed my mask. . . .

Is it not rather ugly, one may ask? One collects material possessions not only for security, comfort or vanity, but for beauty as well. Is your sea-shell house not ugly and bare? No, it is beautiful, my house. It is bare, of course, but the wind, the sun, the smell of the pines blow through its bareness. The unfinished beams in the roof are veiled by cobwebs. They are lovely, I think, gazing up at them with new eyes; they soften the hard lines of the rafters as grey hairs soften the lines in a middle-aged face. I no longer pull out grey hairs or sweep down cobwebs. As for the walls, it is true they looked forbidding at first. I felt cramped and enclosed by their blank faces. I wanted to knock holes in them, to give them another dimension with pictures or windows. So I dragged home from the beach grey arms of driftwood, worn satin-smooth by wind and sand. I gathered trailing green vines with floppy red-tipped leaves. I picked up the whitened skeletons of conchshells, their curious hollowed-out shapes faintly reminiscent of abstract sculpture. With these tacked to walls and propped up in corners, I am satisfied.

Anne Morrow Lindbergh, *Gift From the Sea* (New York: Pantheon Bks., 1955), pp. 30–34.

Everything frayed, worn: clothes, curtains, chairs, sofas. It would have horrified me seven years ago, me with my passion for meticulous order, daintiness, in things about me. Now the contrary has taken place. I feel as if a touch of vulgarity clung to the spick-and-span and a certain charm, a tender, affectionate homeliness to the worn, the show of wear and tear, to the slightly musty, dusty, and rag-fair feel of things.

Bernard Berenson, Diary, February 13, 1947, in Bernard Berenson, *Sunset and Twilight,* ed. Nicky Mariano (New York: Harcourt, 1963), p. 5.

Table conversation usually is lively, especially when Schweitzer, who is a gifted raconteur, tells about some occurrence from his rich experience. . . . After supper, the moment the table has been cleared, the conversation dies down. Schweitzer has already looked through his hymnal and his Bible. When he announces the number of the hymn to be sung, you hear an old minister's voice. He has a particular churchy tone for this, which he never uses otherwise. Hymn books are distributed, he gets up heavily and goes to the piano. Then he starts improvising his prelude to the evening's choice. Often the same hymn is sung, but he never plays the same prelude. The style seems to depend on his mood. Sometimes he improvises in eighteenth-century style. The next evening his prelude may be classical or even romantic. His improvisations have reminded me of Schumann, Mendelssohn, or Beethoven, but they never are Schumann, Mendelssohn, or Beethoven—they have always passed through Schweitzer.

The piano must be decades old, decades of tropical humidity. It is completely out of tune even by equatorial standards, but this does not disturb Dr. Schweitzer. He is attached to it as he is attached to all the objects which have accompanied him through his life. He is not a modern man who will discard things as mere things. They seem to have become beings to him, beings he started to love long ago and which become ever dearer as time goes on. What does it matter that certain keys of this piano are stuck and that no one else can play it at all? He knows which keys have died and his improvisation neatly circumvents them. What does it matter that some benefactor sends a new piano which is standing in a corner? It is all right for the nurses to play on. He remains married to his old one.

Frederick Franck, *Days with Albert Schweitzer* (London: Davies, 1959), pp. 29–30.

———◆———

My attachments are all local, purely local. I have no passion (or have had none since I was in love, and then it was the spurious engendering of poetry and books,) for groves and valleys. The rooms where I was born, the furniture which has been before my eyes all my life, a book-case which has followed me about like a faithful dog, (only exceeding him in knowledge,) wherever I have moved, old chairs, old tables, streets, squares, where I have sunned myself, my old school,—these are my mistresses.

Charles Lamb, letter to William Wordsworth, January 30, 1801, *Letters of Charles Lamb*, ed. William Macdonald (London: Dent, 1903), vol. I, pp. 190–91.

———◆———

Now I became alarmed [at Advance Base in the Antarctic]. . . . Great waves of fear, a fear I had never known before, swept through me and settled deep within. But it wasn't the fear of suffering or even of death itself. It was a terrible anxiety over the consequences to those at home if I failed to return. I had done a damnable thing in going to Advance Base, I told myself. Also, during those hours of bitterness, I saw my whole life pass in review. I realized how wrong my sense of values had been and how I had failed to see that the simple, homely, unpretentious things of life are the most important.

Richard E. Byrd, *Alone* (New York: Putnam, 1938), pp. 177–78.

LITTLE THINGS

◆

"Life is a great bundle of little things." It is very many years since I read that saying of Oliver Wendell Holmes, but there is no saying I oftener have occasion to repeat to myself. There is the whole universe to dream over, and one's life is spent in the perpetual doing of an infinite series of little things. It is a hard task, if one loses the sense of the significance of little things, the little loose variegated threads which are yet the stuff of which our picture of the universe is woven. . . .

For each of these insignificant little things of life stretches far beyond itself—like a certain Impromptu of Schubert's, which begins as though it might be a cradle song in a nursery and ends like the music of the starry sphere which carries the world on its course.

Havelock Ellis, *Impressions and Comments*, 1st series (London: Constable, 1914), pp. 229–30.

Yesterday afternoon I went to the Cliff with Henry Thoreau. Warm, pleasant, misty weather, which the great mountain amphitheatre seemed to drink in with gladness. A crow's voice filled all the miles of air with sound. A bird's voice, even a piping frog, enlivens a solitude and makes world enough for us. At night I went out into the dark and saw a glimmering star and heard a frog, and Nature seemed to say, Well do not these suffice? Here is a new scene, a new experience. Ponder it, Emerson, and not like the foolish world, hanker after thunders and multitudes and vast landscapes, the sea or Niagara.

Ralph Waldo Emerson, Journal, April 26, 1838, *The Heart of Emerson's Journals*, ed. Bliss Perry (Boston: Houghton, 1926), p. 127.

Once you begin to study it, all Nature is equally interesting and equally charged with beauty. I was shown a picture by Cézanne of a blank wall of a house, which he had made instinct with the most delicate lights and colours. Now I often amuse myself when I am looking at a wall or a flat surface of any kind by trying to distinguish all the different colours and tints which can be discerned upon it, and considering whether these arise from reflections or from natural hue. You would be astonished the first time you tried this to see how many and what beautiful colours there are even in the most commonplace objects, and the more carefully and frequently you look the more variations do you perceive.

Sir Winston Churchill, "Painting as a Pastime," *Thoughts and Adventures* (London: Thornton Butterworth, 1942), p. 316.

On fine days, when the grass was dry, I used to lie down on it and draw the blades as they grew, with the ground herbage of buttercup or hawkweed mixed among them, until every square foot of meadow, or mossy bank, became an infinite picture and possession to me, and the grace and adjustment to each other of growing leaves, a subject of more curious interest to me than the composition of any painter's masterpiece.

John Ruskin, *Praeterita*, 2d ed. (New York: Merrill and Baker, n.d.), vol. II, p. 365.

I have myself heard her speak of what she has somewhere written about—the rapture of the sight of some primroses growing in a railway cutting.

Theodore Watts-Dunton, "Christina Georgina Rossetti," *Old Familiar Faces* (London: Jenkins, 1916), p. 187.

———◆———

The side of our observation ridge was thickly covered with White Pine, but the summit was an open field and there Herman rejoiced exceedingly when he found Nodding Ladies'-tresses in bloom. He pointed to them in triumph, but I'm afraid I was not enthusiastic. They were not much to look at in my opinion.

"Sir!" thundered Herman. "They are orchids!"

Perhaps so, but I much preferred something more pleasing to the eye even if of more humble stock. I loved the Common Dandelion, for instance, and the Common Daisy. If the Common Dandelion were rare and expensive, how it would be praised for its matchless beauty! But it grows everywhere in our region and I have seen it bravely blooming eleven out of twelve months in the year, wherefor—as Prince Hal said of the wisdom that cries out in the streets—no man regards it. . . .

We found November fields dotted with shining yellow Dandelions and we came upon meadows that still offered us Red Clover in full rich flower. I must register distinct approval of Red Clover. It is beautiful; it is fragrant; it is good for the soil; cattle relish it; bumblebees feed from its florets; Rabbits munch it with zest; it gives a fine touch of color to the meadows and it flourishes merrily from May to November. It is one of the common things—like air and water and sunsets and the march of the constellations at night—that we haven't sense enough to appreciate no matter how essential or beneficial or decorative they may be.

John Kieran, *Footnotes on Nature* (New York: Doubleday, 1947), pp. 222, 233.

———◆———

Some years after his death, I met at Beverly Farms Miss Caroline H. King, who had been a friend of [James Russell] Lowell in his youth . . . She wrote to me, "Lowell took great pleasure in our piazza with its peeps at the sea. He always said that a wide, unbroken view, with no suggestions and surprises, was prosaic," and she remembered his annoyance when some visitors, after having been to the end of "the point", as it was called, suggested cutting down some trees to enlarge the view of the sea. "Lowell," she said, "turned to my father, with whom he often talked New England dialect, and broke out indignantly: 'Idiots! Talking about the *pint*; this is twice as good, I call it the quart. Why will people always want the whole at once? Bits are so much better.'"

Robert Underwood Johnson, *Remembered Yesterdays* (Boston: Little, Brown, 1923), p. 332.

———◆———

It is when we weary of this mesmerism of Rome and the bewilderment of its perspectives, when we begin to feel these waves close over us, that we instinctively look for some small corner or object to hold on to, firmly. It may be only a restaurant where it is pleasant to be recognised by a waiter. It may be a corner of a garden that is 'our' corner. We might even—I did—form a preference for one cabby. For several days in sequence I used to sit in the Borghese gardens, under the ilexes, on a broken column that was too casual and unimportant ever to invite identification, yet a veritable fragment of Rome on which to knock out my pipe.

Sean O'Faolain, *A Summer in Italy* (London: Eyre & Spottiswoode, 1949), p. 143.

———◆———

In China he [Stanley Spencer] could not eat the food and was so rushed from one sight to another that he could not think. He was afraid of being lost and dared not lag behind the party to look at what had struck him. He liked the interpreters but found the guides too didactic. While they held forth on the Meridian Gate he became absorbed in a wild flower on the wall.

Maurice Collis, *Stanley Spencer* (London: Harvill, 1962), p. 229.

WITH A CERTAIN EASE

———◆———

Nothing was more amazing in Morris than the way in which he always seemed at leisure, and always was ready for enjoyment. Neither in work nor in play was he wasteful; he had learned, in a way that few can, the great secret of not doing, whether it took the guise of work or of amusement, what he did not want to do. The so-called claims of society, so far as they did not represent anything for which he really cared, he quite simply and unaffectedly ignored. He never throughout his life belonged to a club. The drudgery of business he could not wholly escape, but he never allowed it either to absorb his time or to master his intelligence. That neglect of detail which is one of the secrets of success came to him naturally. For the intricacies of business he had no taste and little patience. "I keep fifteen clerks doing my accounts," he once observed, when inveighing against the artificial complexity of modern commerce, "and yet I cannot find out how much money I have got." If he had insisted on finding out, he might perhaps have known, but at the cost of this striking quality of detachment from routine. And for one so simple in his pleasures as he was, the routine of pleasure was as little worth its price to him as the routine of business.

J. W. Mackail, *The Life of William Morris*, 2d ed. (London: Longmans, 1901), vol. I, pp. 221–22.

———◆———

One of the first sweet and novel pleasures a man experiences in the wilds of Africa, is the almost perfect independence; the next thing is the indifference to all things earthly outside his camp; and that, let people talk as they may, is one of the most exquisite, soul-lulling pleasures a mortal can enjoy. . . .

No luxury in civilisation can be equal to the relief from the tyranny of custom.

Sir Henry Morton Stanley, Note-Book, 1876, *The Autobiography of Sir Henry Morton Stanley*, ed. Dorothy Stanley (Boston: Houghton, 1909), pp. 532–33.

Who, on calling to mind the occasions of his highest social enjoyments, does not find them to have been wholly informal, perhaps impromptu? How delightful a picnic of friends, who forget all observances save those dictated by good nature! How pleasant the little unpretended gatherings of book-societies, and the like; or those purely accidental meetings of a few people well known to each other! Then, indeed, we may see that "a man sharpeneth the countenance of his friend." Cheeks flush and eyes sparkle. The witty grow brilliant, and even the dull are excited into saying good things. There is an overflow of topics; and the right words to put it in, spring up unsought. Grave alternates with gay; now serious converse, and now jokes, anecdotes, and playful raillery. Every one's best nature is shown; every one's best feelings are in pleasurable activity; and, for the time, life seems well worth having. Go now and dress for some half-past eight dinner, or some ten o'clock "at home"; and present yourself in spotless attire, with every hair arranged to perfection. How great the difference! The enjoyment seems in the inverse ratio of the preparation. These figures, got up with such finish and precision, appear but half alive. They have frozen each other by their primness; and your faculties feel the numbing effects of the atmosphere the moment you enter it. All those thoughts, so nimble and so apt awhile since, have disappeared—have suddenly acquired a preternatural power of eluding you. If you venture a remark to your neighbour, there comes a trite rejoinder, and there it ends. No subject you can hit upon outlives half a dozen sentences. Nothing that is said excites any real interest in you; and you feel that all you say is listened to with apathy. . . . You see the hostess standing about the doorway, keeping a factitious smile on her face, and racking her brain to find the requisite nothings with which to greet her guests as they enter. You see numberless traits of weariness and embarrassment; and, if you have any fellow-feeling, these cannot fail to produce a sense of discomfort. What, now, is the secret of this perpetual miscarriage and disappointment? Does not the fault lie with all these needless adjuncts—these elaborate dressings, these set forms, these expensive preparations, these many devices and arrangements that imply trouble and raise expectation? Who that has lived thirty years in the world has not discovered that Pleasure is coy; and must not be too directly pursued, but must be caught unawares? An air from a street-piano, heard while at work, will often gratify more than the choicest music played at a concert by the most accomplished musicians. A single good picture seen in a dealer's window, may give keener enjoyment than a whole exhibition gone through with catalogue and pencil. By the time we have got ready our elaborate apparatus by which to secure happiness, the happiness is gone. It is too subtle to be contained in these receivers, garnished with compliments, and fenced round with etiquette. The more we multiply and complicate appliances, the more certain are we to drive it away.

Herbert Spencer, "Manners and Fashion," *The Westminster Review*, April, 1854: *Essays: Scientific, Political & Speculative* (London: Williams and Norgate, 1901), vol. III, pp. 39–43.

◆

A melancholic patient is filled through and through with intensely painful emotion about himself. He is threatened, he is guilty, he is doomed, he is annihilated, he is lost. His mind is fixed as if in a cramp on these feelings of his own situation, and in all the books on insanity you may read that the usual varied flow of his thoughts has ceased. His associative processes, to use the technical phrase, are inhibited; and his ideas stand stock-still, shut up to their one monotonous function of reiterating inwardly the fact of the man's desperate estate. . . .

Now from all this we can draw an extremely practical conclusion. If, namely, we wish our trains of ideation and volition to be copious and varied and effective, we must form the habit of freeing them from the inhibitive influence of reflection upon them, of egoistic preoccupation about their results. Such a habit, like other habits, can be formed. Prudence and duty and self-regard, emotions of ambition and emotions of anxiety, have, of course, a needful part to play in our lives. But confine them as far as possible to the occasions when you are making your general resolutions and deciding on your plans of campaign, and keep them out of the details. When once a decision is reached and execution is the order of the day, dismiss absolutely all responsibility and care about the outcome. *Unclamp*, in a word, your intellectual and practical machinery, and let it run free; and the service it will do you will be twice as good. Who are the scholars who get 'rattled' in the recitation-room? Those who think of the possibilities of failure and feel the great importance of the act. Who are those who do recite well? Often those who are most indifferent. *Their* ideas reel themselves out of their memory of their own accord. Why do we hear the complaint so often that social life in New England is either less rich and expressive or more fatiguing than it is in some other parts of the world? To what is the fact, if fact it be, due unless to the over-active conscience of the people, afraid of either saying something too trivial and obvious, or something insincere, or something unworthy of one's interlocutor, or something in some way or other not adequate to the occasion? How can conversation possibly steer itself through such a sea of responsibilities and inhibitions as this? On the other hand, conversation does flourish and society is refreshing, and neither dull on the one hand nor exhausting from its effort on the other, wherever people forget their scruples and take the brakes off their hearts, and let their tongues wag as automatically and irresponsibly as they will. . . .

Just as a bicycle-chain may be too tight, so may one's carefulness and conscientiousness be so tense as to hinder the running of one's mind.

William James, *Talks to Teachers* (New York: Holt, 1912), pp. 219–22.

———◆———

At last [in rewriting the first volume of his history of the French Revolution] he [Thomas Carlyle] began to feel himself like a man trying to swim without water; and doing nothing. "I filled page after page," he said afterwards, "but ran the pen over every line as the page was finished."

This was early in May, before he had reached the middle of the volume. Looking out of the window, "half-hearted and dejected," he noticed a bricklayer building a wall.—"With his trowel he'd lay a great splash of mortar upon the last layer, and then brick after brick upon this, striking each with the butt of his trowel, as if to give it his benediction and farewell; and all the while singing or whistling as blithe as a lark. . . ."

What he used to say he learned from watching the brick layers and masons was that a wall need not be mathematically perpendicular, but only perpendicular enough to be strong. He had to learn to get done once and for all. "The bricklayer does not insist on all being smooth as *marble*, but only on having a certain *degree* of smoothness and straightness; and so he gets a wall done." This was a thing he dwelt upon when he resumed his work.

David Alec Wilson, *Carlyle to "The French Revolution"* (1826–1837). (London: Kegan Paul, 1924), p. 384.

HOME

At the Headquarters of Balfourier's Division we saw a German prisoner who had just been brought in—a Prussian Guard. He was wounded in the arm, and evidently in pain. The Lord Chief Justice spoke to him, and ascertained that he came from Berlin. The prisoner behaved with great dignity, being neither surly nor communicative, but evidently feeling his position keenly. He had every appearance of an educated man. "Well," said the French General, "you need not worry. You will be taken to the hospital, and looked after just as well as our own men." "Your men are well treated by us, too," replied the German. The General shrugged his shoulders. "At any rate," he said, "for you it is now only a question of time. When the war is over you will be free to return to your home." "Ah!" said the prisoner, with weary longing, "home is the only thing that matters in life!"

David Lloyd George, *War Memoirs of David Lloyd George* (London: Nicholson, 1933), vol. I, pp. 159–60.

I put not least among the pleasures of travel, indeed, the supreme pleasure of returning home. In my experience one starts out with zest. The dropping of the Liverpool pilot off Holyhead, at night, in a dark and rolling sea—the first I ever saw climbed nimbly down an endless rope-ladder, wearing, in defiance of wind and weather, a little hard felt bowler hat—is a glorious experience, alone repaying every effort made on behalf of the holiday. One journeys onward, with sensations deepening and accumulating into memory of unsurpassed delight. One arrives. That arrival . . . is the climax of travel. But then, upon the return journey, home is not merely a place to which one relapses. To reach home again is in every sense a major arrival. Marvel-filled as is the outward journey, that which brings us back again contains the greatest marvel of all. For we learn afresh, at each return, that when travelling is over there is no place in the world which has quite the same appeal to our sense of the marvellous as the place we left a few days, a few weeks, a few months earlier with such anticipations of what we should see with our backs to our native land.

Frank Swinnerton, "Perpetual Romance," *Tokefield Papers*, 2d ed. (London: Hamish Hamilton, 1949), pp. 161–62.

———◆———

Every journey homeward is a sentimental journey. Or so, I fancy, it must be for anyone whose good fortune it is to journey homeward to Cornwall. At least, it always is for me: I know the ground so well by now, that I look forward to the familiar landmarks, so often observed before, here a hill or a wood, there a farm-house or a pond, with a start of recognition, always with expectancy, and with a certain contented satisfaction when it has flashed by and been left behind. . . .

Travelling by night in a sleeper was a new experience, and hard to settle into . . . And at last, all such thoughts were lulled to rest by the insistent rhythm of the wheels, beating out "Home again! Home again!" into the strange spaces of the night. So that when the guard came in the morning to wake me, bringing my tea, for we had already crossed the boundary and were in Cornwall, it seemed so short a time since I had left Oxford. . . .

It was Lostwithiel again, so soon: there were the trees by the river, and I saying softly over them "O, lovely! O, lovely!" to the unawakened dawn. Here was a field of clover sloping steeply to a combe. The seeping mists were folded under the arms of the trees in the woods asleep.

To be home again: the trees are more lovely; the fields greener, the gorse more golden; the birds sing sweeter; all the land is a dream.

A. L. Rowse, "The Sentimental Journey," *West-Country Stories* (London: Macmillan, 1945), pp. 161, 163.

———◆———

I am not impressed by the raptures of home-coming travellers when they single out the white cliffs, the comfortable slopes of the Downs, the dazzling scribble of buttercups and daisies outside the train windows; for when I have been some time away from England, then even what I usually dislike here can bring me a flash of delight. I welcome with joy the glum railway sidings, the platforms that exist in a perpetual November, the *Daily Piffler* and the *Weekly Blatherer* on the bookstalls, the mournful muck of the refreshment room, the gimcrack bungalows, the little towns that have never once been gay and gaudy, the hoardings given up to second-rate musical comedies, the vast gloom and decay of London. What a civilisation! What a mess! What a country! But I'm home . . . I'm home. . . .

J. B. Priestley, *Delight* (London: Heinemann, 1949), p. 54.

◆

Let the young married man . . . resolve not to be seduced from his home; let him never go, in one single instance, unnecessarily from his own fire-side. Habit is a powerful thing; and if he begin right, the pleasure that he will derive from it will induce him to continue right. That is not being "tied to the apron-strings," which means quite another matter . . . It is being at the husband's place, whether he have children or not. And is there any want of matter for conversation between a man and his wife? Why not talk of the daily occurrences to her as well as to anybody else, and especially to a company of tippling and noisy men? If you excuse yourself by saying that you go to read the newspaper, I answer buy the newspaper, if you must read it; the cost is not half of what you spend per day at the pot-house; and then you have it your own, and may read it at your leisure, and your wife can read it as well as yourself, if read it you must. And, in short, what must that man be made of who does not prefer sitting by his own fireside with his wife and children, reading to them, or hearing them read, to hearing the gabble and balderdash of a club or a pot-house company! . . .

Men must frequently be from home at all hours of the day and night. Sailors, soldiers, merchants, all men out of the common track of labour, and even some in the very lowest walks, are sometimes compelled by their affairs, or by circumstances, to be from their homes. But what I protest against is the habit of spending leisure hours from home, and near to it, and doing this without any necessity, and by choice: liking the next door, or any house in the same street, better than your own. When absent from necessity, there is no wound given to the heart of the wife; she concludes that you would be with her if you could, and that satisfies; she laments the absence, but submits to it without complaining. Yet, in these cases, her feelings ought to be consulted as much as possible; she ought to be fully apprized of the probable duration of the absence, and of the time of return; and if these be dependent on circumstance, those circumstances ought to be fully stated; for you have no right to keep her mind upon the rack, when you have it in your power to put it in a state of ease. Few men have been more frequently taken from home by business, or by a necessity of some sort, than I have; and I can positively assert, that, as to my return, I never once disappointed my wife in the whole course of our married life. If the time of return was contingent I never failed to keep her informed from day to day: if the time was fixed or when it became fixed, my arrival was as sure as my life. Going from London to Botley once, with Mr. Finnerty, whose name I can never pronounce without an expression of my regard for his memory, we stopped at Alton, to dine with a friend, who, delighted with Finnerty's talk, as everybody else was, kept us till ten or eleven o'clock, and was proceeding to the other bottle, when I put in my protest, saying, "We must go; my wife will be frightened." "Blood, man," said Finnerty, "you do not mean to go home to-night!" I told him I did; and then sent my son, who was with us, to order out the post-chaise. We had twenty-three miles to go, during which we debated the question, whether Mrs. Cobbott would be up to receive us, I contending for the affirmative, and he for the negative. She was up, and had a nice fire for us to sit down at. She had not committed the matter to a servant; her servants and children were all in bed; and she was up, to perform the duty of receiving her husband and his friend. "You did not expect him?" said Finnerty. "To be sure I did," said she; "he never disappointed me in his life."

William Cobbett, *Advice to Young Men and (Incidentally) to Young Women*, 1829 (London: Davies, 1926), Letter IV, pp. 170–72.

———◆———

For an old man or woman who is seriously ill but may recover, the best place is usually the hospital. For one who is dying the best place, or at any rate the happiest place, is his own home. Although it will add greatly to his work, to the number of visits he must make for small medical attentions or merely for friendship, the doctor should try to keep the dying man at home, and to encourage his relatives to give him this last solace. For most people the home is associated with the experiences and the surroundings that make his personality. The pattern on the wallpaper, the shaft of sunlight coming through the window, the school groups and wedding photographs on the wall, the creak of the door, the postman's knock, the recurring noises of the street outside, all these make a familiar pattern in a mind that is drowsing over the past and wondering about the future. He wants a book, a gramophone record, flowers in the vase that used to stand on his desk, his own red silk handkerchief. They are all at hand. He would miss them in hospital.

Sir Heneage Ogilvie, "Journey's End," *No Miracles Among Friends* (London: Parrish, 1959), pp. 168–69.

On this his last journey Sir Walter [Scott] was attended by his two daughters, Mr. Cadell, and myself—and also by Dr. James Watson, who (it being impossible for Dr. Fergusson to leave town at that moment) kindly undertook to see him safe at Abbotsford. . . .

Mr. Laidlaw was waiting at the porch, and assisted us in lifting him into the dining-room, where his bed had been prepared. He sat bewildered for a few moments, and then resting his eye on Laidlaw, said—'Ha! Willie Laidlaw! O man, how often have I thought of you!' By this time his dogs had assembled about his chair—they began to fawn upon him and lick his hands, and he alternately sobbed and smiled over them, until sleep oppressed him.

Dr. Watson having consulted on all things with Mr. Clarkson and his father, resigned the patient to them, and returned to London. None of them could have any hope, but that of soothing irritation. Recovery was no longer to be thought of . . .

And yet something like a ray of hope did break in upon us next morning. Sir Walter awoke perfectly conscious where he was, and expressed an ardent wish to be carried out into his garden. We procured a Bath chair from Huntly-Burn, and Laidlaw and I wheeled him out before his door, and up and down for some time on the turf, and among the rose-beds then in full bloom. The grandchildren admired the new vehicle, and would be helping in their way to push it about. He sat in silence, smiling placidly on them and the dogs their companions, and now and then admiring the house, the screen of the garden, and the flowers and trees. By and by he conversed a little, very composedly, with us—said he was happy to be at home—that he felt better than he had ever done since he left it, and would perhaps disappoint the doctors after all.

He then desired to be wheeled through his rooms, and we moved him leisurely for an hour or more up and down the hall and the great library: 'I have seen much,' he kept saying, 'but nothing like my ain house—give me one turn more!'

John Gibson Lockhart, *Memoirs of Sir Walter Scott*, 1837–1838 (London: Macmillan, 1900), vol. V, chap. LXXXIII, pp. 421–23.

RITUAL

When he leaves the table, he takes his old hat from its hook . . .
Crossing the yard, we look up at the stars.

"In nature most people search for the unusual, the unexpected," he
tells me. "But it's the monotony of nature that's most dear to me. Like
the monotony of my daily routine. I look forward to knowing what will
happen on Monday and that the same thing will happen on Tuesday
and again on Wednesday. I am not much of a traveler. To pack up and
live out of a suitcase is something I do only when I have to."

Erica Anderson, *Albert Schweitzer's Gift of Friendship* (New
York: Harper, 1964), p. 86.

The pleasure of doing a thing in the same way at the same time
every day, and savouring it, should be noted.

Arnold Bennett, Journal, April 14, 1913, *The Journals of Arnold
Bennett 1911–1921*, ed. Newman Flower (London: Cassell, 1932), p.
61.

I came every day to walk slowly up and down the plain road, by
the starry flowers under the ash-green boughs . . .

A friend said, "Why do you go the same road every day? Why not
have a change and walk somewhere else sometimes? Why keep on up
and down the same place?" I could not answer; till then it had not oc-
curred to me that I did always go one way; as for the reason of it I
could not tell; I continued in my old mind while the summers went
away. Not till years afterwards was I able to see why I went the same
round and did not care for change. I do not want change: I want the
same old and loved things . . .

Why, I knew the very dates of them all—the reddening elm, the
arum, the hawthorn leaf, the celandine, the may; the yellow iris of the
waters, the heath of the hillside. The time of the nightingale—the place
to hear the first note; onwards to the drooping fern and the time of the

redwing—the place of *his* first note, so welcome to the sportsman as the acorn ripens and the pheasant come to the age of manhood, feeds himself; onwards to the shadowless days—the long shadowless winter . . . Past the shadowless winter, when it is all shade, and therefore no shadow; onwards to the first coltsfoot and on to the seed-time again; I knew the dates of all of them. I did not want change; I wanted the same flowers to return on the same day, the titlark to rise soaring from the same oak to fetch down love with a song from heaven to his mate on the nest beneath. No change, no new things . . .

Richard Jefferies, "Wild Flowers," *The Open Air* (London: Chatto, 1909), pp. 41–44.

———◆———

I welcome every new day with new gratitude. I almost wonder at myself, when I think of the pleasure which the dawn gives me, after having witnessed it so many years. This blessed light of heaven, how dear it is to me! and this earth which I have trodden so long, with what affection I look on it! I have but a moment ago cast my eyes on the lawn in front of my house, and the sight of it, gemmed with dew and heightening by its brilliancy the shadows of the trees which fall upon it, awakened emotions more vivid, perhaps, than I experienced in youth.

William Ellery Channing, letter, 1839, in William Henry Channing, *Memoirs of William Ellery Channing* (London: Routledge, n.d.), vol. II, p. 479.

———◆———

One of the symbols of this saving continuity—and no less a symbol because it was sometimes resisted—was the whole ceremony of church-going. It came at the end of that long Sunday afternoon and was undertaken often enough in no very willing or pious spirit. Left to oneself, one might have chosen the garden, not the sermon, and yet, when the decision was made and the little procession had set out, the power of ritual asserted itself—not yet the ritual of the Church, but that of the fields, the bells, the angle of the sun, of other figures approaching down the convergent lanes of the hill opposite. In the church-yard, if the five-minute bell had not yet begun, there was a pause for neighbourly conversation, and it was possible to wander among the graves and read again an inscription which, long ago, had been learned by heart. Inside the church itself was a mingling of daylight and lamplight, a pallor of glass which would presently darken, a low gleam of stone and wood; and all these things bespoke the hour and the month, and were part of the order of the seasons.

Charles Morgan, "The Village Church," *Reflections in a Mirror*, 2d series (London: Macmillan, 1946), p. 52.

———————◆———————

In time of peace the world is self-contained. The villagers come home at dusk from their fields. The grain is stored up in the barns. The folded linen is piled up in the cupboards. In time of peace each thing is in its place, easily found. Each friend is where he belongs, easily reached. All men know where they will sleep when night comes. Ah, but peace dies when the framework is ripped apart. When there is no longer a place that is yours in the world. When you know no longer where your friend is to be found. Peace is present when man can see the face that is composed of things that have meaning and are in their place.

Antoine de Saint-Exupéry, *Flight to Arras*, tr. by Lewis Galantière (New York: Reynal, 1942), p. 116.

WORK

———————◆———————

One day I had occasion to go into Sir Thomas's music room about 5 P.M., believing it to be empty. He [Sir Thomas Beecham] had first been rehearsing his orchestra and then was on the stage from 11 A.M., with a break of about half an hour for a lunch of something like milk and biscuits, continuing to work all afternoon.

He was due to conduct *Die Meistersinger* at 7:30, and to my astonishment there he sat deep in an orchestral score.

"Why, Sir Thomas, I thought you were having a rest."

"So I am—study rests me."

"I know—but I mean a real rest before the evening."

"Oh; a REST? I haven't had a rest for about thirty-five years—shouldn't know what to do with it if I had one!"

Josephine O'Donnell, *Among the Covent Garden Stars* (London: Stanley Paul, 1936), pp. 285–86.

———◆———

. . . I am persuaded that . . . there is not half so much danger of overwork as of underwork. And also that the life which leans to the first is at once more fruitful and more enjoying than the life which leans to the second. . . .

There are three or four of my friends who might fairly be described as work-drunken. . . . Two of them are not physically robust, but, save at times of immense pressure, they are the most cheerful and gentle men I know. They never brood, they are generally hopeful; they have little relaxation, but what they have is relished with an intensity of joy. They are the people who keep young in the true sense of the word. They have the spirit that secures the happiness because it does not shrink from the unhappiness of working days. They have their times of full sunshine given to happy memories, happy experiences, and happy hopes. I think of others who are underworked, and I will not say that I have not sometimes envied them their leisure, but I have never envied them long, nor have I ever felt that the envy was rational.

Sir William Robertson Nicoll ("Claudius Clear"), " 'Work-Drunkenness,' " *The Day Book of Claudius Clear*, 3d ed. (London: Hodder, n.d.), pp. 255, 260–61.

———◆———

"To execute great things," says Vauvenargues, "a man must live as though he had never to die." Agassiz lived in this way. . . . He never had an hour in his life when he was not pleasantly occupied; and he innocently wondered, when the people he met in society sometimes complained of being bored with life. Every contrivance to kill time appeared to him the funniest of all jokes. "Time!" he was wont to exclaim; "my only trouble is that I have not enough time for my work. I cannot understand why anybody should be idle; much less can I understand why anybody should be oppressed by having time hang on his hands. There is never a moment, except when I am asleep, that I am not joyfully occupied. Please give to me the hours which you say are a bore to you, and I will receive them as the most precious of presents. For my part, I wish the day would never come to an end." His recreations were only variations of his occupations. He told me that he had never known a dull hour in his whole life.

Edwin Percy Whipple, "Recollections of Agassiz," *Recollections of Eminent Men* (Boston: Ticknor, 1887), pp. 98–99.

———◆———

The School of Physics could give us no suitable premises, but for lack of anything better, the Director permitted us to use [as a radium laboratory] an abandoned shed which had been in service as a dissecting room of the School of Medicine. Its glass roof did not afford complete shelter against rain; the heat was suffocating in summer, and the bitter cold of winter was only a little lessened by the iron stove, except in its immediate vicinity. There was no question of obtaining the needed proper apparatus in common use by chemists. We simply had some old pine-wood tables with furnaces and gas burners. We had to use the adjoining yard for those of our chemical operations that involved producing irritating gases; even then the gas often filled our shed. With this equipment we entered on our exhausting work.

Yet it was in this miserable old shed that we passed the best and happiest years of our life, devoting our entire days to our work. Often I had to prepare our lunch in the shed, so as not to interrupt some particularly important operation. Sometimes I had to spend a whole day mixing a boiling mass with a heavy iron rod nearly as large as myself. I would be broken with fatigue at the day's end. Other days, on the contrary, the work would be a most minute and delicate fractional crystallization, in the effort to concentrate the radium. I was then annoyed by the floating dust of iron and coal from which I could not protect my precious products. But I shall never be able to express the joy of the untroubled quietness of this atmosphere of research and the excitement of actual progress with the confident hope of still better results. The feeling of discouragement that sometimes came after some unsuccessful toil did not last long and gave way to renewed activity. We had happy moments devoted to a quiet discussion of our work, walking around our shed.

One of our joys was to go into our workroom at night; we then perceived on all sides the feebly luminous silhouettes of the bottles or capsules containing our products. It was really a lovely sight and one always new to us. The glowing tubes looked like faint, fairy lights.

Marie Curie, *Pierre Curie* (New York: Macmillan, 1923), pp. 186–87.

I must say something of his [Charles Darwin's] manner of working: one characteristic of it was his respect for time; he never forgot how precious it was. This was shown, for instance, in the way in which he tried to curtail his holidays; also, and more clearly, with respect to shorter periods. He would often say, that saving the minutes was the way to get work done; he showed this love of saving the minutes in the difference he felt between a quarter of an hour and ten minutes' work; he never wasted a few spare minutes from thinking that it was not worth while to set to work. I was often struck by his way of working up to the very limit of his strength, so that he suddenly stopped in dictating, with the words, "I believe I mustn't do any more." The same eager desire not to lose time was seen in his quick movements when at work. I particularly remember noticing this when he was making an experiment on the roots of beans, which required some care in manipulation; fastening the little bits of card upon the roots was done carefully and necessarily slowly, but the intermediate movements were all quick; taking a fresh bean, seeing that the root was healthy, impaling it on a pin, fixing it on a cork and seeing that it was vertical, &c.; all these processes were performed with a kind of restrained eagerness. He always gave one the impression of working with pleasure, and not with any drag. I have an image, too, of him as he recorded the result of some experiment, looking eagerly at each root, &c., and then writing with equal eagerness. I remember the quick movement of his head up and down as he looked from the object to the notes.

Francis Darwin, reminiscences of his father, Charles Darwin, in *The Life and Letters of Charles Darwin*, ed. Francis Darwin (New York: Appleton, 1898), vol. I, p. 121.

What is this impulse sometimes called the "instinct of workmanship"? Not an instinct, of course, in the technical sense—more like a dominant passion in some men: but a verifiable trait in most men, under whatever name. A carpenter earning high wages tells me he is dissatisfied because he is hurried in his work: "a man never gets a chance to do his best." Why does he want a chance to do his best—he will earn no more by it? Or what is it that keeps the business man going when he has heaped up all he can use? Not greed. Not ambition exactly. Something more like a modified instinct of workmanship. There is something *there to be done*: it seems to him that he must be the one to do it. What is it that makes a good housekeeper, or a good captain of a ship? Something that exceeds every definable duty. The officer who studied instructions and fulfilled them all would never, on that ground, become the captain of a ship. The man who becomes captain is the man who finds his orders in the ship itself and its mission, and who does whatever at any time there is no one else to do. The work of the ship is his work: something objective, something not in him is issuing requirements, and he is there to fulfil them. To a sound instinct it is never a particular stimulus alone, *it is reality that commands*. The living instinct of man has in it an element of the mystical: it is responding to the world in its invisible unity.

William Ernest Hocking, *The Self: Its Body and Freedom* (New Haven: Yale Univ. Press, 1928), pp. 170–71.

———◆———

Everybody is an artist who enjoys his job and takes pride in making the best of it, putting his whole self into it—having what the Italians call *passione*. It matters not how humble or petty, shopkeeper or the higher occupations, from domestic servant to President of the U.S.A. or Prime Minister of England. It is the zest, the delight in his work, that something extra which he puts into it, that blesses him and those who benefit by him. Contrary to the person who enjoys his task so much that he puts payments, compensations, rewards, honours, last, the man or woman who does not enjoy his work wants to be exorbitantly paid for what he dislikes or even hates doing. So I always have found innkeepers and workmen more exorbitant in their charges the worse they had served me.

Bernard Berenson, Diary, September 1, 1948, in Bernard Berenson, *Sunset and Twilight*, ed. Nicky Mariano (New York: Harcourt, 1963), p. 97.

———◆———

He made the common remark on the unhappiness which men who have led a busy life experience, when they retire in expectation of enjoying themselves at ease, and that they generally languish for want of their habitual occupation, and wish to return to it. He mentioned as strong an instance of this as can well be imagined. 'An eminent tallow-chandler in London, who had acquired a considerable fortune, gave up the trade in favour of his foreman, and went to live at a country-house near town. He soon grew weary, and paid frequent visits to his old shop, where he desired they might let him know their *melting-days*, and he would come and assist them; which he accordingly did. Here, Sir, was a man, to whom the most disgusting circumstance in the business to which he had been used was a relief from idleness.'

James Boswell, *The Life of Samuel Johnson*, 1791, ed. George Birkbeck Hill (New York: Harper, n.d.), vol. II, p. 386.

◆

Rest, with nothing else, results in rust. It corrodes the mechanisms of the brain. The rhubarb that no one picks goes to seed. . . .

The time of retirement should be reorganized and renamed. It is the time for embarking on a new career, the last career perhaps, but not necessarily a less enjoyable one; not, perhaps, a less useful one to society. Disease and disability may overtake men at any age, of course, and force them to withdraw from work. But the capacity of the human brain for certain purposes often increases right through the years that are marked for standard retirement. . . .

I do not urge that the time for a man to retire from his primary career should be postponed—not at all. A second career can quite well begin by the age of sixty. It should start by then at the latest, even if formal retirement takes place at sixty-five or later. His preparation for a second career should be undertaken long before that, preferably in the forties. Better yet that it should come with him from school days. . . .

No one can deny that the human brain passes through certain inexorable changes. Senescence will come in time, inevitably. The brain has a specialized capacity for the beginning of languages during the first decade of life. After that time it is ready for expansion of vocabulary. It is ready for mathematics, rationalization, independent thought. At sixty the body has certainly passed beyond its greatest strength, and physical demands should be lessened and changed. But the brain, quite often, is ready for its best performance in certain fields. . . .

A genius is not a man who was made in some other image; he is just a man driven to constructive action by a great enthusiasm. Enthusiasm feeds on challenge. The ordinary brain is good enough for most men and most purposes. Its best tonic is use; the worst treatment is discouragement and disuse. . . .

To most men, there should come a time for shifting harness, for lightening the load one way and adjusting it for greater effort in another. That is the time for the second career, time for the old dog to perform new tricks. The new career may bring in little or no money; it may be concerned only with good works. It may, on the other hand, bring in

support that is much needed. It can be a deligh
at last to a well-earned job instead of a well-earne

The problem to set before the wise men of tod
can each individual be given the chance to work
is not to the swift nor the battle to the strong. It
work of the old man's hands will serve society best—

Wilder Penfield, "The Second Career," *The S*
Other Essays and Addresses (Boston: Little, Brown, 19   ~4–17.

◆————

In early youth we are accustomed to divide life broadly into work
and play, regarding the first as duty or necessity and the second as pleasure. One of the great differences between childhood and manhood is
that we come to like our work more than our play. It becomes to us if
not the chief pleasure at least the chief interest of our lives, and even
when it is not this, an essential condition of our happiness. Few lives
produce so little happiness as those that are aimless and unoccupied.
Apart from all considerations of right and wrong, one of the first conditions of a happy life is that it should be a full and busy one, directed
to the attainment of aims outside ourselves. . . .

An ideal life would be furnished with abundant work of a kind that
is congenial both to our intellects and our characters and that brings with
it much interest and little anxiety. Few of us can command this. Most
men's work is largely determined for them by circumstances, though in
the guidance of life there are many alternatives and much room for
skilful pilotage. But the first great rule is that we must do something—
that life must have a purpose and an aim—that work should be not
merely occasional and spasmodic, but steady and continuous. Pleasure is
a jewel which will only retain its lustre when it is in a setting of work,
and a vacant life is one of the worst of pains, though the islands of
leisure that stud a crowded, well-occupied life may be among the things
to which we look back with the greatest delight.

William Edward Hartpole Lecky, *The Map of Life* (London:
Longmans, 1899), pp. 19–21.

PART TWO

Recreations

EAGER LEISURE

◆

. . . she [Mrs. Poyser] was standing at the house door with her knitting, in that eager leisure which came to her when the afternoon cleaning was done . . .

George Eliot, *Adam Bede*, 1859 (London and Edinburgh: Chambers, n.d.), chap. XXXII, p. 330.

◆

What a boon is Sunday! I can get out of bed just when the spirit moves me, dress and bath leisurely, even with punctilio. How nice to dawdle in the bath with a cigarette, to hear the holiday sound of Church bells! Then comes that supreme moment when, shaven, clean, warm and hungry for breakfast and coffee, I stand a moment before the looking-glass and comb out my towzled hair with a parting as straight as a line in Euclid. That gives the finishing touch of self-satisfaction, and I go down to breakfast ready for the day's pleasure. I hate this week-day strain of having to be always each day at a set time in a certain place.

W. N. P. Barbellion, Journal, February 28, 1915, *The Journal of a Disappointed Man* (London: Chatto, 1919), p. 178.

◆

What a book could be written on the subject of fine Sundays in nineteenth-century French painting! The impressionists are particularly great there, reaching the summit of their art when they paint our French Sundays, so typical of our people. There is candor in them and gaiety, color, a gracious ease, tenderness, and silences and clear intelligent faces; there are the couples who are faithful to each other, the first call to love, conscious desire but always tinged with romanticism, the eternal Lisette or Mimi Pinson, the little working girls, sunlit kisses, lunch on the grass, repose, work forgotten, unabashed relaxation.

René Gimpel, *Dairy of an Art Dealer* (London: Hodder, 1966), p. 312.

Happily it is possible to go away, if not to home, at any rate to some country retreat at the end of the week, and to combine the best of dry fly fishing with this on Saturday. Where this can be done, the prospect of the escape on Saturday till Monday is a great consolation in all moments of leisure during the week. It is borne about with us like a happy secret; it draws the thoughts towards it continually, as Ruskin says that the luminous distance in a picture attracts the eye, or as the gleam of water attracts it in a landscape.

If our work will let us escape on Friday evening, it is luxury; but even if we belong only to those in the middle state of happiness, who work till midnight or later on Friday, and can have the whole of Saturday and Sunday in the country, we may still be splendidly well off, provided that we are careful to miss nothing. The earliest trains leave Waterloo, the usual place of departure for the Itchen or the Test, either at or just before six o'clock in the morning. To leave London it is possible once a week, even after late hours, to get up in time for these early trains, and if you have no luggage (and you need have none if you go to the same place week after week), you will not find it difficult to get to the station. . . . I pass over the scene at Waterloo station, which at this hour is very different from the usual one, and the journey, on which perhaps one sleeps a little, though I have found that, while it is very easy to sleep sitting up in the late hours of the evening, it is necessary to lie down, if one wishes to sleep in the early hours of the morning. At some time between eight and nine o'clock, you step out of the train, and are in a few minutes among all the long-desired things. Every sense is alert and everything seen or heard is noted with delight. You are grateful for the grass on which you walk, even for the soft country dust about your feet.

Edward Grey (Viscount Grey of Falloden), *Fly Fishing* (London: Dent, 1934), pp. 33–34.

———◆———

For the first time in my life, when I had finished the last sentence [of the second volume of *Modern Painters*], I was really tired. In too long readings at Oxford I got stupid and sleepy, but not fatigued: now, however, I felt distinctly that my head could do no more; and with much satisfied thankfulness, after the revise of the last sheet was sent to printer, found myself on the bows of the little steamer, watching their magical division of the green waves between Dover and Calais.

Little steamers they all were, then; nor in the least well appointed, nor aspiring to any pride of shape or press of speed; their bits of sails worn and patched like those of an old fishing-boat. . . . The immeas-

urable delight to me of being able to loiter and swing about just over the
bowsprit and watch the plunge of the bows, if there was the least swell
or broken sea to lift them, with the hope of Calais at breakfast, and the
horses' heads set straight for Mont Blanc to-morrow, is one of the few
pleasures I look back to as quite unmixed.

John Ruskin, *Praeterita*, 2d ed. (New York: Merrill and Baker,
n.d.), vol. II, pp. 338–40.

⬥

Indeed the Royal Thames Yacht Club, of which he [Bret Harte]
was a member, became his favourite resort when he wanted any dis-
traction from his own home. This selection seemed to me so odd—for
he had no love of yachting—that I questioned him concerning it. "Why,
my dear fellow," he said, "don't you see? I never use a club until I am
tired of my work and want relief from it. If I go to a literary club I am
asked all sorts of questions as to what I am doing, and my views on somebody's last book, and to these I am expected to reply at length. Now my
good friends in Albemarle Street talk of their yachts, don't want my
advice about them, are good enough to let me listen, and I come away
refreshed by their conversation."

T. Edgar Pemberton, *The Life of Bret Harte* (London: Pearson,
1903), pp. 334–35.

⬥

One of the shining moments of my day is that when, having returned a little weary from an afternoon walk, I exchange boots for slippers, out-of-doors coat for easy, familiar, shabby jacket, and, in my deep,
soft-elbowed chair, await the tea-tray. Perhaps it is while drinking tea
that I most of all enjoy the sense of leisure. In days gone by, I could but
gulp down the refreshment, hurried, often harassed, by the thought of
the work I had before me; often I was quite insensible of the aroma, the
flavour, of what I drank. Now, how delicious is the soft yet penetrating odour which floats into my study, with the appearance of the teapot!
What solace in the first cup, what deliberate sipping of that which follows! What a glow does it bring after a walk in chilly rain! The while, I
look around at my books and pictures, tasting the happiness of their
tranquil possession. I cast an eye towards my pipe; perhaps I prepare it,
with seeming thoughtfulness, for the reception of tobacco. And never,

surely, is tobacco more soothing, more suggestive of humane thoughts, than when it comes just after tea—itself a bland inspirer.

In nothing is the English genius for domesticity more notably declared than in the institution of this festival—almost one may call it so—of afternoon tea. Beneath simple roofs, the hour of tea has something in it of sacred; for it marks the end of domestic work and worry, the beginning of restful, sociable evening. The mere chink of cups and saucers tunes the mind to happy repose. . . .

I like to look at my housekeeper when she carries in the tray. Her mien is festal, yet in her smile there is a certain gravity, as though she performed an office which honoured her. She has dressed for the evening; that is to say, her clean and seemly attire of working hours is exchanged for garments suitable to fireside leisure; her cheeks are warm, for she has been making fragrant toast. Quickly her eye glances about my room, but only to have the pleasure of noting that all is in order; inconceivable that anything serious should need doing at this hour of the day. She brings the little table within the glow of the hearth, so that I can help myself without changing my easy position. If she speaks, it will only be a pleasant word or two; should she have anything important to say, the moment will be *after* tea, not before it; this she knows by instinct. Perchance she may just stoop to sweep back a cinder which has fallen since, in my absence, she looked after the fire; it is done quickly and silently. Then, still smiling, she withdraws, and I know that she is going to enjoy her own tea, her own toast, in the warm, comfortable, sweet-smelling kitchen.

George Gissing, *The Private Papers of Henry Ryecroft*, 1903, (New York: Boni & Liveright, 1918), chap. V, pp. 198–201.

———◆———

There were times when I could not afford to sacrifice the bloom of the present moment to any work, whether of the head or hands. I love a broad margin to my life. Sometimes, in a summer morning, having taken my accustomed bath, I sat in my sunny doorway from sunrise till noon, rapt in a revery, amidst the pines and hickories and sumachs, in undisturbed solitude and stillness, while the birds sang around or flitted noiseless through the house, until by the sun falling in at my west window, or the noise of some traveller's wagon on the distant highway, I was reminded of the lapse of time. I grew in those seasons like corn in the night, and they were far better than any work of the hands would have been. They were not time subtracted from my life, but so much over and above my usual allowance. I realized what the Orientals mean by contemplation and the forsaking of works. For the most part, I minded not how the hours went. The day advanced as if to light some work of mine; it was morning, and lo, now it is evening, and nothing memorable is accomplished. Instead of singing like the birds, I silently smiled at my incessant good fortune. As the sparrow had its trill, sitting on the hickory before my door, so had I my chuckle or suppressed warble which he might hear out of my nest. My days were not days of the week, bearing the stamp of any heathen deity, nor were they minced into hours and fretted by the ticking of a clock; for I lived like the Puri Indians, of whom it is said that "for yesterday, to-day, and to-morrow they have only one word, and they express the variety of meaning by pointing backward for yesterday, forward for to-morrow, and overhead for the passing day." This was sheer idleness to my fellow-townsmen, no doubt; but if the birds and flowers had tried me by their standard, I should not have been found wanting.

Henry David Thoreau, *Walden, or Life in the Woods*, 1854 (Boston: Houghton, 1929), chap. IV, pp. 123–24.

EATING

◆

Fate cannot harm; I have dined to-day.

Sydney Smith, quoted by John Ruskin, *Praeterita*, 2d ed. (New York: Merrill and Baker, n.d.), p. 99.

◆

So my poor wife rose by five o'clock in the morning, before day, and went to market and bought fowls and many other things for dinner, with which I was highly pleased, and the chine of beef was down also before six o'clock, and my own jack, of which I was doubtfull, do carry it very well. Things being put in order, and the cook come, I went to the office, where we sat till noon and then broke up, and I home, whither by and by comes Dr. Clerke and his lady, his sister, and a she-cozen, and Mr. Pierce and his wife, which was all my guests. I had for them, after oysters, at first course, a hash of rabbits, a lamb, and a rare chine of beef. Next a great dish of roasted fowl, cost me about 30s., and a tart, and then fruit and cheese. My dinner was noble and enough. I had my house mighty clean and neat; my room below with a good fire in it; my dining-room above, and my chamber being made a withdrawing-chamber; and my wife's a good fire also. I find my new table very proper, and will hold nine or ten people well, but eight with great room. After dinner the women to cards in my wife's chamber, and the Dr. and Mr. Pierce in mine, because the dining-room smokes unless I keep a good charcoal fire, which I was not then provided with. At night to supper, had a good sack posset and cold meat, and sent my guests away about ten o'clock at night, both them and myself highly pleased with our management of this day . . .

Samuel Pepys, Diary, January 13, 1663, *The Diary of Samuel Pepys*, ed. Henry B. Wheatley (London: Bell, 1924), vol. III, pp. 12–13.

◆———

It is a curious fact that novelists have a way of making us believe that luncheon parties are invariably memorable for something very witty that was said, or for something very wise that was done. But they seldom spare a word for what was eaten. It is part of the novelist's convention not to mention soup and salmon and ducklings, as if soup and salmon and ducklings were of no importance whatsoever, as if nobody ever smoked a cigar or drank a glass of wine. Here, however, I shall take the liberty to defy that convention and to tell you that the lunch on this occasion began with soles, sunk in a deep dish, over which the college cook had spread a counterpane of the whitest cream, save that it was branded here and there with brown spots like the spots on the flanks of a doe. After that came the partridges, but if this suggests a couple of bald, brown birds on a plate you are mistaken. The partridges, many and various, came with all their retinue of sauces and salads, the sharp and the sweet, each in its order; their potatoes, thin as coins but not so hard; their sprouts, foliated as rosebuds but more succulent. And no sooner had the roast and its retinue been done with than the silent serving-man, the Beadle himself perhaps in a milder manifestation, set before us, wreathed in napkins, a confection which rose all sugar from the waves. To call it pudding and so relate it to rice and tapioca would be an insult. Meanwhile the wineglasses had flushed yellow and flushed crimson; had been emptied; had been filled. And thus by degrees was lit, half-way down the spine, which is the seat of the soul, not that hard little electric light which we call brilliance, as it pops in and out upon our lips, but the more profound, subtle and subterranean glow which is the rich yellow flame of rational intercourse. No need to hurry. No need to sparkle. No need to be anybody but oneself. We are all going to heaven and Vandyck is of the company—in other words, how good life seemed, how sweet its rewards, how trivial this grudge or that grievance, how admirable friendship and the society of one's kind, as, lighting a good cigarette, one sunk among the cushions in the window-seat.

Virginia Woolf, *A Room of One's Own*, 2d ed. (London: Hogarth, 1931), pp. 16–18.

—————◆—————

Recognizing . . . that there are higher pleasures than eating and drinking, let us clearly perceive that three meals a day all one's life not only give in themselves a constantly renewed innocent satisfaction, but provide the necessary foundation for all other satisfactions. Taking food and drink is a great enjoyment for healthy people, and those who do not enjoy eating seldom have much capacity for enjoyment or usefulness of any sort. Under ordinary circumstances it is by no means a purely bodily pleasure. We do not eat alone, but in families, or sets of friends and comrades, and the table is the best center of friendships and of the domestic affections. When, therefore, a workingman says that he has worked all his life to procure a subsistence for himself and his family, he states that he has secured some fundamental satisfactions, namely, food, productive employment, and family life. The satisfaction of eating is so completely a matter of appetite that such distinction as there is between the luxurious and the hardy in regard to this enjoyment is altogether in favor of the hardy. Who does not remember some rough and perhaps scanty meal in camp, or on the march, or at sea, or in the woods, which was infinitely more delicious than the most luxurious dinner during indoor or sedentary life? But that appetite depends on health. Take good care, then, of your teeth and your stomachs, and be ashamed, not of enjoying your food, but of not enjoying it. There was a good deal of sound human nature in the unexpected reply of the dying old woman to her minister's leading question: "Here at the end of a long life, which of the Lord's mercies are you most thankful for?" Her eye brightened as she answered, after a moment's consideration: "My victuals."

Charles W. Eliot, "The Happy Life," *Charles W. Eliot: The Man and His Beliefs*, ed. William Allan Neilson (New York: Harper, 1926), vol. II, pp. 418–19.

At supper this night he talked of good eating with uncommon satisfaction. 'Some people (said he,) have a foolish way of not minding, or pretending not to mind, what they eat. For my part, I mind my belly very studiously, and very carefully; for I look upon it, that he who does not mind his belly will hardly mind anything else.' . . . He used to descant critically on the dishes which had been at table where he had dined or supped, and to recollect very minutely what he had liked. I remember, when he was in Scotland, his praising *'Gordon's palates,'* (a dish of palates at the Honourable Alexander Gordon's) with a warmth of expression which might have done honour to more important subjects. 'As for Maclaurin's imitation of a *made dish*, it was a wretched attempt.' He about the same time was so much displeased with the performances of a nobleman's French cook, that he exclaimed with vehemence, 'I'd throw such a rascal into the river;' and he then proceeded to alarm a lady at whose house he was to sup, by the following manifesto of his skill: 'I, Madam, who live at a variety of good tables, am a much better judge of cookery than any person who has a very tolerable cook, but lives much at home; for his palate is gradually adapted to the taste of his cook; whereas, Madam, in trying by a wider range, I can more exquisitely judge.' When invited to dine, even with an intimate friend, he was not pleased if something better than a plain dinner was not prepared for him. I have heard him say on such an occasion, 'This was a good dinner enough, to be sure; but it was not a dinner to *ask* a man to.' On the other hand, he was wont to express, with great glee, his satisfaction when he had been entertained quite to his mind. One day when we had dined with his neighbour and landlord in Bolt-court, Mr. Allen, the printer, whose old housekeeper had studied his taste in every thing, he pronounced this eulogy: 'Sir, we could not have had a better dinner had there been a *Synod of Cooks.'*

James Boswell, *The Life of Samuel Johnson*, 1791, ed. George Birkbeck Hill (New York: Harper, n.d.), vol. I, pp. 541, 543–44.

He [T. S. Eliot] relished good food and beer and wine, but his specialty was cheese, of which he had tasted a great many varieties. I think I gained a point in his esteem because I came from a region responsible for Wensleydale, "the Mozart of cheeses". At his club the cheeseboard would be produced with great solemnity and the quality or maturity of the cheeses tested before being offered to his guests.

Sir Herbert Read, "T.S.E.—A Memoir," *T. S. Eliot: The Man and His Work*, ed. Allen Tate (New York: Delacorte Press, 1966), p. 33.

◆

I said the two best cooks I had ever known, one a Yorkshire woman, the other Irish . . . were both devout, one a Protestant, the other Catholic.

"Cooking," replied Whitehead demurely, "is one of those arts which most requires to be done by persons of religious nature."

"And a good cook," added his wife, "cooks to the glory of God."

Lucien Price, *Dialogues of Alfred North Whitehead* (Boston: Little, Brown, 1954), p. 250.

BOOKS

◆

The other day, depressed on the Underground, I tried to cheer myself by thinking over the joys of our human lot. But there wasn't one of them for which I seemed to care a button—not Wine, nor Fame, nor Friendship, nor Eating, nor Making Love, nor the Consciousness of Virtue. Was it worth while then going way up in a lift into a world that had nothing less trite to offer?

Then I thought of reading—the nice and subtle happiness of reading. This was enough, this joy not dulled by Age, this polite and unpunished vice, this selfish, serene, life-long intoxication.

Logan Pearsall Smith, "Consolation," *Trivia*, 1902, Book II, reprinted in *All Trivia* (New York: Harcourt, 1934), p. 74.

Were I forced to make a choice between books and pictures in my home, without any hesitation I would say, "Give me the books".

This is no sudden decision, but a well-considered one. I could, if I had to, live without pictures, but without a book I might exist—but not live in the full sense of the word. . . .

Without books I am lost. Never do I go to bed without a book or something to read. My house is over-full of books; they get in the way. Bookshelves are filled, and smaller volumes lay in piles on the same shelves, hiding those behind them, and I give up seeking in despair. Yet, what can be done? . . . For thirty years this old house has sheltered me, and I like it as it is. I get rid of books which I do not want to read again; and I buy more. What is more pleasant on a winter night than undoing a parcel of secondhand books and going through them, looking at this one and that—finally settling down to something interesting—Lord Malmesbury's Memoirs, for instance? Long ago, and living alone, many evenings were spent in this way—the dog on the opposite chair—books scattered on the hearth-rug between us.

Sir Alfred Munnings, *The Finish* (London: Museum Press, 1952), p. 312.

———————◆———————

The greatest happiness which can happen to any one is to cultivate a love of reading. . . . I read four books at a time; some classical book perhaps on Monday, Wednesday, and Friday mornings. The "History of France," we will say, on the evenings of the same days. On Tuesday, Thursday, and Saturday, Mosheim or Lardner, and in the evening of those days, Reynolds' Lectures, or Burns' Travels. Then I have always a standing book of poetry, and a novel to read when I am in the humour to read nothing else. Then I translate some French into English one day, and re-translate it the next; so that I have seven or eight pursuits going on at the same time, and this produces the cheerfulness of diversity, and avoids that gloom which proceeds from hanging a long while over a single book. I do not recommend this as a receipt for becoming a learned man, but for becoming a cheerful one.

Sydney Smith, "A Little Moral Advice . . . ," in Stuart J. Reid, *A Sketch of the Life and Times of the Rev. Sydney Smith* (New York: Harper, 1885), pp. 113–14.

My father had left a small collection of books in a little room upstairs, to which I had access (for it adjoined my own) and which nobody else in our house ever troubled. From that blessed little room, Roderick Random, Peregrine Pickle, Humphrey Clinker, Tom Jones, the Vicar of Wakefield, Don Quixote, Gil Blas, and Robinson Crusoe, came out, a glorious host, to keep me company. They kept alive my fancy, and my hope of something beyond that place and time,—they, and the Arabian Nights, and the Tales of the Genii,—and did me no harm; for whatever harm was in some of them was not there for me; I knew nothing of it. It is astonishing to me now, how I found time, in the midst of my porings and blunderings over heavier themes, to read those books as I did. It is curious to me how I could ever have consoled myself under my small troubles (which were great troubles to me), by impersonating my favourite characters in them—as I did—and by putting Mr. and Miss Murdstone into all the bad ones—which I did too. I have been Tom Jones (a child's Tom Jones, a harmless creature) for a week together. I have sustained my own idea of Roderick Random for a month at a stretch, I verily believe. I had a greedy relish for a few volumes of Voyages and Travels—I forget what, now—that were on those shelves; and for days and days I can remember to have gone about my region of our house, armed with the centre-piece out of an old set of boot-trees— the perfect realisation of Captain Somebody, of the Royal British Navy, in danger of being beset by savages, and resolved to sell his life at a great price. The Captain never lost dignity, from having his ears boxed with the Latin Grammar. I did; but the Captain was a Captain and a hero, in despite of all the grammars of all the languages in the world, dead or alive.

This was my only and my constant comfort. When I think of it, the picture always rises in my mind, of a summer evening, the boys at play in the churchyard, and I sitting on my bed, reading as if for life.

Charles Dickens, *The Personal History of David Copperfield*, 1850 (London: Chapman, n.d.), chap. IV, p. 77.

———◆———

The *Pilgrim's Progress* is a work of pure genius. Reading this evening a passage from it, my early childhood was revived in my memory with a freshness and reality that no ordinary mind could have caused. This book is one of the few that gave me to myself. It is associated with reality. It unites me with childhood, and seems to chronicle my Identity. How I was rapt in it! How gladly did I seat myself, after the day's labours on the farm, in the chimney niche, with the tallow candle in my hand, and pore over its enchanting pages until late in the night! That book was incorporated into the very substance of my youthful being. I thought and spoke through it. It was my most efficient teacher. . . .

The book was, indeed, my dictionary. By it I learned the English tongue. The dialect in which it was written was quite analogous to that of the simple people of my native town.

I read this book many times during my early childhood. It is the first book, almost, that I remember having read. I did not possess a copy; but a cousin, living at a distance of four miles, had a splendid edition, with fine engravings . . . and often did I get it, and keep it long.

Bronson Alcott, Journal, January 8, 1839, *The Journals of Bronson Alcott*, ed. Odell Shepard (Boston: Little, Brown, 1938), p. 111.

———◆———

When only eleven years old, with three pence in my pocket—my whole fortune—I perceived, at Richmond, in a bookseller's window, a little book, marked 'Price Threepence'—Swift's *Tale of a Tub*. Its odd title excited my curiosity; I bought it in place of my supper. So impatient was I to examine it, that I got over into a field at the upper corner of Kew Gardens, and sat down to read, on the shady side of a haystack. The book was so different from anything I had read before—it was something so new to my mind, that, though I could not at all understand some parts of it, still it delighted me beyond measure, and produced, what I have always considered, a sort of birth of intellect. I read on till it was dark, without any thought of supper or bed. When I could see no longer, I put it into my pocket, and fell asleep beside the stack, till the birds awaked me in the morning; and then I started off, still reading my little book. I could relish nothing beside; I carried it about with me wherever I went, till, when about twenty years old, I lost it in a box that fell overboard in the Bay of Fundy.

William Cobbett, *Political Register*, February 19, 1820, in G. D. H. Cole, *The Life of William Cobbett* (London: Home & Van Thal, 1947), p. 17.

It was in the large leisure of his college days that he [James Russell Lowell] formed an acquaintance which ripened into intimacy with the great writers and with those secondary lights that often suit better the ordinary mood. "I was first directed to Landor's works," he says, in 1888, when introducing some letters of Landor to the readers of his own day, "by hearing how much store Emerson set by them. I grew acquainted with them fifty years ago in one of those arched alcoves in the old college library in Harvard Hall, which so pleasantly secluded without wholly isolating the student. That footsteps should pass across the mouth of his Aladdin's Cave, or even enter it in search of treasure, so far from disturbing only deepened his sense of possession. These faint rumors of the world he had left served but as a pleasant reminder that he was the privileged denizen of another beyond 'the flaming bounds of space and time.' There, with my book lying at ease and in the expansion of intimacy on the broad window-shelf, shifting my cell from north to south with the season, I made friendships, that have lasted me for life, with Dodsley's 'Old Plays,' with Cotton's 'Montaigne,' with Hakluyt's 'Voyages,' among others that were not in my father's library. It was the merest browsing, no doubt, as Johnson called it, but how delightful it was!"

Horace Elisha Scudder, *James Russell Lowell* (Boston: Houghton, 1901), vol. I, pp. 31–32.

———◆———

. . . Dominie Sampson was occupied, body and soul, in the arrangement of the late bishop's library, which had been sent from Liverpool by sea, and conveyed by thirty or forty carts from the seaport at which it was landed. Sampson's joy at beholding the ponderous contents of these chests arranged upon the floor of the large apartment, from whence he was to transfer them to the shelves, baffles all description. He grinned like an ogre, swung his arms like the sails of a windmill, shouted 'Prodigious' till the roof rung to his raptures. 'He had never,' he said, 'seen so many books together, except in the College Library;' and now his dignity and delight in being superintendent of the collection, raised him, in his own opinion, almost to the rank of the academical librarian, whom he had always regarded as the greatest and happiest man on earth. Neither were his transports diminished upon a hasty examination of the contents of these volumes. Some, indeed, of belles lettres, poems, plays, or memoirs, he tossed indignantly aside, with the implied censure of 'psha', or 'frivolous'; but the greater and bulkier part of the collection bore a very different character. . . .

Books of theology and controversial divinity, commentaries, and polyglots, sets of the Fathers, and sermons, which might each furnish forth ten brief discourses of modern date, books of science, ancient and modern, classical authors in their best and rarest forms; such formed the late bishop's venerable library, and over such the eye of Dominie Sampson gloated with rapture. He entered them in the catalogue in his best running hand, forming each letter with the accuracy of a lover writing a valentine, and placed each individually on the destined shelf with all the reverence which I have seen a lady pay to a jar of old china. With all this zeal his labours advanced slowly. He often opened a volume when half-way up the library-steps, fell upon some interesting passage, and, without shifting his inconvenient posture, continued immersed in the fascinating perusal until the servant pulled him by the skirts to assure him that dinner waited. He then repaired to the parlour, bolted his food down his capacious throat in squares of three inches, answered aye or no at random to whatever question was asked at him, and again hurried back to the library as soon as his napkin was removed, and sometimes with it hanging round his neck like a pinafore . . .

Sir Walter Scott, *Guy Mannering*, 1815 (London: Macmillan, 1905), chap. XX, pp. 181–83.

———◆———

Before dinner Dr. Johnson seized upon Mr. Charles Sheridan's *Account of the late Revolution in Sweden*, and seemed to read it ravenously, as if he devoured it, which was to all appearance his method of studying. 'He knows how to read better than any one (said Mrs. Knowles;) he gets at the substance of a book directly; he tears out the heart of it.' He kept it wrapt up in the tablecloth in his lap during the time of dinner, from an avidity to have one entertainment in readiness when he should have finished another; resembling (if I may use so coarse a simile) a dog who holds a bone in his paws in reserve, while he eats something else which has been thrown to him.

James Boswell, *The Life of Samuel Johnson*, 1791, ed. George Birkbeck Hill (New York: Harper, n.d.), vol. III, p. 323.

The only exercise in which he can be said to have excelled was that of threading crowded streets with his eyes fixed upon a book. He might be seen in such thoroughfares as Oxford Street and Cheapside walking as fast as other people walked, and reading a great deal faster than any body else could read.

G. Otto Trevelyan, *The Life and Letters of Lord Macaulay* (New York: Harper, 1876), vol. I, p. 118.

———◆———

. . . I can, and do, see him [Dr. William Osler] perfectly as he came up to my room on the third floor of 1351 St. Catherine Street [Montreal], the second or third night after I moved in. I happened to be sitting up in bed reading at physiology. He broke out at once in praise of the habit of reading in bed, but heartily disapproved the physiology—only literature, never medicine. He walked across the room standing with his back to me, his hands in his trousers' pockets, tilting up and down on his toes, and inspecting the little collection of about twenty or thirty books I had ranged on two small hanging shelves; and taking down the 'Golden Treasury' came over, sat on the foot of the bed, and half-recited, half-read, interjecting a running comment, a number of the poems. Then tossing the book to me he said: 'You'll find that much better stuff than physiology for reading in bed.' That same evening, too, he spoke of Sir Thomas Browne and the 'Religio', and probably for the first time, for I don't remember his making any reference to the subject in the lectures at the college. His enthusiasm rose as he spoke, and running downstairs he brought up his copy, pointed out and read several passages and then left me.

Henry V. Ogden, reminiscences of Sir William Osler in 1879, in Harvey Cushing, *The Life of Sir William Osler* (London: Oxford, 1925), vol. I, p. 176.

———◆———

I know men who say they had as lief read any book in a library copy as in one from their own shelf. To me that is unintelligible. For one thing, I know every book of mine by its *scent*, and I have but to put my nose between the pages to be reminded of all sorts of things. My Gibbon, for example, my well-bound eight-volume Milman edition, which I have read and read and read again for more than thirty years— never do I open it but the scent of the noble page restores to me all the exultant happiness of that moment when I received it as a prize. Or my Shakespeare, the Great Cambridge Shakespeare—it has an odour which carries me yet further back in life; for these volumes belonged to my father, and before I was old enough to read them with understanding, it was often permitted me, as a treat, to take down one of them from the bookcase, and reverently to turn the leaves. The volumes smell exactly as they did in that old time, and what a strange tenderness comes upon me when I hold one of them in hand.

George Gissing, *The Private Papers of Henry Ryecroft,* 1903 (New York: Boni & Liveright, 1918), chap. XII, pp. 29–30.

I hate to read new books. There are twenty or thirty volumes that I have read over and over again, and these are the only ones that I have any desire ever to read at all. . . . I do not think altogether the worse of a book for having survived the author a generation or two. I have more confidence in the dead than the living. Contemporary writers may generally be divided into two classes—one's friends or one's foes. Of the first we are compelled to think too well, and of the last we are disposed to think too ill, to receive much genuine pleasure from the perusal, or to judge fairly of the merits of either. . . . But the dust and smoke and noise of modern literature have nothing in common with the pure, silent air of immortality.

When I take up a work that I have read before (the oftener the better), I know what I have to expect. The satisfaction is not lessened by being anticipated. When the entertainment is altogether new, I sit down to it as I should to a strange dish—turn and pick out a bit here and there, and am in doubt what to think of the composition. There is a want of confidence and security to second appetite. New-fangled books are also like made-dishes in this respect, that they are generally little else than hashes and *rifaccimenti* of what has been served up entire and in a more natural state at other times. Besides, in thus turning to a well-known author, there is not only an assurance that my time will not be thrown away, or my palate nauseated with the most insipid or vilest trash, but I shake hands with, and look an old, tried, and valued friend in the face, compare notes, and chat the hours away. It is true, we form dear friendships with such ideal guests—dearer, alas! and more lasting, than those with our most intimate acquaintance. In reading a book which is an old favourite with me (say the first novel I ever read) I not only have the pleasure of imagination and of a critical relish of the work, but the pleasures of memory added to it. It recalls the same feelings and associations which I had in first reading it, and which I can never have again in any other way. Standard productions of this kind are links in the chain of our conscious being. They bind together the different scattered divisions of our personal identity. They are landmarks and guides in our journey through life.

William Hazlitt, "On Reading Old Books," *London Magazine*, February 1821, in *Essays of William Hazlitt*, ed. Frank Carr (London: Scott, n.d.), pp. 150–52.

Beside the waters of oblivion there is a fair place where storied silence breaks only to half-heard, familiar, but always new and strange communions. It is a sound heard almost without hearing, like the lisping of lake-waves or the remonstrance of some coy stream at the overtures of the young wind when the morning or the evening stars sing together. It is the sound of all sounds the most companionable: it is the whispering of the pages of books. You, if it be really you, have heard it in the quietness of your room, and you have been comforted, or, maybe, in the wizard silence of the Bodleian, where it has gone up to the painted beams as incense, incense of sound, the book-homage of ages to the God of the Printed Word who is so much mightier than the God of Battles—unless they be battles of books. Most pleasant and most comfortable of sounds, recalling the happy bookman from his eternity of words to the time that passeth, without requiring his attendance upon temporal affairs.

Holbrook Jackson, "Bookmen," *Occasions* (London: Grant Richards, 1922), p. 170.

MUSIC

After a good concert. First, no matter how good it has been, I am glad it is over and that I need no longer keep still and quiet but can move about, talk, laugh, smoke, and perhaps eat and drink. But the music has done something to me. I feel refreshed inside, loosened up and easy, no longer an angry dwarf but a careless smiling giant. The night looks better than it did when I hurried into the concert hall. It too is larger and looser, and holds more promise in its glitter and distances. I like the look of people, perhaps for the first time that day. Strangers seem pleasant acquaintances; acquaintances turn into friends; and friends now seem well-tried, old and dear. This is the hour, I feel, to give and receive confidences, confessions of the soul. Somehow the world outside the hall seems to reflect the noble patterns of sound. Still held aloft on the shoulders of Bach and Mozart, Beethoven and Brahms, I can take a longer view, a broader outlook, and can believe that the good life is not yet a lost dream. Ten minutes wait for a taxi—and the mood will be gone; but while it lasted and the green sap seemed to be rising in the Tree of Life—what delight!

J. B. Priestley, *Delight* (London: Heinemann, 1949), pp. 226-27.

The concert restored my moral health. I came away in love with people I was hating before and full of compassion for others I usually contemn. A feeling of immeasurable well being—a jolly bonhomie enveloped me like incandescent light. At the close when we stood up to sing the National Anthem we all felt a genuine spirit of camaraderie. Just as when Kings die, we were silent musing upon the common fate, and when the time came to separate we were loath to go our several ways, for we were comrades who together had come thro' a great experience.

W. N. P. Barbellion, Journal, June 29, 1914, *The Journal of a Disappointed Man* (London: Chatto, 1919), p. 128.

Feb. 11, '80.–At a good concert to-night in the foyer of the opera house, Philadelphia—the band a small but first-rate one. Never did music more sink into and soothe and fill me—never so prove its soul-rousing power, its impossibility of statement. Especially in the rendering of one of Beethoven's master septettes by the well-chosen and perfectly-combined instruments (violins, viola, clarionet, horn, 'cello and contra-bass,) was I carried away, seeing, absorbing many wonders. Dainty abandon, sometimes as if Nature laughing on a hillside in the sunshine; serious and firm monotonies, as of winds; a horn sounding through the tangle of the forest, and the dying echoes; soothing floating of waves, but presently rising in surges, angrily lashing, muttering, heavy; piercing peals of laughter, for interstices; now and then weird, as Nature herself is in certain moods—but mainly spontaneous, easy, careless—often the sentiment of the postures of naked children playing or sleeping. It did me good even to watch the violinists drawing their bows so masterly—every motion a study. I allow'd myself, as I sometimes do, to wander out of myself. The conceit came to me of a copious grove of singing birds, and in their midst a simple harmonic duo, two human souls, steadily asserting their own pensiveness, joyousness.

Walt Whitman, *Specimen Days*, 1882, reprinted in Walt Whitman, *Prose Works* (Philadelphia: McKay, n.d.), p. 158.

———◆———

A part of Lord Harrington's new raised corps have taken up their quarters at Olney . . . They have the regimental music with them. The men have been drawn up this morning upon the Market-hill, and a concert, such as we have not heard these many years, has been performed at no great distance from our window. Your mother and I both thrust our heads into the coldest east wind that ever blew in April, that we might hear them to greater advantage. The band acquitted themselves with taste and propriety, not *blairing,* like trumpeters at a fair, but producing gentle and elegant symphony, such as charmed our ears, and convinced us that no length of time can wear out a taste for harmony; and that though plays, balls, and masquerades have lost all their power to please us, and we should find them not only insipid but insupportable, yet sweet music is sure to find a corresponding faculty in the soul, a sensibility that lives to the last, which even religion itself does not extinguish.

William Cowper, letter to Rev. William Unwin, April 27, 1782, *The Works of William Cowper,* 2d ed., ed. John S. Memes (Edinburgh: Fraser, 1835), vol. I, p. 142.

About 11 I home, it being a fine moonshine and so my wife and Mercer come into the garden, and, my business being done, we sang till about twelve at night, with mighty pleasure to ourselves and neighbours, by their casements opening, and so home to supper and to bed.

Samuel Pepys, Diary, May 5, 1666, *The Diary of Samuel Pepys*, ed. Henry B. Wheatley (London: Bell, 1924), vol. V, p. 268.

◆

I hear little music but what I make myself or help to make with the Parson's son and daughter. We, with not a voice among us, go through Handel's Coronation Anthems! Laughable it may seem; yet it is not quite so; the things are so well-defined, simple, and grand, that the faintest outline of them tells; my admiration of the old Giant grows and grows: his is the Music for a Great, Active People. Sometimes too, I go over to a place elegantly called *Bungay*, where a Printer lives who drills the young folks of a manufactory there to sing in Chorus once a week. . . . They sing some of the English Madrigals, some of Purcell, and some of Handel, in a way to satisfy me, who don't want perfection, and who believe that the *grandest* things do not depend on delicate finish. If you were here now, we would go over and hear the Harmonious Blacksmith sung in Chorus, with words, of course. It almost made me cry when I heard the divine Air rolled into vocal harmony from the four corners of a large Hall. One can scarce comprehend the Beauty of the English Madrigals till one hears them done (though coarsely) in this way and on a large scale: the play of the parts as they alternate from the different quarters of the room. . . .

I have written enough for one night: I am now going to sit down and play one of Handel's Overtures as well as I can—Semele, perhaps, a very grand one—then, lighting my lantern, trudge through the mud to Parson Crabbe's.

Edward Fitzgerald, letter to F. Tennyson, December 31, 1850, *Letters of Edward Fitzgerald* (London: Macmillan, 1901), vol. I, p. 265.

◆

But though French soldiers show to ill-advantage on parade, on the march they are gay, alert, and willing, like a troop of fox-hunters. I remember once seeing a company pass through the forest of *Fontainebleau*, on the *Chailly* road, between the *Bas Bréau* and the *Reine*

Blanche. One fellow walked a little before the rest, and sang a loud, audacious marching song. The rest bestirred their feet, and even swung their muskets in time. A young officer on horseback had hard ado to keep his countenance at the words. You never saw anything so cheerful and spontaneous as their gait; school-boys do not look more eagerly at hare and hounds; and you would have thought it impossible to tire such willing marchers.

Robert Louis Stevenson, *An Inland Voyage,* 1878 (New York: Scribner, 1900), chap. XVII, p. 105.

◆

It is well for me that I cannot hear music when I will; assuredly I should not have such intense pleasure as comes to me now and then by haphazard. . . . It happened at times—not in my barest days, but in those of decent poverty—that some one in the house where I lodged played the piano—and how it rejoiced me when this came to pass! I say "played the piano"—a phrase that covers much. For my own part, I was very tolerant; anything that could, by the largest interpretation, be called music, I welcomed and was thankful for; even "five-finger exercises" I found, at moments, better than nothing. For it was when I was labouring at my desk that the notes of the instrument were grateful and helpful to me. Some men, I believe, would have been driven frantic under the circumstances; to me, anything like a musical sound always came as a godsend; it tuned my thoughts; it made the words flow. Even the street organs put me in a happy mood; I owe many a page to them —written when I should else have been sunk in bilious gloom.

More than once, too, when I was walking London streets by night, penniless and miserable, music from an open window has stayed my step. . . .

George Gissing, *The Private Papers of Henry Ryecroft,* 1903 (New York: Boni & Liveright, 1918), chap. XXVI, pp. 126–27.

◆

In former years Raoul Pugno, Bizet, Massenet, men whom he admired and cherished, and during the later years Hahn, were real enchanters for him. The melodies by his "little Hahn" which he caused to be played three times in succession—Hahn, so precocious in genius, so learned and so free from pettiness, so lucid and gently sensual—

positively put him in an ecstasy. Seated in his big armchair he half closed his eyes while his nervous hand clasped the knob of his cane; his half-opened lips seemed to drink in the sound.

Léon Daudet, *Alphonse Daudet* (Boston: Little, Brown, 1898), p. 60.

———◆———

After the war was over—and the San Francisco conference and a few other aftermaths—I settled myself into a farmhouse in Vermont for half of every year and all of some years. . . .

And these years of approximate although intermittent tranquillity happened also to be the ones in which the gramophone, or phonograph (and I do not know the difference), went through so many transformations, as a result of technological advances . . .

What it amounts to is this: the recording devices preserve, perpetuate and disseminate what we might like to hear in a living form, but know we cannot. One would have to go to every concert given in New York for twenty or thirty years, indefatigably, day after day and night after night, to hear even a sizable part of the music I can hear at will on the machine in my sitting room in Vermont. The enormous repertoire and the variant performances, the freedom of choice, the suiting of music to mood, the ability to draw on resources no longer available in public halls, the access to work which is rarely or never heard in the concert hall—all these things enormously enlarge the boundaries of a small room so that it can come at times to be as large as the earth itself. And to hear it *absolutely* alone and unobserved (so that you can conduct it yourself if you will, or follow it with a score or simply yield to it) is a rare and special form of living through music. When I am told that Oswald Spengler spent his last years in Munich, after *The Decline of the West* had more or less faded into the past for him, playing Beethoven records to himself alone, I do believe that I understand how and why. . . .

A twisted old tree in the back yard of that Vermont house catches the moon in its branches—leafy in summer, bare in autumn—when it is warm enough to sit in the doorway at the back and look at it. The machine at the other end of the odd-shaped room plays with great smoothness an uncomplaining continuity of music for as long as you wish. On those warm evenings I have often sat in the back door and watched the moon in the tree . . . while sounds of rare magic fill the air. An entire work, the lifeblood of a master spirit, may be played out upon the warm evening before the moon is released from the branches and sails off to illumine a wider darkness. I know of no better box at such times.

Vincent Sheean, *First and Last Love* (New York: Random House, 1956), pp. 274, 276–77, 289.

When alone listening to the radio or recorded music, I never read, but abandon myself to the sonority, to the rhythm, the cadences, and to the wisps of feeling and reflection and reminiscence, evoked or liberated by the music. For me music is a realm of being, and like art primarily to be enjoyed and absorbed, not to be scalpelled, anatomized, cross-questioned inquisitorially.

Bernard Berenson, Diary, September 24, 1956, in Bernard Berenson, *Sunset and Twilight*, ed. Nicky Mariano (New York: Harcourt, 1963), p. 450.

For there is a music wherever there is a harmony, order, or proportion; and thus far we may maintain the music of the spheres; for those well-ordered motions, and regular paces, though they give no sound unto the ear, yet to the understanding they strike a note most full of harmony. Whosoever is harmonically composed delights in harmony; which makes me much distrust the symmetry of those heads which declaim against all church-music. For myself, not only from my obedience, but my paticular genius, I do embrace it: for even that vulgar and tavern-music, which makes one man merry, another mad, strikes in me a deep fit of devotion, and a profound contemplation of the first composer. There is something in it of divinity more than the ear discovers: it is an hieroglyphical and shadowed lesson of the whole world, and creatures of God; such a melody to the ear, as the whole world well understood, would afford the understanding. In brief, it is a sensible fit of that harmony, which intellectually sounds in the ears of God. I will not say with Plato, the soul is a harmony, but harmonical, and has its nearest sympathy unto music. . . .

Sir Thomas Browne, *Religio Medici*, 1642 (London: Washbourne, 1841), pt. II, pp. 133–34.

I am no musician, and want a good ear, and yet I am conscious of a power in music which I want words to describe. It touches chords, reaches depths in the soul, which lie beyond all other influences—extends my consciousness, and has sometimes given me a pleasure which I may have found in nothing else. Nothing in my experience is more mysterious, more inexplicable. An instinct has always led men to transfer it to heaven, and I suspect the Christian, under its power, has often attained to a singular consciousness of his immortality. Facts of this nature make me feel what an infinite mystery our nature is, and how little our books of science reveal it to us.

William Ellery Channing, letter to J. Blanco White, July 21, 1840, in William Henry Channing, *Memoir of William Ellery Channing* (London: Routledge, n.d.), vol. II, p. 442.

◆

. . . the most remarkable musical experiences of my life happened by accident: one was pagan and the other was Christian. The first happened in Russia . . . it was a glimpse I had on an August evening in Central Russia of a procession of women who had come back from harvesting. They were walking against the skyline, and carrying their scythes and their wooden rakes with them, like the figures in a Greek frieze. As they marched past, they sang: first a solo chanted the phrase, and then the chorus took it up, and then solo and chorus became one, and reached a climax, and died away. It was a wonderful tune; a tune that opened its arms. It had not the usual sad wail that is peculiar to Russian singing; nothing of the unsatisfied yearning and restless questioning, for ever never ending on the dominant: on the contrary, what they sang was a hymn of peace and content and thanksgiving, that satisfied the soul. This sight and this sound seemed to tear away the veil of centuries and to take one back as far as ancient Rome and Greece, and further: further than Virgil and Romulus, further than the mysteries of Eleusis, further than Homer: right back to the Golden Age and the "large utterance of the early Gods."

The second instance happened in Paris during the week of the Epiphany in I forget what year

I strolled one evening into a dark little church. The church was empty, and the organist was playing by himself on an old-fashioned organ that sounded like the piped hurdy-gurdies of the beginning of the nineteenth century. He was playing fluted carols with tinkling runs and bell-like notes and soft lullaby, which had a freshness, a homeliness, a smiling tunefulness, an ineffable radiance and sweetness such as I have never heard before or since. And in that little dark church I felt the wise Kings from the East and the Shepherds of Bethlehem were at prayer, and that the Hosts of Heaven themselves had for the moment ceased to sing "Glory to God in the Highest" to listen to the playing of that organist: for God had come down to earth.

Maurice Baring, "Music," *Lost Lectures* (New York: Knopf, 1932), pp. 206–7.

GARDENS

◆

God Almighty first planted a garden; and, indeed, it is the purest of human pleasures. It is the greatest refreshment to the spirits of man . . .

Sir Francis Bacon, "Of Gardens," *Essays,* 1625 (New York: Macmillan, 1931), essay XLVI, p. 158.

◆

I know no means of calming the fret and perturbation into which too much sitting, too much talking, brings me, so perfect as labor. I have no animal spirits; therefore, when surprised by company and kept in a chair for many hours, my heart sinks, my brow is clouded and I think I will run for Acton woods, and live with the squirrels henceforward. But my garden is nearer, and my good hoe, as it bites the ground, revenges my wrongs, and I have less lust to bite my enemies. I confess I work at first with a little venom, lay to a little unnecessary strength. But by smoothing the rough hillocks, I smooth my temper; by extracting the long roots of the piper-grass, I draw out my own splinters; and in a short time I can hear the bobolink's song and see the blessed deluge of light and colour that rolls around me.

Ralph Waldo Emerson, Journal, June 12, 1839, *The Heart of Emerson's Journals*, ed. Bliss Perry (Boston: Houghton, 1926), p. 143.

A cure for sleeplessness. If you find that after the worries and excitements of a busy day, say after winding up a debate in Parliament at midnight, you are too excited to sleep when you reach your bed, if then counting sheep passing through a gate proves, as with me, of no avail and you share my incapacity for thinking of nothing, visit your rock garden in imagination. I have put myself to sleep night after night in this way before my head had been five minutes on the pillow or I had covered six paces of my small garden.

Sir Austen Chamberlain, *Down the Years* (London: Cassell, 1935), pp. 305–6.

———◆———

We found Matisse living in a small house, with a magnificent, sweeping view beyond his vegetable garden. In one room there was a cage with a lot of fluttering birds. The place was covered with paintings, most of them obviously new ones. I marveled at his production and I asked him, "What is your inspiration?"

"I grow artichokes," he said. His eyes smiled at my surprise and he went on to explain: "Every morning I go into the garden and watch these plants. I see the play of light and shade on the leaves and I discover new combinations of colors and fantastic patterns. I study them. They inspire me. Then I go back into the studio and paint."

This struck me forcefully. Here was perhaps the world's most celebrated living painter. He was approaching eighty and I would have thought that he had seen every combination of light and shade imaginable. Yet every day he got fresh inspiration from the sunlight on an artichoke; it seemed to charge the delicate dynamo of his genius with an effervescent energy almost inexhaustible.

André Kostelanetz, "Matisse and the Music of Discontent," *This I Believe*, ed. Edward P. Morgan (New York: Simon & Schuster, 1952), p. 91.

———◆———

Though he [Charles Darwin] took no personal share in the management of the garden, he had great delight in the beauty of flowers—for instance, in the mass of Azaleas which generally stood in the drawing-room. I think he sometimes fused together his admiration of the structure of a flower and of its intrinsic beauty; for instance, in the case of the big pendulous pink and white flowers of Dielytra. In the same way he had an affection, half-artistic, half-botanical, for the little blue Lobelia. In admiring flowers, he would laugh at the dingy high-art colours, and contrast them with the bright tints of nature. I used to like to hear him admire the beauty of a flower; it was a kind of gratitude to the flower itself, and a personal love for its delicate form and colour. I seem to remember him gently touching a flower he delighted in; it was the same simple admiration that a child might have.

Francis Darwin, reminiscences of his father, Charles Darwin, in *The Life and Letters of Charles Darwin*, ed. Francis Darwin (New York: Appleton, 1898), vol. I, pp. 94–95.

———◆———

How often I admire the taste shown in the garden which, within the house, may be indifferent. Here is an art which is to-day probably more perfect than at any previous time, one which does not break with the past, while it brings a sense of comely order, and a radiant beauty, to cottage and manor alike.

William Rothenstein, *Since Fifty: Men and Memories, 1922–1938* (London: Faber, 1939), p. 171.

———◆———

If the regular City man, who leaves Lloyd's at five o'clock, and drives home to Hackney, Clapton, Stamford Hill, or elsewhere, can be said to have any daily recreation beyond his dinner, it is his garden. He never does anything to it with his own hands; but he takes great pride in it notwithstanding . . . He always takes a walk round it, before he starts for town in the morning, and is particularly anxious that the fish-pond should be kept specially neat. . . .

There is another and a very different class of men, whose recreation is their garden. An individual of this class resides some short distance from town—say in the Hampstead Road, or the Kilburn Road, or any other road where the houses are small and neat, and have little slips of back garden. He and his wife—who is as clean and compact a little body as himself—have occupied the same house ever since he retired from business twenty years ago. They have no family. They once had a son, who died at about five years old. The child's portrait hangs over the mantel-piece in the best sitting-room, and a little cart he used to draw about is carefully preserved as a relic.

In fine weather the old gentleman is almost constantly in the garden;

and when it is too wet to go into it, he will look out of the window at it, by the hour together. He has always something to do there, and you will see him digging, and sweeping, and cutting, and planting, with manifest delight. In spring-time, there is no end to the sowing of seeds, and sticking little bits of wood over them, with labels, which look like epitaphs to their memory; and in the evening, when the sun has gone down, the perserverance with which he lugs a great watering-pot about is perfectly astonishing. The only other recreation he has is the newspaper, which he peruses every day, from beginning to end, generally reading the most interesting pieces of intelligence to his wife during breakfast. The old lady is very fond of flowers, as the hyacinth-glasses in the parlour-window, and geranium-pots in the little front court, testify. She takes great pride in the garden too: and when one of the four fruit-trees produces rather a larger gooseberry than usual, it is carefully preserved under a wine-glass on the sideboard, for the edification of visitors, who are duly informed that Mr. So-and-so planted the tree which produced it, with his own hands. On a summer's evening, when the large watering-pot has been filled and emptied some fourteen times, and the old couple have quite exhausted themselves by trotting about, you will see them sitting happily together in the little summer-house, enjoying the calm and peace of the twilight, and watching the shadows as they fall upon the garden. . . . These are their only recreations, and they require no more. They have within themselves the materials of comfort and content . . .

Charles Dickens, "London Recreations," *Sketches, by Boz,* 1836, chap. IX, (London: Chapman, n.d.), pp. 122–24.

◆

. . . what enthusiasts or slaves must these evening gardeners be. You see them best by train, by any train that runs on a high embankment out of a metropolis, somewhere around seven o'clock. You look down on miles and miles of narrow gardens, all with the open back-door of a house at one end and a summer-house or odd-job hut at the other. You look down on strips of green grass, earth beds, rubble paths, odd rose trees, a clothes line, a radio aerial, a garden ornament, or a rustic bench. Some of these gardens are pathetic, some heroic. One owner commands his domain from a tiny terrace, another hides in a bower of roses, and the Taj Mahal seems to have inspired the ambitious waterpiece of 'Sunnymede.'

But whatever it is one looks down upon at this hour, little Kew, or cramped Chatsworth, or pseudo-Sandringham, there in the middle, as likely as not in his shirt-sleeves, will be seen the cheerful prisoner, stooping, reaching, pulling, or merely grovelling. He has been at the office from nine till six, he has gobbled a high tea, and rushed into the garden, hoping it won't get dark too soon. For miles on miles this is the vista. A nation of shop-keepers? What nonsense! A nation of gardeners, without doubt.

Cecil Roberts, *Gone Rambling* (London: Hodder, 1935), p. 133.

A Garden is a lovesome thing but, Got wot, one does need a seat in it. My predecessor bequeathed to me everything that a cottage garden should have, from raspberry canes to a clothes-line, save only a plank where in the cool of the evening I might sit and contemplate and grow.

Then on the day of the expedition to the Windrush, as we drove through the village of Marcham, a few miles west of Abingdon, I noticed a timber yard with a profusion of newly cut boards stacked for seasoning, trees sliced and sliced again from end to end and the slivers piled alternately with transverse battens to let the air pass through. The edges were untrimmed, their outlines with the bark still on were as the trees had grown.

'Just what I need for a garden seat,' I said.

'All sorts of timbers in there,' said Dick Gower. 'Pointer is the name —he'll cut you anything you want.'

So next day I visited Mr Pointer. 'Elm is what you need,' he said. 'Unless you prefer teak. It lasts longer.'

'Elm will see out my time?' I queried.

He checked a ready agreement. 'I wish you a long life,' he said, 'but I think it will.' . . .

The choice of the timber that I needed was not difficult: a board about seven feet long and eighteen inches wide for the seat; another of the same length for the back; and then two shorter and thicker pieces for the sides.

'That seat won't blow out of your garden,' said Mr Pointer as we roped the boards to the car.

When I inquired the price of what I had bought, Bill, a son of the house, did some complicated sums with his finger in the timber dust that lay on a saw table and calculated a price that would have seemed cheap for a gross of matchsticks.

The making of the seat was elementary. Two rectangular slots cut in each of the sides to take the tongued ends of the seat and back, and the tongues bored to take a peg, and the job was finished save for the smoothing of an edge that might have been dangerous to nylons and the rounding of a few corners.

And then I sat back and the scent of new-sawn timber mingled with the scent of new-mown lawn. A thrush was singing from the pear-tree, two goldfinches were searching among the tulips, a sulphur yellow butterfly flittered past, and behold it was very good.

Robert Gibbings, *Till I End My Song* (London: Dent, 1957), pp. 120, 122–23.

FIRESIDE

In his boyhood he had often thought that nothing could be better than the life of a country minister 'in some place where the winters were long and snowy, and a man was forced to spend much of his days and all his evenings in a fire-lit library.'

Charles Dick, reminiscences of John Buchan, in *John Buchan, by his Wife and Friends* (London: Hodder, 1947), p. 124.

How often, on a December afternoon, when outside the red glow of sunset sinks behind the iron woods, and the ground mists rise, have I entered the old cottage, and, before the blinds are drawn, or the room is lit, have I paused to watch the play of rosy light on walls and ceiling. It flickers under the old rafters, and draws new colours from rugs and cushions. Now of all times can one indulge in reverie before that ruddy glow, a pleasure scarcer and scarcer in these hurried days. The comfortable old arm-chair, the feet on the fender, a cat, if you will, coiled up on a cushion, and a brass kettle singing on the bar, with a glint of light falling on bellows, toasting-fork, and chestnut-roaster—spoils of visits to the antique shops—these are the symbols of home, and induce that pleasant melancholy of the reminiscent mind. You cannot, however you try, catch the same spirit before an electric stove or a gas-fire; and a room with only radiator-heating is a room without a soul. And when to an open coal-fire one can add the blazing log, with its bright crackle and swift glow, then human comfort seems complete. . . .

In the country, with houses so scattered, the individual chimney is incapable of doing any damage either to nature or society. The friendly smoke curling up from my chimney into the bright air rather enhances than detracts from the scene. Wherefore I pile on the logs, stir up the coals, and watch the blaze without any misgivings. Similarly the chimney of my neighbour down the lane is a signal, not of offence, but of good cheer, for whenever I see an increased volume rising from his slightly tilted old chimney I have a vision of him sitting by his hearth in warm content, what time the gale roars through the beechwoods above and the leaves do a dance of death in the garden.

Cecil Roberts, *Gone Rambling* (London: Hodder, 1935), pp. 147–49.

—◆—

But twilight comes; and the lover of the fireside, for the perfection of the moment, is now alone. He was reading a minute or two ago, and for some time was unconscious of the increasing dusk till, on looking up, he perceived the objects out of doors deepening into massy outline, while the sides of his fireplace began to reflect the light of the flames, and the shadow of himself and his chair fidgeted with huge obscurity on the wall. Still wishing to read, he pushed himself nearer and nearer to the window, and continued fixed on his book, till he happened to take another glance out of doors, and on returning to it could make out nothing. He therefore lays it aside, and restoring his chair to the fireplace, seats himself right before it in a reclining posture, his feet apart upon the fender, his eyes bent down towards the grate, his arms on the chair's elbows, one hand hanging down, and the palm of the other turned up and presented to the fire—not to keep it from him, for there is no glare or scorch about it—but to intercept, and have a more kindly feel of its genial warmth. It is thus that the greatest and wisest of mankind have sat and meditated. . . .

The evening is beginning to gather in. The window, which represents a large face of watery grey, intersected by strong lines, is perceptibly becoming darker, and as that becomes darker the fire assumes a more glowing presence. The contemplatist keeps his easy posture, absorbed in his fancies, and everything around him is still and serene. . . . At length the darker objects in the room become mingled: the gleam of the fire strikes with a restless light the edges of the furniture, and reflects itself in the blackening window; while his feet take a gentle move on the fender, and then settle again . . . This is the only time, perhaps, at which sheer idleness is salutary and refreshing.

Leigh Hunt, "A Day by the Fire," *The Reflector*, 1812, reprinted in *Leigh Hunt as Poet and Essayist*, ed. Charles Kent (London: Warne, n.d.), pp. 87–88.

———◆———

When they all tired of blind-man's buff, there was a great game at snap-dragon, and when fingers enough were burned with that, and all the raisins were gone, they sat down by the huge fire of blazing logs to a substantial supper, and a mighty bowl of wassail, something smaller than an ordinary wash-house copper, in which the hot apples were hissing and bubbling with a rich look, and a jolly sound, that were perfectly irresistible.

'This,' said Mr. Pickwick, looking round him, 'this is, indeed, comfort.'

'Our invariable custom,' replied Mr. Wardle. 'Everybody sit down with us on Christmas Eve, as you see them now—servants and all; and here we wait, until the clock strikes twelve, to usher Christmas in, and beguile the time with forfeits and old stories. Trundle, my boy, rake up the fire.'

Up flew the bright sparks in myriads as the logs were stirred. The deep red blaze sent forth a rich glow, that penetrated into the farthest corner of the room, and cast its cheerful tint on every face.

Charles Dickens, *The Posthumous Papers of the Pickwick Club*, 1837 (London: Collins, 1953), chap. XXVIII, p. 397.

———◆———

I remember once talking to a great Arctic explorer. It was a day of piercing cold—what we in London call piercing cold—and there was a glorious and tremendous fire on the hearth. Before this fire the great man stood, displayed, as I think the heralds say, in his enjoyment of the light, of the glow, of the crackling coals, and the genial heat. His face beamed like the blaze behind it, brightened like the light of the flames that danced on the dull walls. "You know," said he, "that nobody who has not been up to his waist in the freezing slush of the Arctic can enjoy a fire like this."

Arthur Machen, "Where Are the Fogs of Yesteryear?" *Dog and Duck* (New York: Knopf, 1924), pp. 90–91.

We struggled with the wind, and often rested as we went along. A hail shower met us before we reached the Tarn, and the way often was difficult over the snow; but at the Tarn the view closed in. We saw nothing but mists and snow: and at first the ice on the Tarn below us cracked and split, yet without water, a dull grey white. We lost our path, and could see the Tarn no longer. We made our way out with difficulty, guided by a heap of stones which we well remembered. We were afraid of being bewildered in the mists, till the darkness should overtake us. We were long before we knew that we were in the right track, but thanks to William's skill we knew it long before we could see our way before us. There was no footmark upon the snow either of man or beast. . . . The Vale of Grasmere, when the mists broke away, looked soft and grave, of a yellow hue. It was dark before we reached home. . . . My inside was sore with the cold . . . O how comfortable and happy we felt ourselves, sitting by our own fire, when we had got off our wet clothes and had dressed ourselves fresh and clean.

Dorothy Wordsworth, Grasmere Journal, January 23, 1802, *Journals of Dorothy Wordsworth*, ed. E. de Selincourt (London: Macmillan, 1941), vol. I, p. 101.

WALKING

———◆———

One of the pleasantest things in the world is going a journey; but I like to go by myself. I can enjoy society in a room; but out of doors, nature is company enough for me. I am never less alone than when alone.

"The fields his study, nature was his book."

I cannot see the wit of walking and talking at the same time. When I am in the country, I wish to vegetate like the country. I am not for criticising hedge-rows and black cattle. I go out of town in order to forget the town and all that is in it. . . . The soul of a journey is liberty, perfect liberty, to think, feel, do, just as one pleases. We go a journey chiefly to be free of all impediments and of all inconveniences; to leave ourselves behind, much more to get rid of others. . . . Give me the clear blue sky over my head, and the green turf beneath my feet, a winding road before me, and a three hours' march to dinner—and then to thinking! It is hard if I cannot start some game on these lone heaths. I laugh, I run, I leap, I sing for joy. From the point of yonder rolling cloud, I plunge into my past being, and revel there, as the sun-burnt Indian plunges headlong into the wave that wafts him to his native shore. Then long-forgotten things, like "sunken wrack and sumless treasuries," burst upon my eager sight, and I begin to feel, think, and be myself again. Instead of an awkward silence, broken by attempts at wit or dull common-places, mine is that undisturbed silence of the heart which alone is perfect eloquence. . . . Is not this wild rose sweet without a comment? Does not this daisy leap to my heart set in its coat of emerald? Yet if I were to explain to you the circumstance that has so endeared it to me, you would only smile. . . . I want to see my vague notions float like the down of the thistle before the breeze, and not to have them entangled in the briars and thorns of controversy. For once, I like to have it all my own way; and this is impossible unless you are alone . . .

William Hazlitt, *Table Talk*, 1822 (London: Bell, 1889), chap. XIX, pp. 249–51.

. . . for him the most satisfying days were when he wandered far afield alone, retreading forgotten footpaths and hidden lanes, stopping at remote and primitive inns where strangers were rare. This of all his pleasures was the deepest and the most comprehensive. For to Edward Thomas walking was not merely exercise, though he swung along with a long slow stride—a tall, slim, powerful figure: striking, too, with his fine head and uncovered hair bleached by the wind and rain and sun. Nor was he as he walked only the nature lover intent on observing birds and flowers and clouds and all the life of the hedges and copses, though his keen eye missed little of what his minute knowledge of these things knew to be there. Nor was he only the æsthete satisfying his eye with the beauty of the contours of the hills, the symmetry of the trees, and the grouping of villages. Nor was he only the wayfarer meeting fellow-travellers on the roads and in the inns, talking to them, and listening to their slow shrewd talk. Nor was he only the artist transmuting all this into words. He was all these and much more. By the English country his soul was revived when it was faint with despair, and comforted as some are by religion or music. Solitary on the bare downs, or in the sheltered valleys, on the ancient tracks above which the kestrel has always circled and hovered, and where the sheep have nibbled for such ages that the very grass and flowers have adapted their growth to evade the ceaseless menace of their teeth; or leaning over a gate to talk to the ploughman who, with such skilful ease, swings his plough at the end of the furrow; or wandering among the epitaphed tombstones of the village churchyard; or sitting in a meadow by a stream reading Traherne or Chaucer, or in the evening at the inn, or anywhere where the rural life of England continued in the traditional ways—there he could throw off his melancholy brooding and be content.

Introduction by Helen Thomas to Edward Thomas, *The South Country*, 1909 (London: Dent, 1932), pp. vii–viii.

———◆———

The secret beauties of Nature are unveiled only to the cross-country walker. Pan would not have appeared to Pheidippides on a road. On the road we never meet the "moving accidents by flood and field": the sudden glory of a woodland glade; the open back-door of the old farmhouse sequestered deep in rural solitude; the cow routed up from meditation behind the stone wall as we scale it suddenly; the deep, slow, south-country stream that we must jump, or wander along to find the bridge; the northern torrent of molten peat-hag that we must ford up to the waist, to scramble, glowing warm-cold, up the farther fox-glove bank; the autumnal dew on the bracken and the blue straight smoke of the cottage in the still glen at dawn; the rush down the mountain side, hair flying, stones and grouse rising at our feet; and at the bottom, the plunge in the pool below the waterfall, in a place so fair that kings should come from far to bathe therein—yet is it left, year in year out, unvisited save by us and "troops of stars." These, and a thousand other blessed chances of the day, are the heart of Walking, and these are not of the road.

Yet the hard road plays a part in every good walk, generally at the beginning and at the end. Nor must we forget the "soft" road, mediating as it were between his hard artificial brother and wild surrounding nature. The broad grass lanes of the low country, relics of mediæval wayfaring; the green, unfenced moorland road; the derelict road already half gone back to pasture; the common farm track—these and all their kind are a blessing to the walker . . . For they unite the speed and smooth surface of the harder road with much at least of the softness to the foot, the romance and the beauty of cross-country routes.

Sir George Macaulay Trevelyan, "Walking," *Clio, a Muse and Other Essays* (London: Longmans, 1913), pp. 69–71.

———◆———

Someone once told him [George Moore] that Zola was so bored on his constitutionals that he was obliged to count up figures in his head or estimate the distance between lamp-posts. It surprised him. "I am never like that," he said; and on solitary walks he was always thinking about something in particular, or watching for an incident that would excite his inward comment and set him speculating or telling himself a story.

Joseph Hone, *The Life of George Moore* (London: Gollancz, 1936), pp. 192–93.

———◆———

My vicinity affords many good walks; and though for so many years I have walked almost every day, and sometimes for several days together, I have not yet exhausted them. An absolutely new prospect is a great happiness, and I can still get this any afternoon. Two or three hours' walking will carry me to as strange a country as I expect ever to see. A single farm-house which I had not seen before is sometimes as good as the dominions of the King of Dahomey. There is in fact a sort of harmony discoverable between the capabilities of the landscape within a circle of ten miles' radius, or the limits of an afternoon walk, and the threescore years and ten of human life. It will never become quite familiar to you.

Henry David Thoreau, "Walking," *Excursions,* 1863 (Boston: Houghton, 1899), chap. VI, p. 259.

Nor must I forget to say a word on bivouacs. You come to a milestone on a hill, or some place where deep ways meet under trees; and off goes the knapsack, and down you sit to smoke a pipe in the shade. You sink into yourself, and the birds come round and look at you; and your smoke dissipates upon the afternoon under the blue dome of heaven; and the sun lies warm upon your feet, and the cool air visits your neck and turns aside your open shirt. If you are not happy, you must have an evil conscience. You may dally as long as you like by the roadside. It is almost as if the millennium were arrived, when we shall throw our clocks and watches over the housetop, and remember time and seasons no more. Not to keep hours for a lifetime is, I was going to say, to live for ever. You have no idea, unless you have tried it, how endlessly long is a summer's day, that you measure out only by hunger, and bring to an end only when you are drowsy.

Robert Louis Stevenson, "Walking Tours," *Virginibus Puerisque and Other Papers,* 1881 (New York: Scribner, 1909), chap. X, pp. 155–56.

FISHING

No life, my honest scholar, no life so happy and so pleasant as the life of a well-governed angler; for when the lawyer is swallowed up with business, and the statesman is preventing or contriving plots, then we sit on cowslip-banks, hear the birds sing, and possess ourselves in as much quietness as these silent silver streams, which we now see glide so quietly by us. Indeed, my good scholar, we may say of angling, as Dr. Boteler said of strawberries, 'Doubtless God could have made a better berry, but doubtless God never did;' and so, if I might be judge, God never did make a more calm, quiet, innocent recreation than angling.

Izaak Walton, *The Compleat Angler*, 1653 (London: Oxford, 1915), pt. I, chap. V, p. 120.

That Presidents have taken to fishing in an astonishing fashion seems to me worthy of investigation. I think I have discovered the reason: it is the silent sport. One of the few opportunities given a President for the refreshment of his soul and the clarification of his thoughts by solitude lies through fishing. As I have said in another place, it is generally realized and accepted that prayer is the most personal of all human relationships. Everyone knows that on such occasions men and women are entitled to be alone and undisturbed.

Next to prayer, fishing is the most personal relationship of man; and of more importance, everyone concedes that the fish will not bite in the presence of the public, including newspapermen.

Fishing seems to be one of the few avenues left to Presidents through which they may escape to their own thoughts, may live in their own imaginings, find relief from the pneumatic hammer of constant personal contacts, and refreshment of mind in rippling waters.

Herbert Hoover, *Fishing For Fun—And To Wash Your Soul* (New York: Random House, 1963), p. 76.

And here comes one of the paradoxes of fishing. By some strange trick of the memory, the fish which you take or lose seem in retrospect only a bit of high light in the general picture. The exaltation of an instant of perfect skill, the heartbreaking sense of clumsiness or stupidity when you lose a salmon, lessen their poignancy in the presence of the beauty which is always waiting upon the angler. . . .

And between dawn and dark what infinite variations of air and light and color and wind play upon the mind of the fisherman as if it were an opal! The wind caresses him one moment, and torments him the next, tossing his fly into treetops or breaking the brittle hook against a rock. But the water is the true opal. In the upper reaches of many of our New England streams the water flowing from a peat bog or cedar swamp has the tone of a very dark sherry; in full sunlight, flecked by shadows, it becomes one of Emerson's leopard-colored rills; as it pours over granite ledges it changes to something strangely austere and pure. No two successive hours are alike to the angler, for the brook or river is changing its form and hue in every instant, and his mind and mood and artistry are affected by every yard of the gliding, Protean stream. He is watching it, not with the sentimentalist's preoccupation with pure beauty, but rather with the fisherman's trained perception of the effect of wind and light, of deeper or darker-colored water, of eddy or shallow, upon the next cast of his fly. The paradox is that this very preoccupation with angling seems to make him more sensitive to the enfolding beauty of the landscape.

He must, of course, to perceive it fully, have a certain capacity for philosophical detachment, a kind of Oriental superiority to failure or success. Perhaps that is what being a "born fisherman" means. . . .

The mystery of fly-fishing, after all, is what is called by the younger generation a "complex." One of its strands—not the subtlest—is mere joy in manual dexterity. Another is the exquisite artificiality with which the means are adapted to the end. There is the pleasure of accurate observation of bewildering living creatures. There is moving water, and all the changes of the sky, shadow and sunlight and raindrops upon trees and flowers, and the old, inexhaustible, indescribable beauty of the world. There are a few fish. There is at times the zest of companionship and at other times the satisfaction of solitude. There are gentle memories of some "excellent angler, now with God." . . . There are no scales for weighing such imponderable things as these, but surely next to the happiness of one's own home and work is the happiness of sitting in the bow of a canoe, rod in hand, as the guide paddles you noiselessly around the bend of an unknown river.

Bliss Perry, *Pools and Ripples* (Boston: Little, Brown, 1927), pp. 50–51, 53–55, 59–60.

. . . greatest of all the attractions of a day's float-fishing, next of course to the glorious and exciting looking-forward to it, are the sights and sounds and scents which the angler enjoys.

I grant you the fly-fisherman, as he moves slowly and quietly up or down the river enjoys these too, but to a less extent. He has ever to mind his step, to watch his fly, to keep a look-out for branches of trees behind him, or submerged snags in front of him. These divert his attention. But the silent, immobile angler has his eyes and ears less occupied and he sees and hears more. The sound of moorhens and coots playing games of touch-last amongst the reed beds, with loud cries and laughter. Across the lake may be a heron, still and grey, watching and waiting. A pair of mallard come suddenly wheeling out of the sky to pitch with a gliding splash on the lake's surface. A kingfisher flashes by, a streak of azure. On more than one occasion I have experienced the indescribable delight of seeing close before me a kingfisher perched on my rod, a sight once seen never to be forgotten.

There is that characteristic scent of wild mint which, if you are an angler, never fails to bring back the memory of happy peaceful hours spent fishing quietly by some pond side or slow-moving river.

All the inhabitants of the waterside soon become accustomed to the silent figure seated on the bank.

Philip Gosse, "On Angling," *Traveller's Rest* (London: Cassell, 1937), pp. 146–47.

———◆———

Very pleasant the evening is after a successful day in hot, bright weather in June. Let us suppose that the angler has caught some three brace of trout in the day, and a brace and a half in the evening on good water. He will then have had plenty of interest and excitement, moments of anxiety and even of disappointment, but all contributing at the end to give a delightful satisfactory feeling of successful effort. . . . What he thinks about in the evening will not be only of angling, but of the scenes in which he has spent the day. I am often ashamed to think how much passes unnoticed in the actual excitement of angling, but the general impression of light and colour and surroundings is not lost; some is noted at the time, and some sinks into one's mind unconsciously and is found there at the end of the day, like a blessing given by great bounty to one who was too careless at the time to deserve it. May is the month of fresh leaves and bright shrubs, but June is the month in which the water meadows themselves are brightest. The common yellow iris, ragged robin, and forget-me-not make rough damp places gay, and the clear water in the little runnels among the grass sparkles in the sun. . . . Though the sun may be as hot as midsummer, everything in the first half of June seems young and fresh and active. Birds are singing still, and for a week or two it seems as if the best of spring and summer, warmth and songs, luxuriance and freshness, were spread abroad so abundantly that it is almost too much. The cup of happiness is full and runs over. Such may be one's last thoughts in the quiet of approaching night after sounds have ceased, and in the perfect enjoyment of 'that still spirit shed from evening air.'

Edward Grey (Viscount Grey of Falloden), *Fly Fishing* (London: Dent, 1934), pp. 43–44.

◆

Summer is not considered the best of times for the fresh-water fisherman. Trout lakes are generally too warm and the fish are deep and lazy. Streams are low and clear, the fish are likely to be shy and difficult. . . .

I am willing to concede that the lakes may be off in the hot weather, and even that the abundance of salt water can have its attractions. But summer days are golden days and for me summer streams are golden streams. . . .

Most of all I love the streams themselves at low water. They are stripped of fat then, to bone and muscle. One can see the shape and interplay of the bones and watch the flow of sinew and muscle over and around them. Little runs and riffles that were hidden under the force of the snow run-off are suddenly clear and sparkling. Great rocks that scarcely creased the current surface now break it to white water or stand boldly out in the air from the pool bottom. Little glides that were lost and lapped in torrent flow are suddenly glides again to shelter a fish and welcome the kiss of a fly. The trees along the banks are heavy with green and hushed. It is a peaceful time for no one hunts and the ruffed grouse and the merganser broods are safe and undisturbed. The river warblers, yellow and Audubon, sit tight on their nests or feed their fledglings. Robins are busy with second broods and the hermit thrushes look over their nest rims with anxious eyes, but stay there crouched and still until the passerby is gone.

Along the streams, we fish: kingfisher, heron, merganser, water ouzel and I, with perhaps a sharp-eyed mink or a playful nuisance of an otter to make an occasional diversion. The sun lights the river clear to the pool bottoms and sometimes shows up the shapes or casts the shadows of fish against them. The water feels and sounds different—it is kindly and welcoming, willing for once to commune its secrets. One moves slowly, carefully and attentively, for it is a good time to experiment and learn. . . .

I would not discount the other seasons. Each has its own values, sharp and positive and clear. But if fishing is the quiet sport of the contemplative man, then summer is the time of times for it, when the mind and body are relaxed and easy, the sun is warm and bright, the colors strong and the days long. A man should think when he is fishing, of all manner and shapes of things, flowing as easily through his mind as the light stream among its rocks. And the mind thinks best when the body is comfortable. All summer is not sunlight and the gray days and the stormy days may be the days when the fish rise best. But for me summer is low water and high sun, visible fish and difficult fish. And I know no lovelier time.

Roderick Haig-Brown, *Fisherman's Summer* (Toronto: Collins, 1959), pp. 12–13, 15.

———◆———

I soon fell into conversation with the old angler, and was so much entertained that, under pretext of receiving instructions in his art, I kept company with him almost the whole day; wandering along the banks of the stream, and listening to his talk. He was very communicative, having all the easy garrulity of cheerful old age; and I fancy was a little flattered by having an opportunity of displaying his piscatory lore; for who does not like now and then to play the sage?

He had been much of a rambler in his day, and had passed some years of his youth in America, particularly in Savannah, where he had entered into trade and had been ruined by the indiscretion of a partner. He had afterwards experienced many ups and downs in life, until he got into the navy, where his leg was carried away by a cannon ball, at the battle of Camperdown. This was the only stroke of real good fortune he had ever experienced, for it got him a pension, which, together with some small paternal property, brought him in a revenue of nearly forty pounds. On this he retired to his native village, where he lived quietly and independently; and devoted the remainder of his life to the "noble art of angling."

I found that he had read Izaak Walton attentively, and he seemed to have imbibed all his simple frankness and prevalent good humor. Though he had been sorely buffeted about the world, he was satisfied that the world, in itself, was good and beautiful. . . .

On parting with the old angler I inquired after his place of abode, and happening to be in the neighborhood of the village a few evenings afterwards, I had the curiosity to seek him out. . . .

I found him seated on a bench before the door, smoking his pipe in the soft evening sunshine. His cat was purring soberly on the threshold, and his parrot describing some strange evolutions in an iron ring that swung in the centre of his cage. He had been angling all day, and gave me a history of his sport with as much minuteness as a general would talk over a campaign; being particularly animated in relating the manner in which he had taken a large trout, which had completely tasked all his skill and wariness, and which he had sent as a trophy to mine hostess of the inn. . . .

On inquiring further about him, I learnt that he was a universal favorite in the village, and the oracle of the tap-room; where he delighted the rustics with his songs, and, like Sinbad, astonished them with his stories of strange lands, and shipwrecks, and sea-fights. He was much noticed too by gentlemen sportsmen of the neighborhood; had taught several of them the art of angling; and was a privileged visitor to their kitchens. The whole tenor of his life was quiet and inoffensive, being principally passed about the neighboring streams, when the weather and season were favorable; and at other times he employed himself at home, preparing his fishing tackle for the next campaign, or manufacturing rods, nets, and flies, for his patrons and pupils among the gentry.

Washington Irving, "The Angler," *The Sketch Book*, author's rev. ed. (New York: George P. Putnam, 1849), pp. 416–17, 419–21.

———◆———

Sometimes, after staying in a village parlor till the family had all retired, I have returned to the woods, and, partly with a view to the next day's dinner, spent the hours of midnight fishing from a boat by moonlight, serenaded by owls and foxes, and hearing, from time to time, the creaking note of some unknown bird close at hand. These experiences were very memorable and valuable to me,—anchored in forty feet of water, and twenty or thirty rods from the shore, surrounded sometimes by thousands of small perch and shiners, dimpling the surface with their tails in the moonlight, and communicating by a long flaxen line with mysterious nocturnal fishes which had their dwelling forty feet below, or sometimes dragging sixty feet of line about the pond as I drifted in the gentle night breeze, now and then feeling a slight vibration along it, indicative of some life prowling about its extremity, of dull uncertain blundering purpose there, and slow to make up its mind. At length you slowly raise, pulling hand over hand, some horned pout squeaking and squirming to the upper air. It was very queer, especially in dark nights, when your thoughts had wandered to vast and cosmogonal themes in other spheres, to feel this faint jerk, which came to interrupt your dreams and link you to Nature again. It seemed as if I might next cast my line upward into the air, as well as downward into this element, which was scarcely more dense. Thus I caught two fishes as it were with one hook.

Henry David Thoreau, *Walden, or Life in the Woods,* 1854 (Boston: Houghton, 1929), chap. IX, pp. 194–95.

PART THREE

Oneself and Others

TOLERANCE

———◆———

I must learn to bear even with those things which offend my susceptibilities and with companions who are uncongenial to me, and I must bear with them calmly and peaceably, otherwise there is no merit in it and God is not pleased. I will always try to find some virtue in people, even when none is apparent. Above all, I must say to myself that perhaps others, because of my innumerable faults, may have to make great efforts to put up with me. Humility then, always humility, joined to cheerfulness of soul, unalterable and blessed.

Pope John XXIII, "Spiritual Notes," in the Roman Seminary, April 22, 1903, *Journal of a Soul* (Montreal: Palm, 1965), p. 120.

———◆———

Curious, odd compounds are these fellow-creatures, at whose mercy you will be; full of fads and eccentricities, of whims and fancies; but the more closely we study their little foibles of one sort and another in the inner life which we see, the more surely is the conviction borne in upon us of the likeness of their weaknesses to our own. The similarity would be intolerable, if a happy egotism did not often render us forgetful of it. Hence the need of an infinite patience and of an ever-tender charity toward these fellow-creatures; have they not to exercise the same toward us?

Sir William Osler, "Aequanimitas," *Aequanimitas, With other Addresses*, 2d ed. (London: H. K. Lewis, 1930), pp. 6–7.

———◆———

People we love must be loved as they are. It is a want both of wisdom and courage on our part—a sort of drug—this wilful blindness, to blame them, because they fail our vision of them.

Mrs. Patrick Campbell, *My Life and Some Letters* (London: Hutchinson, n.d.), p. 281.

What a vile antithesis is that between a man and his faults! If I love a man, I do not love his faults, for they are abstractions, but I love the man *in* his faults. Are they not truly himself? He is often more himself in his faults than in his virtues.

Mark Rutherford, "Notes," *More Pages From a Journal* (London: Oxford, 1910), pp. 228–29.

◆

A basic temptation: the flatly unchristian refusal to love those whom we consider, for some reason or other, unworthy of love. And, on top of that, to consider others unworthy of love for even very trivial reasons. Not that we hate them of course: but we just refuse to accept them in our hearts, to treat them without suspicion and deal with them without inner reservations. In a word, we reject those who do not please us. We are of course "charitable toward them." An interesting use of the word "charity" to cover and to justify a certain coldness, suspicion, and even disdain. But this is punished by another inexorable refusal: we are bound by the logic of this defensive rejection to reject any form of happiness that even implies acceptance of those we have decided to reject. This certainly complicates life, and if one is sufficiently intolerant, it ends by making all happiness impossible.

This means that we have to get along without constantly applying the yardstick of "worthiness" (who is worthy to be loved, and who is not). And it almost means, by implication, that we cease to ask even indirect questions about who is "justified," who is worthy of acceptance, who can be tolerated by the believer! What a preposterous idea that would be! And yet the world is full of "believers" who find themselves entirely surrounded by people they can hardly be expected to "tolerate," such as Jews, Negroes, unbelievers, heretics, Communists, pagans, fanatics, and so on.

God is asking of me, the unworthy, to forget my unworthiness and that of all my brothers, and dare to advance in the love which has redeemed and renewed us all in God's likeness. And to laugh, after all, at all preposterous ideas of "worthiness."

Thomas Merton, *Conjectures of a Guilty Bystander* (New York: Doubleday, 1966), pp. 156–57.

It was his habit to say that 'nine out of every ten people improve on acquaintance' . . .

Frank Swinnerton, "Arnold Bennett," *Tokefield Papers*, 2d ed. (London: Hamish Hamilton, 1949), pp. 130–31.

———◆———

I think it was in 1947 or 1948. It was in the Smoking Room of the House of Commons, and all things said there are confidential. But this saying was to the credit of all, and can do no harm: so I will risk it. Rather late at night Churchill was leaving the Smoking Room. As he passed a little group of us—all Parties—we said, "Good night, sir!" He stopped and beamed upon us—that wonderful genial beam! There is no face I know that can express so humorously, so grimly, so many emotions. His glance fell on my friend—nay, the friend of most of us—Richard Stokes, the Socialist Member for Ipswich. Dick Stokes never loses his temper (which is a most unfair handicap to those who disagree with him), and says the most frightful things with a smile so youthful and warming that I think of him always as a junior Pickwick. All the war he was attacking Churchill, fearlessly, continuously, about tanks (among other things). I never knew enough about tanks to know whether he was talking sense or not, but certainly he was a formidable enemy to Churchill and his Ministers. Now Churchill came back and put a hand on his shoulder and said: "Of course, I've forgiven you. Indeed, I agree with very much that you are saying about the Germans. Very good." He moved away a few paces and said, as if we might be surprised by what he had said, "Such hatred as I have left in me—and it isn't much—I would rather reserve for the future than the past." He beamed again and moved off a pace or two, but stopped again, and made that inimitable sound . . . ["half grunt, half chuckle"] and he said: "H'm. A judicious and thrifty disposal of bile."

Here, once again, is "the little more" that means so much. You or I might have said that we reserved our small store of hatred for the future. But only one man in this world would have thought of adding, "a judicious and thrifty disposal of bile", and left his company both moved and mirthful.

Sir Alan Patrick Herbert, "Churchill's Humour," in *Churchill by his Contemporaries*, ed. Charles Eade (London: Hutchinson, 1953), pp. 432–33.

. . . it is almost a definition of a gentleman to say he is one who never inflicts pain. This description is both refined and, as far as it goes, accurate. He is mainly occupied in merely removing the obstacles which hinder the free and unembarrassed action of those about him; and he concurs with their movements rather than takes the initiative himself. His benefits may be considered as parallel to what are called comforts or conveniences in arrangements of a personal nature: like an easy chair or a good fire, which do their part in dispelling cold and fatigue, though nature provides both means of rest and animal heat without them. The true gentleman in like manner carefully avoids whatever may cause a jar or a jolt in the minds of those with whom he is cast;—all clashing of opinion, or collision of feeling, all restraint, or suspicion, or gloom, or resentment; his great concern being to make every one at their ease and at home. He has his eyes on all his company; he is tender towards the bashful, gentle towards the distant, and merciful towards the absurd; he can recollect to whom he is speaking; he guards against unseasonable allusions, or topics which may irritate; he is seldom prominent in conversation, and never wearisome. He makes light of favours while he does them, and seems to be receiving when he is conferring. He never speaks of himself except when compelled, never defends himself by a mere retort, he has no ears for slander or gossip, is scrupulous in imputing motives to those who interfere with him, and interprets every thing for the best. He is never mean or little in his disputes, never takes unfair advantage, never mistakes personalities or sharp sayings for arguments, or insinuates evil which he dare not say out. From a long-sighted prudence, he observes the maxim of the ancient sage, that we should ever conduct ourselves towards our enemy as if he were one day to be our friend.

John Henry Cardinal Newman, *The Idea of a University*, 1873 (London: Longmans, 1901), chap. VIII, pp. 208–10.

———◆———

I enjoy life because I am endlessly interested in people and their growth. My interest leads me continually to widen my knowledge of people, and this in turn compels me to believe that the normal human heart is born good. That is, it is born sensitive and feeling, eager to be approved and to approve, hungry for simple happiness and the chance to live. It neither wishes to be killed nor to kill. If through circumstances it is overcome by evil, it never becomes entirely evil. There remain in it elements of good, however recessive, which continue to hold the possibility of restoration.

I believe in human beings but my faith is without sentimentality. I know that in environments of uncertainty, fear and hunger, the human being is dwarfed and shaped without his being aware of it, just as the plant struggling under a stone does not know its own condition. Only when the stone is removed can it spring up freely into the light. But the power to spring up is inherent, and only death puts an end to it.

I feel no need for any other faith than my faith in human beings. Like Confucius of old, I am so absorbed in the wonder of earth and the life upon it that I cannot think of heaven and the angels. I have enough for this life. If there is no other life, then this one has been enough to make it worth being born, myself a human being.

Pearl Buck, "Roll Away the Stone," *This I Believe*, ed. Edward P. Morgan (New York: Simon & Schuster, 1952), p. 21.

———◆———

Yesterday was my fifty-fifth birthday. . . .

One sits more easily to life as one grows older, the self-torture of youth far behind now, still distant the pains and physical ignominy of old age. Since I am no longer sodden with guilt for things done and left undone, I can accept other people for what they are, not needing to turn them into mirrors, props, blue-prints or Aunt Sallies. During the ten years after 1940 . . . I was never long free from the sense of guilt, oppressive with disaster like the atmosphere before a storm that will not break, until I learnt how guilt may be a kind of self-indulgence, or at least a futile surrogate for the moral action one cannot, dare not take. If I understand people a bit better now, it is largely because my view of them is less fogged by the steam of introspection, and seldom interrupted by the old, frantic gesticulations of a mind drowning in self-pity or self-disgust.

The intolerant young man I used to be would view with suspicion the measure of inner peace I have achieved. He would probably say I had "taken the bribe"—a phrase we were addicted to in the Thirties, meaning a surrender to the *status quo*, a going over to reaction, complacence, hypocrisy. . . . Let him say what he will, then, this awkward young customer. He had yet to learn that intolerance of others—their habits or ideas—more often than not springs from the inability to accept one's self. . . .

C. Day Lewis, *The Buried Day* (London: Chatto, 1960), pp. 239–40.

To ask that one's own higher self should forgive one's own tres-
passes is the hardest prayer to answer that we can ever offer up. If we
can breathe this prayer, and find it truly answered in a harmony of exalted comprehension and acceptance, then we have learnt what forgiveness is. There is no other way to learn forgiveness. We cannot forgive
others in any comprehensible sense unless we have first learnt how to
forgive ourselves.

Havelock Ellis, *Impressions and Comments*, 3d series (Boston:
Houghton, 1924), pp. 96–97.

———◆———

/ It seems to me to be a duty which we owe to society, to feel
pleased with ourselves. Not satisfied, but pleased. For there are various
kinds of self-love, and the best of these is adorable. It is not the self-
infatuation of the very young, which is rather trying in large quantities;
it is not the self-satisfaction of the vulgarly successful; it is not the self-
complacency of the unco' guid. It is not smug, but bland. It is consider-
ate, innocent, childlike. It is a testimony to innocence.

Those who are pleased with themselves are ready to be pleased with
simple things and agreeable things. And this readiness to be pleased is
what endears them to us—this, and their expectation that we shall be
equally pleased. It springs from true modesty, for it is impossible to be
pleased with oneself if one is always measuring oneself with others, always (so to speak) bringing oneself into the false and alarming glare of
self-examination. Those who are pleased with themselves take life very
much as they find it. And life treats them very well. Misery of long
duration is unknown to them. They are buoyant and carefree. They
know that if they tumble they will pick themselves up again, as they
have always done before. And, being confident, they rarely tumble. They
come into the room, to the battle, smiling; and they make us smile in
return. How can we be severe with them?

A very little boy of my acquaintance, at the age of something between
three and four, was once exceedingly naughty. His aunt became angry
with him, and sent him to bed as a punishment. On his way to bed he
put his small, round, rosy face round the edge of the door, and looked at
his aunt with an ingratiating smile—with *the* ingratiating smile. She,
although still rather stern, could not resist that pleasant glance. 'Come
and let me give you a kiss before you go,' said the aunt. The little boy
came toward her. 'I *thought* you'd have to,' he said. His punishment
was not cancelled; he duly went to bed; but there was no anger upon

either side, and the little boy left the field with honour. When he grows up, that child will be pleased with himself. He will have—as he now has —noticeable charm. Nothing will ever go seriously amiss with him. The pleasure he takes in himself will be communicated to others. He will be liked, and his path through the years will be a smooth one. This is not all. Wherever he goes, he will carry happiness.

That, it seems to me, is the real reason why it is a duty to be pleased with oneself. We live among other people, and our attitude to ourselves should be such as to give pleasure to others. Pleasure can be given to others by thoughtfulness, by kindness, by various generosities; but in the long run thoughtfulness, etc., tend to pall, since they are acts of grace, and do not create bonhomie. If all the benefactions are upon one side, or if retaliatory benefactions are made out of a sense of duty ('She gave me this, so I must give *her* something'), love suffers a strain. Whereas those who are pleased with themselves are, as it were, broadcasting benefactions which are so little obvious that the return is made instinctively. The beam in the smile of our friends is a beam of light. Its refractions are innumerable, and are not to be calculated in number or extent. All we know is that our hearts are eased and our spirits raised, and the true cause of our happiness is this pervasive sense of pleasure, which is the truest charm against care and constraint that man has yet discovered.

Frank Swinnerton, "On Thinking Well of Oneself," *Tokefield Papers*, 2d ed. (London: Hamish Hamilton, 1949), pp. 62–63.

GOOD HUMOR

◆

Up, and to church, and home and dined with my wife and Deb. alone, but merry and in good humour, which is, when all is done, the greatest felicity of all. . . .

Samuel Pepys, Diary, June 21, 1668: *The Diary of Samuel Pepys*, ed. Henry B. Wheatley (London: Bell, 1924), vol. VIII, p. 51.

'Life,' said a gaunt widow, with a reputation for being clever—
'life is a perpetual toothache.'

In this vein the conversation went on: the familiar topics were discussed of labour-troubles, epidemics, cancer, tuberculosis, and taxation.

Near me there sat a little old lady who was placidly drinking her tea,
and taking no part in the melancholy chorus. 'Well, I must say,' she
remarked, turning to me, and speaking in an undertone, 'I must say I
enjoy life.'

'So do I,' I whispered.

'When I enjoy things,' she went on, 'I know it. Eating, for instance,
the sunshine, my hot-water bottle at night. Other people are always
thinking of unpleasant things.'

'It makes a difference,' she added, as she got up to go with the others.

'All the difference in the world!' I answered.

Logan Pearsall Smith, "Interruption," *More Trivia*, 1921, reprinted in *All Trivia* (New York: Harcourt, 1934), p. 114.

It was in Butcher-row that this meeting happened. Mr. Edwards,
who was a decent-looking elderly man in grey clothes, and a wig of many
curls, accosted Johnson with familiar confidence, knowing who he was,
while Johnson returned his salutation with a courteous formality, as to a
stranger. But as soon as Edwards had brought to his recollection their
having been at Pembroke-College together nine-and-forty years ago, he
seemed much pleased . . .

'You are a philosopher, Dr. Johnson [said Edwards]. I have tried too
in my time to be a philosopher; but, I don't know how, cheerfulness was
always breaking in.'

James Boswell, *The Life of Samuel Johnson*, 1791, ed. George
Birkbeck Hill (New York: Harper, n.d.), vol. III, pp. 344, 346.

To him she [Goethe's mother] transmitted her love of story-
telling, her animal spirits, her love of everything which bore the stamp
of distinctive individuality, and her love of seeing happy faces around
her. "Order and quiet," she says in one of her charming letters to
Freiherr von Stein, "are my principal characteristics. Hence I despatch

at once whatever I have to do, the most disagreeable always first, and I gulp down the devil without looking at him. When all has returned to its proper state, then I defy any one to surpass me in good humour." Her heartiness and tolerance are the causes, she thinks, why every one likes her. "I am fond of people, and *that* every one feels directly—young and old. I pass without pretension through the world, and that gratifies men. I never *bemoralize* any one—*always seek out the good that is in them, and leave what is bad to him who made mankind, and knows how to round off the angles.* In this way I make myself happy and comfortable."

G. H. Lewes, *The Life and Works of Goethe* (London: Nutt, 1855), vol. I, p. 13.

———◆———

Mrs. Bates, the widow of a former vicar of Highbury, was a very old lady, almost past every thing but tea and quadrille. She lived with her single daughter in a very small way, and was considered with all the regard and respect which a harmless old lady, under such untoward circumstances, can excite. Her daughter enjoyed a most uncommon degree of popularity for a woman neither young, handsome, rich, nor married. Miss Bates stood in the very worst predicament in the world for having much of the public favour; and she had no intellectual superiority to make atonement to herself, or frighten those who might hate her, into outward respect. She had never boasted either beauty or cleverness. Her youth had passed without distinction, and her middle of life was devoted to the care of a failing mother, and the endeavour to make a small income go as far as possible. And yet she was a happy woman, and a woman whom no one named without good-will. It was her own universal good-will and contented temper which worked such wonders. She loved every body, was interested in every body's happiness, quick-sighted to every body's merits; thought herself a most fortunate creature, and surrounded with blessings in such an excellent mother and so many good neighbours and friends, and a home that wanted for nothing. The simplicity and cheerfulness of her nature, her contented and grateful spirit, were a recommendation to every body and a mine of felicity to herself.

Jane Austen, *Emma*, 1816 (London: Dent, 1906), vol. I, chap. III, pp. 15–16.

But the marvel of Agassiz, and a never-ceasing source of wonder and delight to his friends and companions, was the union in his individuality of this solidity, breadth, and depth of mind with a joyousness of spirit, an immense overwhelming geniality of disposition, which flooded every company he entered with the wealth of his own opulent nature. Placed at the head of a table, with a shoulder of mutton before him, he so carved the meat that every guest was flattered into the belief that the host had given him the best piece. His social power exceeded that of the most brilliant conversationists and of the most delicate epicures; for he was not only fertile in thoughts, but wise in wines and infallible in matters of fish and game. It was impossible to place him in any company where he was out of place. The human nature *in* him fell into instinctive relations with every kind and variety of human nature outside of him. His wide experience of life had brought him into familiar contact with emperors, kings, and nobles, with scientists and men of letters, with mechanics, farmers, and day-laborers,—in short, with men divided by race, rank, wealth, and every other distinction from other men; and by the felicity of his cosmopolitan nature he placed himself on an easy equality with them all,—never cringing to those conventionally above him, never "condescending" to those intellectually below him, but cordially welcoming everybody he met on the common ground of human brotherhood. Himself a strong man, his test of manhood was entirely independent of conventional rules. When he discovered a real *man*, it was indifferent to him whether he occupied a palace or a hovel; and certainly no man of science ever equalled him in captivating the representatives of all grades of rank and intelligence by sheer force of human sympathy. The French, or Austrian, or Brazilian emperor, the peasant of the Alps, the "rough" of our Western plains, agreed at least in one opinion,—that Agassiz was a grand specimen of manhood.

Edwin Percy Whipple, "Recollections of Agassiz," *Recollections of Eminent Men* (Boston: Ticknor, 1887), pp. 83–84.

GOOD COMPANY

◆

We walked in the evening in Greenwich Park. He asked me, I suppose, by way of trying my disposition, 'Is not this very fine?' Having no exquisite relish of the beauties of Nature, and being more delighted with 'the busy hum of men,' I answered, 'Yes, Sir; but not equal to Fleet-street.' JOHNSON. 'You are right, Sir.'

James Boswell, *The Life of Samuel Johnson*, 1791, ed. George Birkbeck Hill (New York: Harper, n.d.), vol. I, p. 533.

◆

I ought before this to have replied to your very kind invitation into Cumberland. With you and your sister I could gang anywhere; but I am afraid whether I shall ever be able to afford so desperate a journey. Separate from the pleasure of your company, I don't much care if I never see a mountain in my life. I have passed all my days in London, until I have formed as many and intense local attachments as any of you mountaineers can have done with dead Nature. The lighted shops of the Strand and Fleet Street; the innumerable trades, tradesmen, and customers, coaches, waggons, playhouses; all the bustle and wickedness round about Covent Garden; the very women of the Town; the watchmen, drunken scenes, rattles; life awake, if you awake, at all hours of the night; the impossibility of being dull in Fleet Street; the crowds, the very dirt and mud, the sun shining upon houses and pavements, the print-shops, the old book-stalls, parsons cheapening books, coffee-houses, steams of soups from kitchens, the pantomimes—London itself a pantomime and a masquerade—all these things work themselves into my mind, and feed me, without a power of satiating me. The wonder of these sights impels me into night-walks about her crowded streets, and I often shed tears in the motley Strand from fulness of joy at so much life. All these emotions must be strange to you; so are your rural emotions to me. But consider, what must I have been doing all my life, not to have lent great portions of my heart with usury to such scenes?

Charles Lamb, letter to William Wordsworth, January 30, 1801, *Letters of Charles Lamb*, ed. William Macdonald (London: Dent, 1903), vol. I, p. 190.

During the last few years of Sydney Smith's life, the Athenæum
Club formed one of his favourite resorts, and there he might frequently
have been seen chatting pleasantly with friends old and new. The chief
literary club of the metropolis, with its noble library and unusual social
advantages, had naturally powerful attractions for such a man, and, being himself of an eminently "clubable" disposition, he was extremely
popular within its walls. The social intercourse which he enjoyed in London was rendered still more agreeable because it was in marked contrast
with his ordinary life at Combe-Florey; and the quietude of a country
life in a secluded Somerset parsonage—which to a lively man with
flagging physical powers must otherwise have grown irksome and monotonous—was brightened on the dullest day by the recollection that in the
course of a month or two his work at St. Paul's would take him back
once more to the crowded town. Sydney Smith felt as much at home in
Piccadilly as Dr. Johnson was in Fleet Street, and he sympathized with
the great moralist's sententious verdict, that the man who is tired of London is tired of life. "I have no relish for the country," is his amusing
confession to a lady friend, "it is a kind of healthy grave. I am afraid you
are not exempt from the delusions of flowers, green turf, and birds; they
all afford slight gratification, but are not worth an hour of rational conversation; and rational conversation in sufficient quantities is only to be
had from the congregation of a million of people in one spot."

Stuart J. Reid, A *Sketch of the Life and Times of the Rev. Sydney Smith* (New York: Harper, 1885), pp. 348–49.

———◆———

Talk has none of the freezing immunities of the pulpit. It cannot, even if it would, become merely æsthetic or merely classical like
literature. A jest intervenes, the solemn humbug is dissolved in laughter,
and speech runs forth out of the contemporary groove into the open
fields of nature, cheery and cheering, like schoolboys out of school. And
it is in talk alone that we can learn our period and ourselves. In short,
the first duty of a man is to speak; that is his chief business in this
world; and talk, which is the harmonious speech of two or more, is by
far the most accessible of pleasures. It costs nothing in money; it is all
profit; it completes our education, founds and fosters our friendships,
and can be enjoyed at any age and in almost any state of health.

Robert Louis Stevenson, "Talk and Talkers," *Memories and Portraits,* 1887 (New York: Scribner, 1909), chap. X, p. 266.

In contradiction to those, who, having a wife and children, prefer domestic enjoyments to those which a tavern affords, I have heard him [Dr. Samuel Johnson] assert, that a tavern-chair was the throne of human felicity.—'As soon,' said he, 'as I enter the door of a tavern, I experience an oblivion of care, and a freedom from solicitude: when I am seated, I find the master courteous, and the servants obsequious to my call; anxious to know and ready to supply my wants: wine there exhilarates my spirits, and prompts me to free conversation and an interchange of discourse with those whom I most love: I dogmatise and am contradicted, and in this conflict of opinions and sentiments I find delight.'

Sir John Hawkins, *The Works of Samuel Johnson, LL. D. Together with His Life* . . . (London: Buckland, 1787), vol. I, p. 87.

———◆———

Schlosser, who was ten years his [Goethe's] senior, not only awakened emulation by his own superior knowledge and facility, but further aided him by introducing him to a set of literary friends, where poetic discussions formed the staple of conversation. This circle met at the house of one Schönkopf, a *Weinhändler* and *Hauswirth*, living in the Brühl, No. 79. To translate these words into English equivalents would only mislead the reader. Schönkopf kept neither an hotel, nor a public house, but what in Germany is a substitute for both. He sold wine, and kept a table d'hôte; occasionally also let bedrooms to travellers. His wife, a lively, cultivated woman, belonging to a noble family in Frankfurt, drew Frankfurt visitors to the house; and with her Goethe soon became on terms of intimacy, which would seem surprising to the English reader who only heard of her as an innkeeper's wife. He became "one of the family", and fell in love with the daughter. I must further beg the reader to understand that in Germany, to this day, there is a wide difference between the dining customs and our own. The English student, clerk, or bachelor, who dines at an eating house, chop house, or hotel, goes there simply to get his dinner and perhaps look at the *Times*. Of the other diners he knows nothing, cares little. It is rare that a word is interchanged between him and his neighbour. Quite otherwise in Germany. There the same society is generally to be found at the same table. The *table d'hôte* is composed of a circle of *habitués*, varied by occasional visitors, who in time become, perhaps, members of the circle.

Even with strangers conversation is freely interchanged; and in a little while friendships are formed over these dinner tables, according as natural tastes and likings assimilate, which, extending beyond the mere hour of dinner, are carried into the current of life. Germans do not rise so hastily from the table as we; for time with them is not so precious; life is not so crowded; time can be found for quiet after-dinner talk. The cigars and coffee, which appear before the cloth is removed, keep the company together; and in that state of suffused comfort which quiet digestion creates, they hear without anger the opinions of antagonists. In such a society must we imagine Goethe in the Schönkopf establishment, among students and men of letters, all eager in advancing their own opinions, and combating the "false taste" which was not their own.

G. H. Lewes, *The Life and Works of Goethe* (London: Nutt, 1855), vol. I, pp. 59–60.

———◆———

And before long my closest friend was Joseph Wood Krutch, hereinafter to be known as Joe.

Many times since then I have to tried to date the moment when I knew this to be true. I think it was one evening when the two of us stood in the vestibule of a subway train bound for Times Square, to a restaurant, a theater, or both. The train was noisy so that we had to shout, but the circumstance seemed unimportant. The important thing was that we had a great deal to say to each other, and that each was really interested in what the other said; also, that each was eager to speak when it came his turn, and was confident that what he said would be worth hearing. We like those who inspire us to talk well, to talk indeed our best, which in their presence becomes something better than it ever was before, so that it surprises and delights us too. We like least those persons in whose presence we are dull. For we can be either, and company brings it out; that is what company is for. Joe Krutch from this moment was famous company for me, and the conversation begun then has never stopped. It has ranged without apology from the grandest to the meanest subjects; it has a natural facility in rising or in sinking; but the point is, we have never run out of things to say.

Mark Van Doren, *The Autobiography of Mark Van Doren* (New York: Harcourt, 1958), pp. 72–73.

I had him [Dr. Oliver Wendell Holmes] several days quite to myself, and there were few subjects which we did not discuss. We mostly agreed, but even where we did not, it was a real pleasure to differ from him. We discussed the greatest and the smallest questions, and on every one he had some wise and telling remarks to pour out. I remember one long conversation while we were sitting in an old wainscoted room at All Souls' [Cambridge], ornamented with the arms of former fellows. It had been at first the library of the college, then one of the fellows' rooms, and lastly a lecture-room. We were deep in the old question of the true relation between the Divine and the Human in man, and here again, as on all other questions, everything seemed to be clear and evident to his mind. Perhaps I ought not to repeat what he said to me when we parted: "I have had much talk with people in England; with you I have had a real conversation." We understood each other, and wondered how it was that men so often misunderstood one another.

F. Max Müller, *Auld Lang Syne* (New York: Scribner, 1898), pp. 183–84.

COMPANIONABLE SILENCE

———◆———

For those who have managed that things shall run smoothly over the domestic rug there is no happier time of life than these long candlelight hours of home and silence. No spoken content or uttered satisfaction is necessary. The fact that is felt is enough for peace.

Anthony Trollope, *Orley Farm*, 1862 (London: Oxford, 1935), vol. I, chap. XXI, p. 205.

There was one older man, an excellent fisher and skilled in all kinds of woodcraft, who was pleased to look upon my house as a building erected for the convenience of fishermen; and I was equally pleased when he sat in my doorway to arrange his lines. Once in a while we sat together on the pond, he at one end of the boat, and I at the other; but not many words passed between us, for he had grown deaf in his later years, but he occasionally hummed a psalm, which harmonized well enough with my philosophy. Our intercourse was thus altogether one of unbroken harmony, far more pleasing to remember than if it had been carried on by speech.

Henry David Thoreau, *Walden, or Life in the Woods,* 1854, (Boston: Houghton, 1929), chap. IX, p. 193.

——————◆——————

Went out this afternoon to call on C. and his wife. They are certainly the most cultivated people I know. They travel a good deal, and each of them can speak two or three languages besides English. They read the best books, and do not read those which are bad. Some friends were there, and I was entertained with intelligent criticism of literature, music, and pictures, and learned much that was worth knowing. But I came away unsatisfied, and rather dazed. On my way back— it was a singularly warm, clear evening in February—I turned in to see an old lady who lives near me. She was sitting wrapped up at her wide-open window, looking at the light that was still left in the south-west. I said, of course, that I hoped she would not take cold. 'Oh no,' she replied, 'I often sit here, and so long as I keep myself warm I come to no harm. I cannot read by candlelight, and I am thankful that this room faces the south. I know the stars much better than when I was young.' I took the chair beside her, and for ten minutes neither of us spoke, but I was not conscious for an instant of the disagreeable feeling that silence must be broken, and search be made for something with which to break it. If two persons are friends in the best sense of the word, they are not uncomfortable if they do not talk when they are together. Presently she told me that she had received news that morning of the birth of a grand-daughter. She was much pleased. The mother already had two sons and desired a girl. I stayed for about half an hour, and went home in debt to her for peace.

Mark Rutherford, "Notes," *More Pages From a Journal* (London: Oxford, 1910), pp. 248–49.

June 9–10 [1865].—I have been sitting late to-night by the bed-side of a wounded captain, a special friend of mine, lying with a pain-ful fracture of left leg in one of the hospitals, in a large ward partially vacant. The lights were put out, all but a little candle, far from where I sat. The full moon shone in through the windows, making long, slanting silvery patches on the floor. All was still, my friend too was silent, but could not sleep; so I sat there by him, slowly wafting the fan, and occupied with the musings that arose out of the scene, the long shadowy ward, the beautiful ghostly moonlight on the floor, the white beds, here and there an occupant with huddled form, the bed-clothes thrown off.

Walt Whitman, *Specimen Days*, 1882, reprinted in Walt Whit-man, *Prose Works* (Philadelphia: McKay, n.d.), p. 75.

———◆———

I have sat with [James Matthew] Barrie night after night in his flat high up over the Thames by Adelphi Terrace. He sits tucked up in his chair, puffing at his pipe, absorbed, silent. Now he stirs a little as though about to speak; but does not. Yet a great peace broods over this communion of silence. Now perhaps a word or two: sentences as short as in his plays—consummate master of compression that he is—a kind word, a whimsical word, never once in all the years we have sat and kept silence together has Barrie uttered an unworthy or an unkind thought. Only poets know such reticence. Barrie can talk and talk well when he likes; he can encourage by what he says, but most by that strange gift he has—not of telling you but of making you feel his sym-pathy. Silence with Barrie is no empty silence. It is eloquent. He can be silent in many languages. His silence can freeze, but it can also thaw the heart which is numb. Wizard of words, no doubt, but owner of that more occult wizardry—expressive silence.

Now I come to think of it, the good Samaritan never said a word to the man he succoured.

Lillah McCarthy (Lady Keeble) *Myself and My Friends* (Lon-don: Thornton Butterworth, 1933), pp. 97–98.

Reader, would'st thou know what true peace and quiet mean; would'st thou find a refuge from the noises and clamours of the multitude; would'st thou enjoy at once solitude and society; would'st thou possess the depth of thine own spirit in stillness, without being shut out from the consolatory faces of thy species; would'st thou be alone and yet accompanied; solitary, yet not desolate; singular, yet not without some to keep thee in countenance; a unit in aggregate; a simple in composite:—come with me into a Quakers' Meeting. . . .

For a man to refrain even from good words, and to hold his peace, it is commendable; but for a multitude it is great mastery. . . .

There are wounds which an imperfect solitude cannot heal. By imperfect I mean that which a man enjoyeth by himself. The perfect is that which he can sometimes attain in crowds, but nowhere so absolutely as in a Quakers' Meeting. . . .

Nothing-plotting, nought-caballing, unmischievous synod! convocation without intrigue: parliament without debate! what a lesson dost thou read to council, and to consistory! . . .

How far the followers of these good men in our days have kept to the primitive spirit, or in what proportion they have substituted formality for it, the Judge of Spirits can alone determine. I have seen faces in their assemblies upon which the dove sate visibly brooding. Others, again, I have watched, when my thoughts should have been better engaged, in which I could possibly detect nothing but a blank inanity. But quiet was in all, and the disposition to unanimity, and the absence of the fierce controversial workings.—If the spiritual pretensions of the Quakers have abated, at least they make few pretences. Hypocrites they certainly are not, in their preaching. It is seldom, indeed, that you shall see one get up amongst them to hold forth. . . .

More frequently the Meeting is broken up without a word having been spoken. But the mind has been fed. You go away with a sermon not made with hands. You have been in the milder caverns of Trophonius; or as in some den, where that fiercest and savagest of all wild creatures, the Tongue, that unruly member, has strangely lain tied up and captive. You have bathed with stillness.—O, when the spirit is sore fretted, even tired to sickness of the janglings and nonsense-noises of the world, what a balm and a solace it is to go and seat yourself for a quiet half-hour upon some undisputed corner of a bench among the gentle Quakers!

Charles Lamb, "A Quakers' Meeting," *Elia—Essays* . . . , 1823 (London: Cassell, 1907,) chap. IX, pp. 62–66.

At no time did my father ever appear so free from care as when communing with nature. With him it was indeed communion. He did not, as many do when living in the presence of fine scenery, show any impatience to leave one scene in order to seek another; no restless desire to be on the top of a mountain, or away into some distant valley; but he would linger in and about the place his heart had fixed to visit. All he desired was there before him; it was almost a lesson to look at his countenance at such moments. . . .

I remember walking a whole day with him, rambling about the neighborhood of Cladich; scarcely a word was uttered. Now and then he would point out a spot, which sudden sun-gleams made for a moment what he called a "sight of divine beauty;" and then again, perhaps when some more extended and lengthened duration of light overspread the whole landscape, making it a scene of matchless loveliness, gently touching my arm, he signified, by a motion of his hand, that I too must take in and admire what he did not express by words; silence at such moments was the key to more intense enjoyment. We sat down to rest on an eminence at the head of Loch Awe, when the mid-day sun glittered over every island and promontory, streaking the green fields with lines of gold. Not a sound escaped his lips . . .

Mary [Wilson] Gordon, *'Christopher North': A Memoir of John Wilson* (Edinburgh: Edmonston and Douglas, 1862), vol. II, pp. 270–71.

———◆———

He [Kenneth Grahame] had a marvellous gift of silence. We all know the old rustic who said, "Sometimes I sets and thinks and sometimes I just sets." Kenneth Grahame had reduced "just setting" to a fine art. He would slowly become part of the landscape and a word from him would come as unexpectedly as a sudden remark from an oak or a beech. He could not have been thinking . . . No, he was "just setting"; in other words he was on the threshold of Nirvana; his brain was receptive but at rest, a great peace was with him and about him and his companion was drawn into it.

Graham Robertson, reminiscences of Kenneth Grahame, in Patrick R. Chalmers, *Kenneth Grahame* (London: Methuen, 1933), p. 97.

ALONE

———◆———

It is a difficult lesson to learn today—to leave one's friends and family and deliberately practice the art of solitude for an hour or a day or a week. For me, the break is the most difficult. Parting is inevitably painful, even for a short time. It is like an amputation, I feel. A limb is being torn off, without which I shall be unable to function. And yet, once it is done, I find there is a quality to being alone that is incredibly precious. Life rushes back into the void, richer, more vivid, fuller than before. It is as if in parting one did actually lose an arm. And then, like the star-fish, one grows it anew; one is whole again, complete and round —more whole, even, than before, when the other people had pieces of one.

For a full day and two nights I have been alone. I lay on the beach under the stars at night alone. I made my breakfast alone. Alone I watched the gulls at the end of the pier, dip and wheel and dive for the scraps I threw them. A morning's work at my desk, and then, a late picnic lunch alone on the beach. And it seemed to me, separated from my own species, that I was nearer to others: the shy willet, nesting in the ragged tide-wash behind me; the sand piper, running in little un-frightened steps down the shining beach rim ahead of me; the slowly flapping pelicans over my head, coasting down wind; the old gull, hunched up, grouchy, surveying the horizon. I felt a kind of impersonal kinship with them and a joy in that kinship. Beauty of earth and sea and air meant more to me. I was in harmony with it, melted into the universe, lost in it, as one is lost in a canticle of praise, swelling from an unknown crowd in a cathedral. "Praise ye the Lord, all ye fishes of the sea—all ye birds of the air—all ye children of men—Praise ye the Lord!"

Yes, I felt closer to my fellow men too, even in my solitude. For it is not physical solitude that actually separates one from other men, not physical isolation, but spiritual isolation. It is not the desert island nor the stony wilderness that cuts you from the people you love. It is the wilderness in the mind, the desert wastes in the heart through which one wanders lost and a stranger. When one is a stranger to oneself then one is estranged from others too. If one is out of touch with oneself, then one cannot touch others. How often in a large city, shaking hands with my friends, I have felt the wilderness stretching between us. Both of us were wandering in arid wastes, having lost the springs that nourished us—or having found them dry. Only when one is connected to one's own core is one connected to others, I am beginning to discover. And, for me, the core, the inner spring, can best be refound through solitude.

I walked far down the beach, soothed by the rhythm of the waves, the sun on my bare back and legs, the wind and mist from the spray on my hair. Into the waves and out like a sandpiper. And then home, drenched, drugged, reeling, full to the brim with my day alone; full like the moon before the night has taken a single nibble of it; full as a cup poured up to the lip.

Anne Morrow Lindbergh, *Gift From the Sea* (New York: Pantheon Bks., 1955), pp. 42–45.

◆

There are places and moments in which one is so completely alone that one sees the world entire.

Jules Renard, Journal, December 1900, *The Journal of Jules Renard*, ed. and trans. Louise Bogan and Elizabeth Roget (New York: Braziller, 1964), p. 130.

◆

Last night I looked out about eleven. The moon already a day past its full had risen an hour or more previously. It was strong enough to light up the entire sky in a way that made it look as if it were a mother-of-pearl shell. Yet the same moon was low enough to strike the cypresses and stone pines sideways, so that these threw long shadows over the inner garden and the snow-covered roof of the orangery. Not a light visible, not a sound, but far from estranging as 'real' nature would be (the high mountains for instance); it was cosy, friendly, silent, because everybody had gone to rest, leaving the world to moonlight and to me.

Bernard Berenson, Diary, February 1, 1942, in Bernard Berenson, *Rumour and Reflection* (London: Constable, 1952), p. 88.

Sunday, Aug. 27 [1877].—Another day quite free from mark'd prostration and pain. It seems indeed as if peace and nutriment from heaven subtly filter into me as I slowly hobble down these country lanes and across fields, in the good air—as I sit here in solitude with Nature— open, voiceless, mystic, far removed, yet palpable, eloquent Nature. I merge myself in the scene, in the perfect day. Hovering over the clear brook-water, I am sooth'd by its soft gurgle in one place, and the hoarser murmurs of its three-foot fall in another. Come, ye disconsolate, in whom any latent eligibility is left—come get the sure virtues of creek-shore, and wood and field. Two months (July and August, '77) have I absorb'd them, and they begin to make a new man of me. Every day, seclusion—every day at least two or three hours of freedom, bathing, no talk, no bonds, no dress, no books, no *manners*.

Shall I tell you, reader, to what I attribute my already much-restored health? That I have been almost two years, off and on, without drugs and medicines, and daily in the open air. Last summer I found a particularly secluded little dell off one side by my creek, originally a large dug-out marl-pit, now abandon'd, fill'd with bushes, trees, grass, a group of willows, a straggling bank and a spring of delicious water running right through the middle of it, with two or three little cascades. Here I retreated every hot day, and follow it up this summer. Here I realize the meaning of that old fellow who said he was seldom less alone than when alone. Never before did I get so close to Nature; never before did she come so close to me.

Walt Whitman, *Specimen Days*, 1882, reprinted in Walt Whitman, *Prose Works* (Philadelphia: McKay, n.d.), p. 103.

———◆———

I find it wholesome to be alone the greater part of the time. To be in company, even with the best, is soon wearisome and dissipating. I love to be alone. I never found the companion that was so companionable as solitude. We are for the most part more lonely when we go abroad among men than when we stay in our chambers. A man thinking or working is always alone, let him be where he will. . . .

Society is commonly too cheap. We meet at very short intervals, not having had time to acquire any new value for each other. We meet at meals three times a day, and give each other a new taste of that old musty cheese that we are. We have had to agree on a certain set of rules, called etiquette and politeness, to make this frequent meeting tolerable and that we need not come to open war. We meet at the post-office, and at the sociable, and about the fireside every night; we live thick and are in each other's way, and stumble over one another, and I think that we thus lose some respect for one another. Certainly less frequency would suffice for all important and hearty communications. Consider the girls in a factory,—never alone, hardly in their dreams. It would be better if there were but one inhabitant to a square mile, as where I live. The value of a man is not in his skin, that we should touch him. . . .

I have a great deal of company in my house; especially in the morning, when nobody calls. Let me suggest a few comparisons, that some one may convey an idea of my situation. I am no more lonely than the loon in the pond that laughs so loud, or than Walden Pond itself. What company has that lonely lake, I pray? And yet it has not the blue devils, but the blue angels in it, in the azure tint of its waters. The sun is alone, except in thick weather, when there sometimes appear to be two, but one is a mock sun. God is alone,—but the devil, he is far from being alone; he sees a great deal of company; he is legion. I am no more lonely than a single mullein or dandelion in a pasture, or a bean leaf, or sorrel, or a horse-fly, or a humblebee. I am no more lonely than the Mill Brook, or a weathercock, or the north star, or the south wind, or an April shower, or a January thaw, or the first spider in a new house.

Henry David Thoreau, *Walden, or Life in the Woods*, 1854 (Boston: Houghton, 1929), chap. V, pp. 150–52.

A man can best speak of his own experience. The writer's admittedly is peculiar. For years he was in the habit of spending his winter evenings lecturing to his neighbours in small country towns and villages. It cannot be at all a common form of vocation . . . But more than most it is a seasonal one, for who would listen to a lecture when he might be sitting in the sun or enjoying himself out of doors? . . .

So it came about that for the author of these idle thoughts the coming of winter always spelt a new life, or rather an old life revived after a summer's lapse. The leisurely hours of study between tea and dinner had now to cease; instead, the stroke of five became an alarum to depart. It was now his lot to rise from the fire, collect great-coat and lecture-notes, and grope his way to the garage. An hour or more's driving through the chill-seeming hostility of a winter's night would bring him to hall or institute, where the frugality of the illumination and the uncompromising hardness of the chairs only heightened the impression of earnest endeavour which the audience always politely contrived to convey.

It sounds, I dare say, a comfortless picture. Yet strangely those evenings of sober discourse—a parliament of half-hesitant, deeply thought-
ful countrymen round a stove—were as stimulating as any in my re-
membrance. And the homeward journeys afterwards are as pleasant to
recall, for solitude, the ranging silver beam of headlight on hedgerow
and sleeping meadow, and the hazards of wintry weather made them
partake of some peculiar and inexpressible romance. Now, far to south
or north, the light of a distant town would make an arc of dim fire in
the sky, now the moon would rise cold and vibrant to ride visible clouds,
now wisps of white fog enfold road and bonnet and transform the guid-
ing beam into an impenetrable wall of emptiness. Six times in nine
years a fox ran swiftly across the car's course, and twice an owl slept un-
scathed in the midst of a lane, and the swift wheels passed on either
side of him. Such hours of moving isolation afforded time for thought
and meditation seldom allowed by the conditions of modern life. There
are compensations in the hurry-scurry of an age of transport, and the
solitude of the wheel by night may give the peace and inward content
which in former times men sought for in the wilderness.

Sir Arthur Bryant, "Hunter's Moon," *Historian's Holiday* (London: Collins, 1951), pp. 32–33.

Among the sadder and smaller pleasures of this world I count
this pleasure: the pleasure of taking up one's pen. . . .
Note what the action means. You are alone. Even if the room is
crowded (as was the smoking-room in the G.W.R. Hotel, at Paddington,
only the other day, when I wrote my "Statistical Abstract of Christen-
dom"), even if the room is crowded, you must have made yourself alone
to be able to write at all. You must have built up some kind of wall and
isolated your mind. You are alone, then; and that is the beginning.
If you consider at what pains men are to be alone: how they climb
mountains, enter prisons, profess monastic vows, put on eccentric daily
habits, and seclude themselves in the garrets of a great town, you will
see that this moment of taking up the pen is not least happy in the fact
that then, by a mere association of ideas, the writer is alone.

Hilaire Belloc, "On Nothing," *On Nothing & Kindred Subjects*,
2d ed. (New York: Dutton, 1909), pp. 1–2.

My idea of a home is a house in which each member of the family can on the instant kindle a fire in his or her private room. Otherwise their society is compulsory and wasteful to the individual.

Ralph Waldo Emerson, Journal, September 1866, *The Heart of Emerson's Journals*, ed. Bliss Perry (Boston: Houghton, 1926), p. 318.

———◆———

He was in retreat at 188 Adelaide Road for three months and a half. He has left descriptions of how he lived. 'The room I lived and slept in was the top room of the house, except for a long low attic above. Alone here I felt that I could sort myself out. After sweeping the floor and dusting a bit, I would sit down on one of the two chairs and think and look at the floor. Oh, the joy of just that!'

Maurice Collis, *Stanley Spencer* (London: Harvil, 1962), p. 153.

———◆———

. . . I feel the pleasure of being alone and uninterrupted. Few men, leading a quiet life, and without any strong or highly varied change of circumstances, have seen more variety of society than I—few have enjoyed it more, or been *bored*, as it is called, less by the company of tiresome people. I have rarely, if ever, found any one, out of whom I could not extract amusement or edification; and were I obliged to account for hints afforded on such occasions, I should make an ample deduction from my inventive powers. Still, however, from the earliest time I can remember, I preferred the pleasure of being alone to waiting for visitors, and have often taken a bannock and a bit of cheese to the wood or hill, to avoid dining with company. As I grew from boyhood to manhood I saw this would not do; and that to gain a place in men's esteem I must mix and bustle with them. Pride and an excitation of spirits supplied the real pleasure which others seem to feel in society, and certainly upon many occasions it was real. Still, if the question was, eternal company, without the power of retiring within yourself, or solitary confinement for life, I should say, "Turnkey, lock the cell!"

Sir Walter Scott, Journal, December 27, 1825, *The Journal of Sir Walter Scott* (New York: Harper, 1891), vol. I, pp. 65–66.

PART FOUR

Unexpected Contentment

IN SICKNESS

How are you? Asthmatic, I know you will reply; but as my poor father (who was asthmatic, too, and the jolliest of men) used philosophically to say, "one must have something wrong, I suppose, and I like to know what it is."

Charles Dickens, letter to M. de Cerjat, November 13, 1865, *The Letters of Charles Dickens*, ed. Georgina Hogarth and Mary Dickens, 2d ed. (London: Chapman, 1880), vol. II, p. 240.

If there be a regal solitude, it is a sick-bed. How the patient lords it there; what caprices he acts without controll . . .

How sickness enlarges the dimensions of a man's self to himself! he is his own exclusive object. Supreme selfishness is inculcated upon him as his only duty. 'Tis the Two Tables of the Law to him. He has nothing to think of but how to get well. What passes out of doors, or within them, so he hear not the jarring of them, affects him not. . . .

To the world's business he is dead. He understands not what the callings and occupations of mortals are; only he has a glimmering conceit of some such thing, when the doctor makes his daily call; and even in the lines on that busy face he reads no multiplicity of patients, but solely conceives of himself as *the sick man*. To what other uneasy couch the good man is hastening, when he slips out of his chamber, folding up his thin douceur so carefully, for fear of rustling—is no speculation which he can at present entertain. He thinks only of the regular return of the same phenomenon at the same hour to-morrow.

Household rumours touch him not. Some faint murmur, indicative of life going on within the house, soothes him, while he knows not distinctly what it is. He is not to know anything, not to think of anything. Servants gliding up or down the distant staircase, treading as upon velvet, gently keep his ear awake, so long as he troubles not himself further than with some feeble guess at their errands. . . .

To be sick is to enjoy monarchal prerogatives. Compare the silent tread and quiet ministry, almost by the eye only, with which he is served—with the careless demeanour, the unceremonious goings in and out (slapping of doors, or leaving them open) of the very same attendants, when he is getting a little better—and you will confess, that from the bed of sickness (throne let me rather call it) to the elbow-chair of convalescence, is a fall from dignity, amounting to a deposition.

How convalescence shrinks a man back to his pristine stature! Where is now the space, which he occupied so lately, in his own, in the family's eye?

The scene of his regalities, his sick-room, which was his presence-chamber, where he lay and acted his despotic fancies—how is it reduced to a common bedroom! . . .

Perhaps some relic of the sick man's dream of greatness survives in the still lingering visitations of the medical attendant. But how is he, too, changed with everything else? Can this be he—this man of news—of chat—of anecdote—of everything but physic—can this be he, who so lately came between the patient and his cruel enemy, as on some solemn embassy from Nature, erecting herself into a high mediating party?—Pshaw! 'tis some old woman.

Farewell with him all that made sickness pompous—the spell that hushed the household—the desert-like stillness, felt throughout its inmost chambers—the mute attendance—the inquiry by looks—the still softer delicacies of self-attention—the sole and single eye of distemper alonely fixed upon itself—world-thoughts excluded—the man a world unto himself—his own theatre—

What a speck is he dwindled into!

Charles Lamb, "The Convalescent," *The Last Essays of Elia,* 1833 (London: Cassell, 1907), chap. VIII, pp. 225–28.

———◆———

A long time since I wrote in this book. In September I caught a cold, which meant three weeks' illness.

I have not been suffering; merely feverish and weak and unable to use my mind for anything but a daily hour or two of the lightest reading. The weather has not favoured my recovery, wet winds often blowing, and not much sun. Lying in bed, I have watched the sky, studied the clouds, which—so long as they are clouds indeed, and not a mere waste of grey vapour—always have their beauty. Inability to read has always been my horror; once, a trouble of the eyes all but drove me mad with fear of blindness; but I find that in my present circumstances, in my own still house, with no intrusion to be dreaded, with no task or care to worry me, I can fleet the time not unpleasantly even without help of books. Reverie, unknown to me in the days of bondage, has brought me solace; I hope it has a little advanced me in wisdom.

For not, surely, by deliberate effort of thought does a man grow wise. The truths of life are not discovered by us. At moments unforeseen, some gracious influence descends upon the soul, touching it to an emotion which, we know not how, the mind transmutes into thought. This can happen only in a calm of the senses, a surrender of the whole being to passionless contemplation. I understand, now, the intellectual mood of the quietist.

George Gissing, *The Private Papers of Henry Ryecroft*, 1903, Autumn (New York: Boni & Liveright, 1918), chap. V, pp. 137-38.

◆

It is hard, if people are young and eager for action, to be chained by physical weakness. It is grievous to be forced to lead a life of contemplation when the heart is set upon roaming—to be placed upon a philosophical hillside when you are all afire to be down in the plain amid the sweet, keen trouble of living. Yet a charm clothes all things seen from a hilltop. . . . Through the still air come mysterious calls and echoes—remote as dreams, provocative to the imagination as a half-told romance. Looking into the world of nature from sickroom or garden, one finds out how lovely the near things are; the one tree or field will reveal depth on depth of beauty to the long, concentrated gaze. . . .

Through any window may be seen the same gracious depths of blue air as Buddha contemplated through the interstices of his tree, as Michael Angelo saw through the windows of the Sistine chapel. The long gaze of a sick man may probe as far into the illimitable as they did.

Mary Webb, *The Spring of Joy*, 1928 (London: Cape, 1937), chap. IX, pp. 196-97.

◆

After a fortnight at home, it was discovered suddenly that I had developed a high temperature, and had evidently become afflicted with the same illness responsible for the early disbanding of my school. . . . I lay in bed for nearly three months, in a large room cut off from the rest of the house. . . . Certainly, however, this short period was the most important of my whole childhood, because it gave me that which is granted to so few children: time—apparently endless time—in which to think and still more to feel. In my mind the whole perspective of this illness and the months to follow is immensely magnified, no doubt because of its moment to me. Nor am I the only person by any means to have found a physical crisis of this kind helpful to development. For example, I once asked Sir Edwin Lutyens, who was one of thirteen children, whether any other member of his family shared his genius or had found a similar direction for their gifts. He replied, "No. . . . Any talent I may have was due to a long illness as a boy, which afforded me time to think, and to subsequent ill-health, because I was not allowed to play games, and so had to teach myself, for my enjoyment, to use my eyes instead of my feet. My brothers hadn't the same advantage."

Similarly, I owe an immense debt to those few months of exterior struggle and growing interior calm and reconciliation: and though I endured a great deal of pain and restlessness, I found peace to an extent of which I had never before been conscious. Yet I inhabited no pleasant or comfortable world, though at any rate it was one in which the imagination could flourish without hindrance, was, on the contrary, helped and forced on. . . . During the day, if I were not asleep and the room were not darkened, I lay watching through the broad windows the flights of charcoal-winged rooks flapping their way over the tree-tops into the sky, where, in a splendour of golden light, existed those cloud-continents that one so seldom for long examines, for, in health, the eyes prefer a world that is on their own level. But now I looked at them until, when I turned my glance back to the objects in the room, I could see little of these; I gazed at the shifting and melting castles, the fulgent towers and palaces, shapes that in their turn revealed processions from times past, antique and plumy triumphs of arches and spears and helmets and cars drawn by wild-maned horses, or, with a sudden change of scale, dissolved into superhuman torsos, their golden muscles rippling in the wind, or into the likeness of gods and furies, all these being brought to life by the flickering and hispid sun. I visited countries and kingdoms I was never to see again, equatorial vistas of sand, and snow landscapes with an organisation of their own, more wild in architecture than the forms to which even limestone can lend itself, floating alpine heights built up in a golden flame that was like a lion's steadfast glare, vast cities washed by huge seas, that undulated in answer to the moon's call, through a mist of prismatic spume—metropolises of a thousand spires, a thousand belfries from which, very occasionally, I caught the sound of the solemn but brassy peals rung for immense victories I could not fathom, and then, my eyes dazzling with rainbows, I was forced for a moment to shut them, and so was asleep again.

Sir Osbert Sitwell, *The Scarlet Tree* (London: Macmillan, 1946), pp. 223–25.

... I believe that life cannot be enjoyed by anybody who has not known pain. One of fortune's gifts to me, as precious as any, has been a great deal of acute pain from early childhood onwards. I realize now what an armoury early pain provides for age and how much the threat of it in the background enhances the enjoyment of life while it stays in the background. Let it be understood, I am not suggesting that continuous pain is a boon.

Two or three months after my eighth birthday I almost tore one of my hands in half on a hook. What remains most vividly in my mind of that unpleasant business? Not the agony of having my fingers bent back three times a day to keep my hand from curling up permanently, but the joy of lying on a sofa on sunny May days and having read to me the adventures of Sherlock Holmes which were making their first appearance in the *Strand Magazine*.

Sir Compton Mackenzie, "My Time of Life," *Echoes* (London: Chatto, 1954), pp. 180–81.

When first he [Walt Whitman] came [to stay with George and Mary Stafford on their farm at Timber Creek, New Jersey] he didn't look as though he would live many months. But she found that he chiefly needed rousing and heartening up. She told him of cases of paralytics who lived for twenty years or more after a seizure. It seemed to cheer him.

He gradually improved sufficiently to go outdoors a little and then a little farther. He would hobble as far as the barn and one of the children would carry a chair for him. Later he would venture farther and go down the lane a little. Then he began to take the chair himself. . . .

At first he was rather downcast, but soon became quite happy. He always used to sing in a morning as soon as he rose from bed. After he had been out he would sometimes say: "Susan, folks question sometimes what happiness is. But I have had a happy day."

J. W. Wallace, reminiscences of Walt Whitman, in J. Johnston and J. W. Wallace, *Visits to Walt Whitman in 1890–1891* (London: Allen & Unwin, 1917), pp. 186–87.

No murmur or complaint was heard from this athlete and lover of life, as he sat crippled alike by disease and age. He [George Meredith] was the man who had written, "There is nothing the body suffers that the soul may not profit by." His soul enriched itself with all the pleasures and activities that his once splendid body was now compelled to forgo. Youth never left him, but became transformed into a gracious spiritual repossession of youth's joys, by memory and by seeing others enjoy them in their turn. . . . I have seen him watching the esplanade from a seaside-lodging window. To most of us it would have seemed a very ordinary lodging-house window indeed, but to him, and to those who heard him talk, it was a peephole on glorious life. A girl passing on a bicycle set him prophesying the fuller life that was now setting in for women. A boy leading a pet goat up and down aroused his envy and delight, made him again in spirit a boy, a Crossjay. To listen to him was to be plunged by Esculapius into the healing waters of youth.

Sir George Macaulay Trevelyan, "George Meredith," *Clio, a Muse and Other Essays* (London: Longmans, 1913), pp. 99–100.

◆

My father lived in a small wooden house in western Canada, where he carved himself out a fruit orchard from the hillside and the forest. He had chosen it with one of the most beautiful views in the world, an open valley and a river winding, with mountains beyond, and the Kootenay lake just visible to the north; and built himself a wide window, to look out on three sides. This window, and six Chippendale chairs which he had rescued in a farmer's sale, and a few sketches on the walls, were all the luxury of the place. . . .

Four years before his death, when he was seventy-two, a stroke took away from him the open-air life he loved; and though by the strength of his will he managed, step by step with the passing months, to walk a mile or so with a stick to lean on, most of his time came to be spent in the window that looked out on his view. Here, he told me, the changing clouds and the light of the river would fill his mind with pleasantness for hours at a time and lead his thoughts into endless variation: and I believe this to be true, and that he was happy, for not only did he never complain, but his whole atmosphere was one of serenity and peaceful interest in all things as they came. And later, when I have thought of happiness and what it may be, I have always seen his gentle old head in the window, with the hillside full of tame pheasants and pigeons, and the valley and the mountains beyond. . . .

Freya Stark, "Happiness," *Perseus in the Wind*, 1948, (London: Murray, 1963), chap. III, pp. 21–22.

While he was being put into his wheel chair, the model went outside and took her place on flower-spangled grass. The foliage of the olive trees sifted the rays of light and made an arabesque on her red blouse. In a voice still weak from his suffering [from severe arthritis] during the night, Renoir had the adjustable windows opened or closed, as he wished . . . While one of us prepared his palette he could not help groaning once or twice. Adjusting his stricken body to the hard seat of the wheel chair was painful. But he wanted this "not too soft" seat, which helped him to keep upright and allowed him a certain amount of movement. . . . My father's suffering devastated all of us. . . . Whenever we would try to talk in a cheerful voice, it sounded false.

One of us would put the protecting piece of linen in Renoir's hand, pass him the brush he had indicated with a wink of the eye. "That one, there . . . No, the other one." . . .

The landscape was a microcosm of all the riches in the world. His eyes, nose and ears were assailed by countless contradictory sensations. "It's intoxicating," he kept repeating. He stretched out his arm and dipped his brush into the turpentine. But the movement was painful. He waited a few seconds, as if asking himself: "Why not give up? Isn't it too hard?" Then a glance at the subject restored his courage. He traced on the canvas a mark, in madder red, that only he understood. "Jean, open the yellow curtain a little more." Another touch of madder. Then, in a stronger voice, "It's divine!" We watched him. He smiled and winked, as he called us to witness this conspiracy which had just been arranged between the grass, the olive trees, the model and himself. After a minute or two he would start humming. And a day of happiness would begin for Renoir, a day as wonderful as the one which preceded it, and the one which was to follow.

Jean Renoir, *Renoir, My Father* (Boston: Little, Brown, 1962), pp. 455–56.

———◆———

"Life is sweet, brother."
"Do you think so?"
"Think so!—There's night and day, brother, both sweet things; sun, moon, and stars, brother, all sweet things; there's likewise a wind on the heath. Life is very sweet, brother; who would wish to die?" . . .
"In sickness, Jasper?"
"There's the sun and stars, brother."
"In blindness, Jasper?"

"There's the wind on the heath, brother; if I could only feel that, I would gladly live for ever. . . ."

George Borrow, *Lavengro*, 1851 (London: Nelson, n.d.), chap. XXV, p. 166.

IN SADNESS

◆

Occasional melancholy is not inconsistent with a preponderance of happiness; indeed, it is quite possible to be happy and melancholy at the same time, as a landscape may be both beautiful and sad, or as a piece of music may pass from a major to a minor key and be equally harmonious in both.

Philip Gilbert Hamerton, *The Quest of Happiness* (Boston: Roberts Brothers, 1897), p. 180.

◆

. . . I was flying to California, I had been ill, and I was in a very troubled and frustrated period of my life. Moody, I sat in the big, noisy plane and gazed out of the window. There was the vast light-brown sand of the desert, the majesty of the mountains. It was a scene of continuing but forbidding beauty. There was a grandeur of desolation in the mountains and deserts. To man, this was all waste. It was living and savage but empty of human cultivation. The beauty of this scene was almost deathlike. Rock and sand changed colors as the day dramatically faded. The colors of the sky changed and increased the cast of softening glow upon them. I gazed and gazed. And suddenly I told myself that I had no complaints. I had seen much of the grandeur and beauty of this world. And I was, at the moment, seeing more of it.

James T. Farrell, "Reflections at Fifty," *Reflections at Fifty and Other Essays* (New York: Vanguard, 1954), p. 63.

. . . church bells . . . have always had a queer hypnotic effect on me, not at all easy to describe. I can listen to them for hours on end. It is extremely difficult for me to pass a church where they are ringing; I always want to stay and listen, and usually do. The pleasure I get from them may be tinged with melancholy, but it is not the less pleasurable for that. They evoke scenes and memories. Though they suggest the passing of time, they imply also the continuity of things. Life is short, but it goes on: here to-day, there to-morrow: Shakespeare in 1600, Beethoven in 1800. Again I sense the biographer in me, for with the sound of bells I seem very near to my favourite personalities of the past, who have heard what I am hearing and have felt the same kind of mournful joy.

Hesketh Pearson, *Thinking It Over* (London: Hamish Hamilton, 1938), pp. 36–37.

───────◆───────

I love to wander on these soft gentle mournful autumn days, alone among the quiet peaceful solitary meadows, tracing out the ancient footpaths and mossy overgrown stiles between farm and hamlet, village and town, musing of the many feet that have trodden these ancient and now well nigh deserted and almost forgotten ways and walking in the footsteps of the generations that have gone before and passed away.

Francis Kilvert, Diary, August 31, 1874, *Kilvert's Diary*, ed. William Plomer (London: Cape, 1940), vol. III, pp. 74–75.

───────◆───────

Stendhal said that for him a landscape needed to possess some history or human interest. For me a place must have a genius in the air, a sort of distillation of years, a pathos of perspective, a mist of distance. In a word, it must have ghosts of lost wandering life, now forgotten by the extrovert and contemporary world. Historical and archæological interest is prosaic for me; I do not particularly wish to see the house in which the greatest poet was born; but to walk from Grinzing down to Vienna on a September evening, as twilight deepens and the lights of the city begin to twinkle, and to feel the sense of the past, almost to hear the vanished beauty and song whispering in the rustle of leaf or wind, and in some hurrying footfalls on the roadside; to feel an awareness to all the hearts that have beaten here, the hopes and the strivings in these old houses, huddled in deserted gardens; birth and marriage and death; the comings-home at the day's end, the glow of candlelight and wine and fellowship that surely seemed perennial and everlasting; the security of life at the crest, and now not only dead but lost to a world that must for ever be up and doing—this for me, is to live and to "go places." Every great city is a palimpsest not of facts and events but of atmosphere and feeling, shaped by the irony of transition. That means I cannot enter into an unexplored land, a new land, where nature has not acquired an æsthetic and a pathos. Mountains and grand canyons and plains and mighty rivers are only so much geography in my eyes; mere countour-maps built on a large scale.

Sir Neville Cardus, *Autobiography* (London: Collins, 1947), p. 250.

———◆———

In the course of an excursion through one of the remote counties of England, I had struck into one of those cross roads that lead through the more secluded parts of the country, and stopped one afternoon at a village, the situation of which was beautifully rural and retired. There was an air of primitive simplicity about its inhabitants, not to be found in the villages which lie on the great coach-roads. I determined to pass the night there, and, having taken an early dinner, strolled out to enjoy the neighboring scenery.

My ramble, as is usually the case with travelers, soon led me to the church, which stood at a little distance from the village. Indeed, it was an object of some curiosity, its old tower being completely overrun with ivy, so that only here and there a jutting buttress, an angle of gray wall, or a fantastically carved ornament, peered through the verdant covering. It was a lovely evening. The early part of the day had been dark and showery, but in the afternoon it had cleared up; and though sullen clouds still hung over head, yet there was a broad tract of golden sky in the west, from which the setting sun gleamed through the dripping leaves, and lit up all nature into a melancholy smile. . . .

I had seated myself on a half-sunken tombstone, and was musing, as one is apt to do at this sober-thoughted hour, on past scenes and early friends—on those who were distant and those who were dead—and indulging in that kind of melancholy fancying, which has in it something sweeter even than pleasure. Every now and then, the stroke of a bell from the neighboring tower fell on my ear; its tones were in unison with the scene, and, instead of jarring, chimed in with my feelings . . .

Washington Irving, "The Pride of the Village," *The Sketch Book*, author's rev. ed. (New York: George P. Putnam, 1849), pp. 399–400.

I have said how beautiful New England gravestones are as they fit into the green carpet. On the blue-green carpet which is the Maine coast this is especially so. . . . Life and death can go splendidly hand in hand in the midst of such continuous splendor. Lichened gravestones go well against walls of dark spruces, with stonewalls that keep the wild trees out. Here lie captains who sailed all the seas and took these Welsh slates with them till they should have use for them; here are captains' stones with no captains below them, for the captains sleep in oceans on the other side of the globe. Wild rabbits pause to wonder at the death's-head cherubs in stone here; and Queen Anne's lace imitates the lace-work of weeping willows on ancient slates. . . .

Even when the stonewalls have been cast down by the frost and wild maples and hemlocks have come in at last into the graveyard, it is the right thing to do to forgive the wild things for coming back home. Deer eye these even white and gray stones slanting all parallel in the sweet wild grass they graze. The wild and the tame are friends at last in a dusky green truce. Man forgives the wild that won the battle of two centuries . . .

Robert P. Tristram Coffin, *On the Green Carpet* (Indianapolis: Bobbs, 1951), pp. 190–91.

———◆———

The English burying-place [in Rome] is a green slope near the walls, under the pyramidal tomb of Cestius, and is, I think, the most beautiful and solemn cemetery I ever beheld. To see the sun shining on its bright grass, fresh, when we first visited it, with the autumnal dews, and hear the whispering of the wind among the leaves of the trees which have overgrown the tomb of Cestius, and the soil which is stirring in the sun-warm earth, and to mark the tombs, mostly of women and young people who were buried there, one might, if one were to die, de-sire the sleep they seem to sleep.

Percy Bysshe Shelley, letter to Thomas Love Peacock, December 22, 1818, in Thomas Love Peacock, *Memoirs of Percy Bysshe Shelley* (London: Dent, 1933), p. 415.

When summer opens, I see how fast it matures, and fear it will be short; but after the heats of July and August, I am reconciled, like one who has had his swing, to the cool of autumn. So will it be with the coming of death.

Ralph Waldo Emerson, Journal, May 1846, *The Heart of Emerson's Journal*, ed. Bliss Perry (Boston: Houghton, 1926), p. 218.

———◆———

Everything is sweetened by risk. The pleasant emotion is mixed and deepened by a sense of mortality. Those lovers who have never encountered the possibility of last embraces and farewells are novices in the passion. Sunset affects us more powerfully than sunrise, simply because it *is* a setting sun, and suggests a thousand analogies. A mother is never happier than when her eyes fill over her sleeping child, never does she kiss it more fondly, never does she pray for it more fervently; and yet there is more in her heart than visible red cheek and yellow curl; possession and bereavement are strangely mingled in the exquisite maternal mood, the one heightening the other. All great joys are serious; and emotion must be measured by its complexity and the deepness of its reach. . . . Pleasures which rise beyond the mere gratification of the senses are dependent for their exquisiteness on the number and variety of the thoughts which they evoke. And that joy is the greatest which, while felt to be joy, can include the thought of death and clothe itself with that crowning pathos.

Alexander Smith, "Death and Dying," *Dreamthorp*, 1863 (Boston: Joseph Knight, n.d.), chap. III, pp. 70–71.

———◆———

Death, too, is an enhancer. Through him, life gains its colour, clinging precarious like some Alpine flower that digs its tenuous and tenacious roots in the rock face against the darkness of the drop below. The secret joy of peril comes from the veiled presence, without which most savour goes; and this is no morbid feeling, for the ecstasy belongs not to death itself, but to *life*, suddenly enriched to know itself alive. So after a summer dawn and climb till noon, among clefts and icy triangles or wind-scooped crannies, the mountaineer returning sets foot again on the short turf and flowers; and the breeze that cools him is the same breeze that sways the harebells; the blood that tramples in his ears and runs like chariots through his veins is the kind, swift, temporary stuff by which the smaller things of earth are fed; he is back in the community of his kind and descends, light-footed, among the pastures: but he remembers how in the high silences he has known himself on the edge of Silence and how its wing has brushed him. Once, looking down into a valley of the Lebanon, I have heard below me as it were a swish of silk and seen, within a pebble's drop, an eagle's wings outspread; and so we watch death's flight, in our sunlight.

Freya Stark, "Death," *Perseus in the Wind*, 1948 (London: Murray, 1963), chap. VI, p. 46.

———◆———

When one is nearly seventy, one cannot be sure of the future. 'The years of our life are three score and ten, and even if we are strong enough to reach the age of eighty, yet these years are but toil and vanity; they are soon passed and we also pass away' (cf. Psalm 89: 10–11). So it is no use nursing any illusions: I must make myself familiar with the thought of the end, not with dismay which saps the will, but with confidence which preserves our enthusiasm for living, working and serving. Some time ago I resolved to bear constantly in mind this reverent expectation of death, this joy which ought to be my soul's last happiness when it departs from this life. I need not become wearisome to others by speaking frequently of this; but I must always think of it, because the consideration of death, the *judicium mortis*, when it has become a familiar thought, is good and useful for the mortification of vanity and for infusing into everything a sense of moderation and calm.

Pope John XXIII, "Spiritual notes written during my brief retreat at Oran (Algeria), 6–9 April, 1950 . . ." in *Journal of a Soul* (Montreal: Palm, 1965), p. 276.

———◆———

"It is all right," said Walt Whitman to me as I was leaving his death-bed and hearing his voice for the last time—"It is all right." Of course it was all right, and it will be all right when each and all of us fall into the last eternal sleep. Else it would not be. Our being here is all right, is it not? "Friendly and faithful," says Whitman, "are the arms that have helped me," and friendly and faithful must be the arms that bear us away. If it was good to come, it will be good to go—good in the large, cosmic sense, good in that it is in keeping with the spirit of the All. Not the good of our brief personal successes and triumphs, but good as evolution is good, as the processes of growth and decay are good. If life is good, death must be equally good, as each waits upon the other. From what point of view can we say that death is not all right? Certainly not from the point of view of the universe. Archimedes could have moved the world had he some other world upon which to place his lever, and we must have some other universe to plant our feet upon to condemn death.

John Burroughs, "Accepting the Universe," *Essays in Naturalism* (Boston: Houghton, 1921), pp. 291–92.

———◆———

Why are happy people not afraid of Death, while the insatiable and the unhappy so abhor that grim feature?

Logan Pearsall Smith, "Afterthoughts," *All Trivia* (New York: Harcourt, 1934), p. 168.

———◆———

The Persian Sufi poet Rumi (thirteenth century) writes . . . about death, showing that our attitude toward death is in reality a reflection of our attitude toward ourself and toward our life. He who truly loves life and lives it, is able to accept death without sorrow. . . .

Yet this "friendship" with death is not the same as a pathological death wish. The death wish is merely a refusal of life, an abdication from the difficulties and sorrows of living, a resentment of its joys. The death wish is an incapacity for life. True acceptance of death in freedom and faith demands a mature and fruitful acceptance of life. He who fears death or he who longs for it—both are in the same condition: they admit they have not lived.

Thomas Merton, *Conjectures of a Guilty Bystander* (New York: Doubleday, 1966), p. 214.

BY SURPRISE

◆

Crossing a bare common, in snow puddles, at twilight, under a clouded sky, without having in my thoughts any occurrence of special good fortune, I have enjoyed a perfect exhilaration. I am glad to the brink of fear.

Ralph Waldo Emerson, "Nature," *Nature, Addresses and Lectures* (Boston: Houghton, 1898), p. 15.

◆

Sometimes at breakfast, sometimes in a train or empty bus, or on the moving stairs at Charing Cross, I am happy; the earth turns to gold, and life becomes a magical adventure. Only yesterday, travelling alone to Sussex, I became light-headed with this sudden joy. The train seemed to rush to its adorable destination through a world newborn in splendour, bathed in a beautiful element, fresh and clear as on the morning of Creation. Even the coloured photographs of South Coast watering-places in the railway carriage shone with the light of Paradise upon them.

Logan Pearsall Smith, "Joy," *More Trivia*, 1921, reprinted in *All Trivia* (New York: Harcourt, 1934), pp. 137–38.

◆

Sometimes, in some stillness, the secret is all about us, never held but almost to be perceived. In such moments the individual ceases to be conscious of himself; he has dissolved the familiar, he is part of what he looks at, a part of Happiness: for an instant he has stepped into that ocean of which we are the scattered pools and these moments are never forgotten. They make our lives like journeys through the plain whose vaporous summer hides the mountain ranges; until one day, through some bite of autumn in the air the mist dissolves, and the reality appears unexpected; the hills shine on the horizon, luminous and lightly shadowed like crumpled almond blossom transparent to the sun: the hidden summits are discovered, and ever afterwards we know that they are there.

Freya Stark, "Happiness," *Perseus in the Wind,* 1948 (London: Murray, 1963), chap. III, p. 24.

◆

Magnificent weather. The morning seems bathed in happy peace, and a heavenly fragrance rises from mountain and shore; it is as though a benediction were laid upon us. No vulgar intrusive noise disturbs the religious quiet of the scene. One might believe one's self in a church—a vast temple in which every being and every natural beauty has its place. I dare not breathe for fear of putting the dream to flight—a dream traversed by angels.

> "Comme autrefois j'entends dans lé'ther infini
> La musique du temps et l'hosanna des mondes."

In these heavenly moments the cry of Pauline rises to one's lips. "I feel! I believe! I see!" All the miseries, the cares, the vexations of life, are forgotten; the universal joy absorbs us; we enter into the divine order, and into the blessedness of the Lord. Labor and tears, sin, pain, and death have passed away. To exist is to bless; life is happiness. In this sublime pause of things all dissonances have disappeared. It is as though creation were but one vast symphony, glorifying the God of goodness with an inexhaustible wealth of praise and harmony. We question no longer whether it is so or not. We have ourselves become notes in the great concert; and the soul breaks the silence of ecstasy only to vibrate in unison with the eternal joy.

Henri-Frédéric Amiel, Journal, August 25, 1871, *The Journal Intime of Henri-Frédéric Amiel,* trans. Mrs. Humphrey Ward, 1899 (New York: Burt, n.d.), pp. 241–42.

◆

I do not think I am a credulous person: quite the contrary. Yet once or twice in my life I have had what I can only describe as an illumination . . .

I left [Scunthorpe] . . . and took my seat in the train with the prospect of many hours before me in the dark, dirty and unheated carriage.
I was unconscious of any discomfort. For the past twenty-four hours I
had hardly eaten anything; yet I was not hungry. In fact, I hardly seemed
to inhabit my body at all. Looking out of the window I watched the
snow-covered landscape gliding past. But it was like no landscape I had
ever seen before. It seemed to be bathed in an unearthly light. It was
so beautiful that I was moved to tears. I found myself murmuring the
words of Elephas Lévi: *'Je crois à l'Inconnu que Dieu personifie.'* I
passed the entire journey in this strange exalted state, trance, *samadhi*,
call it what you will, and didn't come to until the train stopped at the
London terminus and the crack of the anti-aircraft guns reminded me of
what is called reality.

That there was a Reality beyond reality I had no doubt. Nor did I
doubt its ultimate beneficence.

James Laver, *Museum Piece* (London: Deutsch, 1963), p. 232.

◆

Contrary to my usual habit of sitting at the desk throughout the
morning hours, I had occasion yesterday to drive into the country town
on an errand. The job done, I set off immediately on the return journey,
troubled because of the loss of a good morning's work according to the
habitual routine. This minor anxiety made me hurry, and I sped along
the main road like a man possessed. So I was: a man possessed, but of
a futile addiction to habit.

Half-way home, I turned off the high road into the lane whose
principal traffic, even in this age of buffer to buffer, is of swallow flight
in summer and the trooping finches in winter. I lost the smell of fuel
and found myself slowing down. Honeysuckle wafts and the almond
tang of wild spiraea (meadow-sweet) came floating in at the open window of the car: a fairy anaesthetic. I passed an ancient farmhouse, tile-
hung and rosy red, set in a garden of madonna lilies, with weeping willows over a pond where a few ducks floated. Beyond that the open
country stretched, over orchards, hop-gardens, and distant hills punc-
tuated with copses and oast-houses.

I came to a standstill. The mood of anxious hurry, the purpose to
get back to work and performance of the daily stint, fell away. Leaning
over the steering-wheel and peering out intently, first at the nearer scene,

then widely at the welkin where distance was playing its subtle deceits on its instrument of invisible air, I felt so powerful a change within me that both mind and body were stirred. At the time I did not try to analyse the emotion. It was too precious to tamper with. It came over me like a caress; a warmth, yet a coolness; an intimacy, yet a universal sensation, as though the whole world were suddenly opened out before me, both in time and space.

Then I was aware of my happiness. It took the form of utmost content. . . .

Everything in front of my windscreen became doubly familiar while I sat there for some five minutes, wrapped in myself, but also embracing the prospect of my beloved countryside. Once again, to the ageing man, everything was new, and the passing moment was an augury of some tremendous adventure about to be experienced, toward the enlargement of my personal horizon. . . .

The important thing is that in these arresting flashes which hold us up, maybe for the fraction of a second, the universe is set blazing before our eyes and we see significances and meanings, relationships and consequences which by the common light of day are obscure to us. These are the times when intuition takes command and inspiration underlines the answers which we have been seeking in vain. . . .

Such grandiloquent thoughts did not follow my miniature adventure yesterday. At the moment, I sat there humbly, utterly unselfconscious, basking in the light of this return to boyhood happiness. My veteran nature melted away under the incandescence, and I sat there for that five-minute spell of rapture, lost in prayerless prayer.

Then I moved my limbs, lifted my head, and drove quietly on, still shining with that light.

Richard Church, "Sweet Content," *Calm October* (London: Heinemann, 1961), pp. 26–29.

———◆———

. . . I went up on the hillside, and lay down in the grass, where a high wind was blowing. Could I never escape from death? Or was it life that would not cease its hostilities? If only I could lose myself in nothing or everything! If only I could become a part of the grass and the wind and the spirit that moved round them, and in them. I thought of the mystics, who had attained Divine consciousness through a surrender of the agonized self. By giving up, by yielding the sense of separateness, by extinguishing the innermost core of identity. I tried with all my strength to find absorption in the Power people called God, or in the vast hollowness of the universe. . . . Then, after long effort, I sank into an effortless peace. Lying there, in that golden August light, I knew, or felt, or beheld, a union deeper than knowledge, deeper than sense, deeper than vision. Light streamed through me, after anguish, and for one instant of awareness, if but for that one instant, I felt pure ecstasy. In a single blinding flash of illumination, I knew blessedness. I was a part of the spirit that moved in the light and the wind and the grass. I was—or felt I was—in communion with reality, with ultimate being. . . . But thinking came long afterwards. There was no thought, there was only blissful recognition, in that timeless awakening. . . . Then the moment sped on; the illumination flashed by me; the wind raced through the grass; the golden light shone and faded.

Ellen Glasgow, *The Woman Within* (New York: Harcourt, 1954), pp. 165–66.

———◆———

In South Africa I recovered an experience which I had not known since my childhood, moments, even hours, of intense exhilaration, when one seemed to be a happy part of a friendly universe. The cause, no doubt, was largely physical, for my long treks made me very fit in body; but not wholly, for I have had the same experiences much later in life when my health was far from perfect. They came usually in the early morning or at sunset. I seemed to acquire a wonderful clearness of mind and to find harmony in discords and unity in diversity, but to find these things not as conclusions of thought, but in a sudden revelation, as in poetry or music. For a little, beauty peeped from the most unlikely wrappings and everything had a secret purpose of joy. It was the mood for poetry had I been anything of a poet.

> "I was all ear
> And took in strains that might create a soul
> Under the ribs of death."

Looking back I find my South African memories studded with those high moments. One especially stands out. I had been ploughing all day in the black dust of the Lichtenburg roads, and had come very late to a place called the Eye of Malmani—Malmani Oog—the spring of a river which presently loses itself in the sands of the Kalahari. We watered our horses and went supperless to bed. Next morning I bathed in one of the Malmani pools—and icy cold it was—and then basked in the early sunshine while breakfast was cooking. The water made a pleasant music, and nearby was a covert of willows filled with singing birds. Then and there came on me the hour of revelation, when, though savagely hungry, I forgot about breakfast. Scents, sights and sounds blended into a harmony so perfect that it transcended human expression, even human thought. It was like a glimpse of the peace of eternity.

John Buchan (Lord Tweedsmuir), *Memory-Hold-the-Door* (Toronto: Musson, 1940), pp. 120–21.

◆

The peace that passes all understanding is the fruit of liberation into eternity . . .

Aldous Huxley, *The Perennial Philosophy* (New York and London: Harper, 1945), p. 194.

PART FIVE

Contentment Out-of-Doors

NATURE

———◆———

This is a delicious evening, when the whole body is one sense, and imbibes delight through every pore. I go and come with a strange liberty in Nature, a part of herself. As I walk along the stony shore of the pond in my shirt-sleeves, though it is cool as well as cloudy and windy, and I see nothing special to attract me, all the elements are unusually congenial to me. The bullfrogs trump to usher in the night, and the note of the whip-poor-will is borne on the rippling wind from over the water. Sympathy with the fluttering alder and poplar leaves almost takes away my breath; yet, like the lake, my serenity is rippled but not ruffled.

Henry David Thoreau, *Walden, or Life in the Woods,* 1854 (Boston: Houghton, 1929), chap. V, p. 143.

———◆———

Throwing open the little wicket-gate, by a step the greensward of the meadow is reached. Though the grass has been mown and the ground is dry, it is better to carry a thick rug, and cast it down in the shadow under the tall horse-chestnut-tree. It is only while in a dreamy, slumbrous, half-mesmerized state that nature's ancient papyrus roll can be read—only when the mind is at rest, separated from care and labour; when the body is at ease, luxuriating in warmth and delicious languor; when the soul is in accord and sympathy with the sunlight, with the leaf, with the slender blades of grass, and can feel with the tiniest insect which climbs up them as up a mighty tree. As the genius of the great musicians, without an articulated word or printed letter, can carry with it all the emotions, so now, lying prone upon the earth in the shadow, with quiescent will, listening, thoughts and feelings rise respondent to the sunbeams, to the leaf, the very blade of grass. Resting the head upon the hand, gazing down upon the ground, the strange and marvellous inner sight of the mind penetrates the solid earth, grasps in part the mystery of its vast extension upon either side, bearing its majestic mountains, its deep forests, its grand oceans, and almost feels the life which in ten thousand thousand forms revels upon its surface. Returning upon itself, the mind joys in the knowledge that it too is a part of this wonder—akin to the ten thousand thousand creatures, akin to the very earth itself.

Richard Jefferies, "Nature and Eternity," *The Hills and the Vale* (London: Duckworth, 1909), pp. 290–91.

———◆———

Here as elsewhere . . . in forenoon I get to feel shut in, no matter how comfortably, how splendidly, in a great Egyptian tomb. Then I go out of doors, here particularly, and see the trees, the sky, the grass, the flowers, and instinctively I stretch up my arms and open the palms of my hands to greet and embrace the beauty I encounter. The ecstasy that overcomes me wafts me away from cares and worries and aches and pains, and for an instant, no matter how brief, I am completely above workaday life. And I take up the rest of the day with less anxiety, less fear of fatigue, of annoyance, of bores . . .

Bernard Berenson, Diary, Vallombrosa, September 24, 1948, in Bernard Berenson, *Sunset and Twilight*, ed. Nicky Mariano (New York: Harcourt, 1963), p. 101.

———◆———

Nurse took me to the window today, and lo! Spring has been at her tricks! We have a good scraplet of garden, which, with those of our neighbors, gives us a delightful glimpse of sky and many a feathery bit of green. . . . How fortunate it is that we have so many aesthetic stomachs, so that when lying in a shaded room, we can chew and re-chew the cud of past contemplations; a slant of light, or a whiff of perfume, or the rustle of wind, and the illusion of the shimmering vista, the murmuring pines and the damp, divine earthiness is before us in perfection.

Alice James, Journal, May 7, 1891, *Alice James: Her Brothers— Her Journal*, ed. Anna Robeson Burr (New York: Dodd, 1934) p. 227.

I have told how after my fifteenth anniversary, when I first began to reflect seriously on my future life, the idea still persisted that my perpetual delight in Nature was nothing more than a condition or phase of my child's and boy's mind, and would inevitably fade out in time. I might have guessed at an earlier date that this was a delusion, since the feeling had grown in strength with the years . . . So powerful it was, so unaccountable, I was actually afraid of it, yet I would go out of my way to seek it. At the hour of sunset I would go out half a mile or so from the house, and sitting on the dry grass with hands clasped round my knees, gaze at the western sky, waiting for it to take me. And I would ask myself: What does it mean? . . .

And that was the life I desired—the life the heart can conceive—the earth life. When I hear people say they have not found the world and life so agreeable or interesting as to be in love with it, or that they look with equanimity to its end, I am apt to think they have never been properly alive nor seen with clear vision the world they think so meanly of, or anything in it—not a blade of grass. Only I know that mine is an exceptional case, that the visible world is to me more beautiful and interesting than to most persons, that the delight I experienced in my communings with Nature did not pass away, leaving nothing but a recollection of vanished happiness to intensify a present pain. The happiness was never lost, but owing to that faculty I have spoken of, had a cumulative effect on the mind and was mine again, so that in my worst times, when I was compelled to exist shut out from Nature in London for long periods, sick and poor and friendless, I could yet always feel that it was infinitely better to be than not to be.

W. H. Hudson, *Far Away and Long Ago* (New York: Dutton, 1918), pp. 322–23, 331–32.

———————◆———————

When I went with Henry each hummock, each pool in the clear stream, each sand bar became a thing of interest and even fascination in which there existed some small pattern of the universe. It was Henry who had taught me how to see and to fathom and understand the incredible and infinite variety of the natural world. Moreover he had taught me how to *love* the things I saw and discovered as well as to see and understand them. The swallows' nests dug deep into the banks, the foxholes, the crayfish moving in his own watery world, the nests of the bass or the killdeer, so alike, one beneath the clear cool water the other on some high, dry gravel bank, had all come through Henry to be a part of my existence, even of my innermost being so that if all else in life failed me, I should still possess a world of infinite beauty and fathomless variety.

Louis Bromfield, *The Wild Country* (New York: Harper, 1948), pp. 124–25.

◆

The best refuge, so far as happiness only is concerned, would be to cherish in ourselves, as much as possible and as long as possible, the true student-spirit, which takes an interest in a pursuit on its own account without reference to any personal success. I have just said that it is extremely difficult to enjoy the practice of an art for itself alone. It is so because the fine arts appeal to others and attempt to awaken their emotions, so that to write what is never to be printed or to paint what is never to be exhibited seems like talking to rocks and trees. But the study of nature is a pursuit that does not of necessity involve an appeal to the sympathy or admiration of any human being, and it is a safe refuge. It has been the one remaining happinesss of many a disappointed artist; it is the delight of all obscure men of science; it makes us, so long as we are engaged in it, independent of the whole human world except our predecessors, who have prepared the way for us, and who, for the most part, were solitary students like ourselves.

Philip Gilbert Hamerton, *The Quest of Happiness* (Boston: Roberts Brothers, 1897), pp. 130–31.

◆

The lover of nature is he whose inward and outward senses are still truly adjusted to each other; who has retained the spirit of infancy even into the era of manhood. His intercourse with heaven and earth becomes part of his daily food. In the presence of nature a wild delight runs through the man, in spite of real sorrows. Nature says,—he is my creature, and maugre all his impertinent griefs, he shall be glad with me. Not the sun or the summer alone, but every hour and season yields its tribute of delight; for every hour and change corresponds to and authorizes a different state of the mind, from breathless noon to grimmest midnight. . . . In the woods, too, a man casts off his years, as the snake his slough, and at what period soever of life, is always a child. In the woods is perpetual youth. Within these plantations of God, a decorum and sanctity reign, a perennial festival is dressed, and the guest sees not how he should tire of them in a thousand years. In the woods, we return to reason and faith. There I feel that nothing can befall me in life,—no disgrace, no calamity (leaving me my eyes), which nature cannot repair. Standing on the bare ground,—my head bathed by the blithe air, and uplifted into infinite space,—all mean egotism vanishes. . . . I am the lover of uncontained and immortal beauty. In the wilderness, I find something more dear and cognate than in streets and villages. In the tranquil landscape, and especially in the distant line of the horizon, man beholds somewhat as beautiful as his own nature.

Ralph Waldo Emerson, "Nature." *Nature, Addresses and Lectures* (Boston: Houghton, 1898), pp. 14–16.

My room [in the Swiss Chalet in the grounds of Gad's Hill] is up among the branches of the trees; and the birds and the butterflies fly in and out, and the green branches shoot in, at the open windows, and the lights and shadows of the clouds come and go with the rest of the company. The scent of the flowers, and indeed of everything that is growing for miles and miles, is most delicious.

Charles Dickens, letter, Gad's Hill, May 25, 1868, in James T. Fields, *Yesterdays with Authors* (Boston: Houghton, 1882), vol. I, p. 189.

I have just been out for a few moments to soak in the sunshine and listen to the birds. It is a perfect day, such as makes one in love with earth. Not a speck in the sky except the pale ghost of the new moon in the east on her way back to life like Alcestis. She will be beautiful over my pine crests this evening.

James Russell Lowell, letter to Lady Lyttleton, May 25, 1890, *Letters of James Russell Lowell*, ed. Charles Eliot Norton (Boston: Houghton, n.d.), vol. III, pp. 283–84.

Yes, in November the soil should be turned over and loosened: to lift it with a full spade gives you a feeling as appetizing and gratifying as if you lifted food with a full ladle, with a full spoon. A good soil, like good food, must not be either too fat, or heavy, or cold, or wet, or dry, or greasy, or hard, or gritty, or raw; it ought to be like bread, like gingerbread, like a cake, like leavened dough; it should crumble, but not break into lumps; under the spade it ought to crack, but not to squelch; it must not make slabs, or blocks, or honeycombs, or dumplings; but, when you turn it over with a full spade, it ought to breathe with pleasure and fall into a fine and puffy tilth. That is a tasty and edible soil, cultured and noble, deep and moist, permeable, breathing and soft—in short, a good soil is like good people, and as is well known there is nothing better in this vale of tears.

Karel Capek, *The Gardener's Year* (London: Allen & Unwin, 1931), pp. 136–38.

———◆———

April 6 [1877]. . . . The soil, too—let others pen-and-ink the sea, the air, (as I sometimes try)—but now I feel to choose the common soil for theme—naught else. The brown soil here, (just between winter-close and opening spring and vegetation)—the rain-shower at night, and the fresh smell next morning—the red worms wriggling out of the ground—the dead leaves, the incipient grass, and the latent life underneath—the effort to start something—already in shelter'd spots some little flowers—the distant emerald show of winter wheat and the rye-fields—the yet naked trees, with clear interstices, giving prospects hidden in summer—the tough fallow and the plow-team, and the stout boy whistling to his horses for encouragement—and there the dark fat earth in long slanting stripes upturn'd.

Walt Whitman, *Specimen Days*, 1882, reprinted in Walt Whitman, *Prose Works* (Philadelphia: McKay, n.d.), p. 100.

———◆———

Certainly a midsummer day in the country, with all its sights and sounds, its singing birds, its skimming swallows, its grazing or ruminating cattle, its drifting cloud-shadows, its grassy perfumes from the meadows and the hillsides, and the farmer with his men and teams busy with the harvest, has material for the literary artist. A good hay day is a good day for the writer and the poet, because it has a certain crispness and pureness; it is positive; it is rich in sunshine; there is a potency in the blue sky which you feel; the high barometer raises your spirits; your thoughts ripen as the hay cures. You can sit in a circle of shade beneath a tree in the fields, or in front of the open hay-barn doors, as I do, and feel the fruition and satisfaction of nature all about you. The brimming meadows seem fairly to purr as the breezes stroke them; the trees rustle their myriad leaves as if in gladness; the many-colored butterflies dance by; the steel blue of the swallows' backs glistens in the sun as they skim the fields; and the mellow boom of the passing bumble-bee but enhances the sense of repose and contentment that pervades the air. The hay cures; the oats and corn deepen their hue; the delicious fragrance of the last wild strawberries is on the breeze; your mental skies are lucid, and life has the midsummer fullness and charm.

John Burroughs, "A Midsummer Idyl," *Under the Maples* (Boston: Houghton, 1921), pp. 70–71.

SUN

◆

Mass before sunrise, without lights, in the novitiate chapel. At such a time there is a beautiful "spirituality" in the predawn light on the altar. Silence in the chapel, and this pearl-gray light on the white altar cloth. Two candles burning with silent life. What more beautiful liturgical sign than to have this light as witness to the greatest Mystery?

Thomas Merton, *Conjectures of a Guilty Bystander* (New York: Doubleday, 1966), p. 247.

◆

I happened to go to the window at about an hour before sunrise. The full moon was still some degrees above the western horizon. To the east the sky was beginning to flush with the dawn. The moon had a dimmed lustre as of old gold and was bedded in its own rays, making a halo like a great wheel, and touched with faint rainbow colour. Under it, the hillside rising to Poggio Gherardo looked greyish-green and the olive trees did not come out singly or in clusters, but as rolls of felt folded back on the ground. The sky had a strange, almost uncanny air, both gay and solemn.

I looked and gazed and breathed deep and recognized that in seventy years and more that I have looked at landscape consciously I had never seen the like effect. While contemplating the scene I did not think of any poet, whether Homer or Wordsworth or Goethe, who might interpret what I felt but could not put into words. For some minutes I was the world seen by my eyes and felt by my senses, the landscape, the freshness of the air, the smells coming up from the garden, the caress of the breeze.

Bernard Berenson, Diary, August 27, 1942, in Bernard Berenson, *Rumour and Reflection* (London: Constable, 1952), pp. 109–10.

I said when I awoke, After some more sleepings and wakings I shall lie on this mattress sick; then, dead; and through my gay entry they will carry these bones. Where shall I be then? I lifted my head and beheld the spotless orange light of the morning beaming up from the dark hills into the wide Universe.

Ralph Waldo Emerson, Journal, October 21, 1837, *The Heart of Emerson's Journals*, ed. Bliss Perry (Boston: Houghton, 1926), p. 117.

Morning, early morning, that is the time to see and know the river. Often before dawn, in dressing-gown and slippers, I creep down the Green Lane to a gate that opens on to mown grass. There, inside the gate, I leave my slippers, and silently on dewy lawn make my way to the water's edge. The night's last stars are high in the western sky: eastward a thin sickle of the ageing moon loses its lustre in the strengthening promise of day. Birds are still silent; there is no sound but the rustle of the distant weir. Scarcely a movement anywhere, moths pale as comfrey drowse their slow way from plant to plant. Bats only are in haste, whirling specks of blackness, on their aerial excursions.

In my small boat I move up-stream past untilled meadows heavy with resting kine. The white lilies of the stream are still folded, glimmering ghosts of their noonday selves. . . .

Slowly the promise of dawn spreads upwards in the east and a whisper of wind stirs the unsheltered pools. From a copse beyond the weir come the soft words of ring-doves, and then as I ship my oars and let the boat float with the stream I hear the harsh cluck of moor-hens. Twelve of their nests I had counted by daylight in that short stretch of river . . .

Now rooks, dark and raucous, are hurrying across the sky and, as if awakened by their chatter, thrushes, chaffinches, and warblers are muttering and chirping. Moving with the current I pass into deep shadows, and then out again into light-struck waters.

Robert Gibbings, *Till I End My Song* (London: Dent, 1957), pp. 125–27.

———◆———

Every morning was a cheerful invitation to make my life of equal simplicity, and I may say innocence, with Nature herself. I have been as sincere a worshipper of Aurora as the Greeks. I got up early and bathed in the pond; that was a religious exercise, and one of the best things which I did. They say that characters were engraven on the bathing tub of King Tching-thang to this effect: "Renew thyself completely each day; do it again, and again, and forever again." I can understand that. Morning brings back the heroic ages. . . . The morning, which is the most memorable season of the day, is the awakening hour. Then there is least somnolence in us; and for an hour, at least, some part of us awakes which slumbers all the rest of the day and night. Little is to be expected of that day, if it can be called a day, to which we are not awakened by our Genius, but by the mechanical nudgings of some servitor, are not awakened by our own newly acquired force and aspirations from within, accompanied by the undulations of celestial music, instead of factory bells, and a fragrance filling the air—to a higher life than we fell asleep from; and thus the darkness bear its fruit, and prove itself to be good, no less than the light. That man who does not believe that each day contains an earlier, more sacred, and auroral hour than he has yet profaned, has despaired of life, and is pursuing a descending and darkening way. After a partial cessation of his sensuous life, the soul of man, or its organs rather, are reinvigorated each day, and his Genius tries again what noble life it can make. All memorable events, I should say, transpire in morning time and in a morning atmosphere. The Vedas say, "All intelligences awake with the morning." Poetry and art, and the fairest and most memorable of the actions of men, date from such an hour. All poets and heroes, like Memnon, are the children of Aurora, and emit their music at sunrise. To him whose elastic and vigorous thought keeps pace with the sun, the day is a perpetual morning. It matters not what the clocks say or the attitudes and labors of men. Morning is when I am awake and there is a dawn in me.

Henry David Thoreau, *Walden, or Life in the Woods,* 1854 (Boston, Houghton, 1929), chap. II, pp. 98–99.

———◆———

The power of the sun and its joy is not felt so early on the downs as on the lower country, and last season it was not until the middle of June that I experienced the blissful sensation and feeling in its fulness. Then a day came that was a revelation; I all at once had a deeper sense and more intimate knowledge of what summer really is to all the children of life; for it chanced that on that effulgent day even the human animal, usually regarded as outside of nature, was there to participate in the heavenly bounty. That I felt the happiness myself was not quite enough, unhuman, or uncivilised, as I generally am, and wish to be. High up the larks were raining down their brightest, finest music; not rising skyward nor falling earthward, but singing continuously far up in that airy blue space that was their home. The little birds that live in the furze, the titlarks, white-throats, linnets, and stonechats, sprang upwards at frequent intervals and poured out their strains when on the wing. Each bird had its characteristic flight and gestures and musical notes, but all alike expressed the overflowing gladness that summer inspired, even as the flowers seemed to express it in their intense glowing colours; and as the butterflies expressed in their fluttering dances, and in the rapturous motions of their wings when at rest. There were many rabbits out, but they were not feeding, and when disturbed ran but fifteen or twenty yards away, then sat and looked at me with their big, round, prominent eyes, apparently too contented with life to suspect harm. But I saw no human creature in the course of a long ramble that morning until I was near the sea, when on approaching a coastguard station I all at once came upon some children lying on the grass on the slope of a down. There were five of them, scattered about, all lying on their backs, their arms stretched crossways, straight out, their hands open. It looked as if they had instinctively spread themselves out, just as a butterfly at rest opens wide its wings to catch the beams. The hot sun shone full on their fresh young faces; and though wide awake they lay perfectly still as I came up and walked slowly past them, looking from upturned face to face, each expressing perfect contentment; and as I successively caught their eyes they smiled, though still keeping motionless and silent . . . Their quietude and composure in the presence of a stranger was unusual, and like the confidence of the wild rabbits on that day was caused by the delicious sensation of summer in the blood.

W. H. Hudson, *Nature in Downland* (London: Longmans, 1901), pp. 168–70.

------◆------

But it is a little awkward to go east. It always seems left-handed. I think this is the feeling of all walkers, and that Thoreau's experience in this respect was not singular. The great magnet is the sun, and we follow him. I notice that people lost in the woods work to the westward. When one comes out of his house and asks himself, "Which way shall I walk?" and looks up and down and around for a sign or a token, does he not nine times out of ten turn to the west? He inclines this way as surely as the willow wand bends toward the water. There is something more genial and friendly in this direction.

John Burroughs, "Winter Sunshine," *Winter Sunshine* (Boston: Houghton, 1917), p. 21.

------◆------

In this hot weather I like to walk at times amid the full glow of the sun. Our island sun is never hot beyond endurance, and there is a magnificence in the triumph of high summer which exalts one's mind.

Among streets it is hard to bear, yet even there, for those who have eyes to see it, the splendour of the sky lends beauty to things in themselves mean or hideous. I remember an August bank-holiday, when, having for some reason to walk across London, I unexpectedly found myself enjoying the strange desertion of great streets, and from that passed to surprise in the sense of something beautiful, a charm in the vulgar vista, in the dull architecture which I had never known. Deep and clear marked shadows, such as one only sees on a few days of summer, are in themselves very impressive, and become more so when they fall upon highways devoid of folk. I remember observing, as something new, the shape of familiar edifices, of spires, monuments. And when at length I sat down somewhere on the Embankment, it was rather to gaze at leisure than to rest, for I felt no weariness, and the sun, still pouring upon me its noontide radiance, seemed to fill my veins with life.

George Gissing, *The Private Papers of Henry Ryecroft*, 1903 (New York: Boni & Liveright, 1918), chap. VIII, pp. 81–82.

◆

The front of the British Museum stands in the sunlight clearly marked against the firm blue of the northern sky. . . .

The shade deepens as I turn from the portico to the hall and vast domed house of books. The half-hearted light under the dome is stagnant and dead. For it is the nature of light to beat and throb; it has a pulse and undulation like the swing of the sea. Under the trees in the woodlands it vibrates and lives; on the hills there is a resonance of light. It beats against every leaf, and, thrown back, beats again; it is agitated with the motion of the grass blades; you can feel it ceaselessly streaming on your face. It is renewed and fresh every moment, and never twice do you see the same ray. Stayed and checked by the dome and book-built walls, the beams lose their elasticity, and the ripple ceases in the motionless pool. The eyes, responding, forget to turn quickly, and only partially see.

It is pleasant to go out again into the portico under the great columns. On the threshold I feel nearer knowledge than when within. The sun shines, and southwards above the houses there is a statue crowning the summit of some building. The figure is in the midst of the light; it stands out clear and white as if in Italy. The southern blue is luminous —the beams of light flow through it—the air is full of the undulation and life of light. There is rest in gazing at the sky: a sense that wisdom does exist and may be found, a hope returns that was taken away among the books. The green lawn is pleasant to look at, though it is mown so ruthlessly. If they would only let the grass spring up, there would be a thought somewhere entangled in the long blades as a dewdrop sparkles in their depths. Seats should be placed here, under the great columns or by the grass, so that one might enjoy the sunshine after books and watch the pigeons. They have no fear of the people, they come to my feet, but the noise of a door heavily swinging-to in the great building alarms them; they rise and float round, and return again. The sunlight casts a shadow of the pigeon's head and neck upon his shoulder; he turns his head, and the shadow of his beak falls on his breast. Iridescent gleams of bronze and green and blue play about his neck. . . .

Richard Jefferies, "Pigeons at the British Museum," *The Life of the Fields* (London: Chatto, 1908), pp. 215–18.

———◆———

It is the unqualified result of all my experience with the sick, that second only to their need of fresh air is their need of light; that, after a close room, what hurts them most is a dark room. And that it is not only light but direct sun-light they want. . . .

To a sleeper in health it does not signify what the view is from his bed. He ought never to be in it excepting when asleep, and at night. Aspect does not very much signify either (provided the sun reach his bed-room some time in every day, to purify the air), because he ought never to be in his bed-room except during the hours when there is no sun. But the case is exactly reversed with the sick, even should they be as many hours out of their beds as you are in yours, which probably they are not. Therefore, that they should be able, without raising themselves or turning in bed, to see out of window from their beds, to see sky and sun-light at least, if you can show them nothing else, I assert to be, if not of the very first importance for recovery, at least something very near it. . . .

One of the greatest observers of human things (not physiological), says, in another language, "Where there is sun there is thought." All physiology goes to confirm this. Where is the shady side of deep vallies, there is cretinism. Where are cellars and the unsunned sides of narrow streets, there is the degeneracy and weakliness of the human race—mind and body equally degenerating. Put the pale withering plant and human being into the sun, and, if not too far gone, each will recover health and spirit.

It is a curious thing to observe how almost all patients lie with their faces turned to the light, exactly as plants always make their way towards the light; a patient will even complain that it gives him pain "lying on that side." "Then why *do* you lie on that side?" He does not know,—but we do. It is because it is the side towards the window. A fashionable physician has recently published in a government report that he always turns his patients' faces from the light. Yes, but nature is stronger than fashionable physicians, and depend upon it she turns the faces back and *towards* such light as she can get. Walk through the wards of a hospital, remember the bed sides of private patients you have seen, and count how many sick you ever saw lying with their faces towards the wall.

Florence Nightingale, *Notes on Nursing* (New York: Appleton, 1860), pp. 84–87.

RAIN

———◆———

At all times I love rain, the early momentous thunderdrops, the perpendicular cataract shining, or at night the little showers, the spongy mists, the tempestuous mountain rain. I like to see it possessing the whole earth at evening, smothering civilization, taking away from me myself everything except the power to walk under the dark trees and to enjoy as humbly as the hissing grass, while some twinkling house-light or song sung by a lonely man gives a foil to the immense dark force. I like to see the rain making the streets, the railway station, a pure desert, whether bright with lamps or not. It foams off the roofs and trees and bubbles into the water-butts. It gives the grey rivers a demonic majesty. It scours the roads, sets the flints moving, and exposes the glossy chalk in the tracks through the woods. It does work that will last as long as the earth. It is about eternal business. In its noise and myriad aspect I feel the mortal beauty of immortal things.

Edward Thomas, *The South Country*, 1909 (London: Dent, 1932), chap. XVI, p. 281.

The weather is rainy, the whole atmosphere gray; it is a time favorable to thought and meditation. I have a liking for such days as these; they revive one's converse with one's self and make it possible to live the inner life; they are quiet and peaceful, like a song in a minor key. We are nothing but thought, but we feel our life to its very center. Our very sensations turn to reverie. It is a strange state of mind; it is like those silences in worship which are not the empty moments of devotion, but the full moments, and which are so because at such times the soul, instead of being polarized, dispersed, localized, in a single impression or thought, feels her own totality and is conscious of herself. She tastes her own substance. She is no longer played upon, colored, set in motion, affected, from without; she is in equilibrium and at rest.

Henri-Frédéric Amiel, Journal, August 22, 1873, *The Journal Intime of Henri-Frédéric Amiel*, trans. Mrs. Humphrey Ward, 1899 (New York: Burt, n.d.), p. 148.

The gentle rain which waters my beans and keeps me in the house to-day is not drear and melancholy, but good for me too. Though it prevents my hoeing them, it is of far more worth than my hoeing. If it should continue so long as to cause the seeds to rot in the ground and destroy the potatoes in the low lands, it would still be good for the grass on the uplands, and, being good for the grass, it would be good for me. . . . I have never felt lonesome, or in the least oppressed by a sense of solitude, but once, and that was a few weeks after I came to the woods, when, for an hour, I doubted if the near neighborhood of man was not essential to a serene and healthy life. To be alone was something unpleasant. But I was at the same time conscious of a slight insanity in my mood, and seemed to foresee my recovery. In the midst of a gentle rain while these thoughts prevailed, I was suddenly sensible of such sweet and beneficent society in Nature, in the very pattering of the drops, and in every sound and sight around my house, an infinite and unaccountable friendliness all at once like an atmosphere sustaining me, as made the fancied advantages of human neighborhood insignificant, and I have never thought of them since. Every little pine needle expanded and swelled with sympathy and befriended me. I was so distinctly made aware of the presence of something kindred to me, even in scenes which we are accustomed to call wild and dreary, and also that the nearest of blood to me and the humanest was not a person nor a villager, that I thought no place could ever be strange to me again . . .

Some of my pleasantest hours were during the long rain-storms in the spring or fall, which confined me to the house for the afternoon as well as the forenoon, soothed by their ceaseless roar and pelting; when an early twilight ushered in a long evening in which many thoughts had time to take root and unfold themselves.

Henry David Thoreau, *Walden, or Life in the Woods,* 1854 (Boston: Houghton, 1929), chap. V, pp. 145–47.

I went out late last night to lock the white gate. The wind had dropped and all was still, save for the occasional slow dripping of the trees after the last heavy shower. Against the clean bright sky every leaf and twig stood out with marvellous distinctness, and as I approached the gate the moonlight streamed in up the avenue, dark with foliage, from the wide empty open Common, like moonlight streaming into a dark house through an open door. The ground was still wet and shining with the rain, and the gigantic shadow of the gate projected by the moonlight was cast far up the avenue in huge bars upon the shining ground.

Francis Kilvert, Diary, May 9, 1875, *Kilvert's Diary,* ed. William Plomer (London: Cape, 1940), vol. III, p. 182.

It was raining hard when I awoke, but I made up my mind to disregard the weather, put on my dripping clothing, glad to know it was fresh and clean; ate biscuits and a piece of dried salmon without attempting to make a tea fire; filled a bag with hardtack, slung it over my shoulder, and with my indispensable ice-axe plunged once more into the dripping jungle. I found my bridge holding bravely in place against the swollen torrent, crossed it and beat my way around pools and logs and through two hours of tangle back to the moraine on the north side of the outlet,—a wet, weary battle but not without enjoyment. The smell of the washed ground and vegetation made every breath a pleasure, and I found *Calypso borealis,* the first I had seen on this side of the continent, one of my darlings, worth any amount of hardship; and I saw one of my Douglas squirrels on the margin of a grassy pool. The drip of the rain on the various leaves was pleasant to hear. More especially marked were the flat low-toned bumps and splashes of large drops from the trees on the broad horizontal leaves of *Echinopanax horridum*, like the drumming of thunder-shower drops on veratrum and palm leaves, while the mosses were indescribably beautiful, so fresh, so bright, so cheerily green, and all so low and calm and silent, however heavy and wild the wind and the rain blowing and pouring above them. Surely never a particle of dust has touched leaf or crown of all these blessed mosses; and how bright were the red rims of the cladonia cups beside them, and the fruit of the dwarf cornel! And the wet berries, Nature's precious jewelry, how beautiful they were!—huckleberries with pale bloom and a crystal drop on each; red and yellow salmon-berries, with clusters of smaller drops; and the glittering, berry-like raindrops adorning the interlacing arches of bent grasses and sedges around the edges of the pools, every drop a mirror with all the landscape in it. . . .

In the gardens and forests of this wonderful moraine one might spend a whole joyful life.

John Muir, *Travels in Alaska* (Boston: Houghton, 1915), pp. 110–11.

❖

The last time I saw him [Charles Dickens]—save at some of the final readings at St. James's Hall—was on the West Pier at Brighton. It was a miserable day, blowing hard and raining, and I thought I had the whole place to myself. But on walking round the head of the pier, behind the curved glass shelter, I beheld the author of "Pickwick!" He had his coat collar turned up and he was looking bronzed and hearty. Quite heedless of rain and flying spray he peered through the mist and gazed upon the huge billows rolling in. He seemed like a sturdy pilot who was steering the pier through a very difficult bit of navigation. I passed slowly, very slowly, by him, raised my hat and went away . . .

J. Ashby-Sterry, reminiscences of Charles Dickens, in *Charles Dickens. A Bookman Extra Number 1914* (London: Hodder, 1914), pp. 105–6.

❖

As soon as I was thoroughly wet through on the way home, I became one with the weather and would not have changed the day. It is only while one is dry that one is out of sympathy with rain; when one is wet through, one minds it no more than the trees do, having become part of the day itself.

Edward Grey (Viscount Grey of Falloden), letter to Katherine Lyttleton, 1900, in Sir George Macaulay Trevelyan, *Grey of Falloden* (London: Longmans, 1937), p. 68.

SEA

◆

For the sea lies all about us. The commerce of all lands must cross it. The very winds that move over the lands have been cradled on its broad expanse and seek ever to return to it. The continents themselves dissolve and pass to the sea, in grain after grain of eroded land. So the rains that rose from it return again in rivers. In its mysterious past it encompasses all the dim origins of life and receives in the end, after, it may be, many transmutations, the dead husks of that same life. For all at last return to the sea—to Oceanus, the ocean river, like the ever-flowing stream of time, the beginning and the end.

Rachel L. Carson, *The Sea Around Us* (New York: Oxford, 1951), p. 216.

◆

What I most love in the sea is its silence: a sentence that may sound strange till it is closely considered. For the loud noises that a man at sea remembers are not of the sea itself—no, not even in a gale of wind—but of battle between the wind and what it encounters: rigging or the ship's side, or canvas, or the play of a loose rope; the pouring of water taken in over the lee or the strain of timbers. The sea of itself is more reserved in its expression and, if it be alone in its vastness, lives in its own communion.

Because the sea lives (while the land lies inert) we cannot think of it as dumb: nor is it. But it speaks in a veiled fashion as do the oracles of the Gods, whereof it is one, the most universal and the most august of the oracles: and indeed the oracles of which we read were mostly not far from the salt and the air of the waves.

The shores are sounding things; but only because they are limits and bonds, not part of the Strength of Ocean. We, being creatures of the land, mostly know Ocean from his beaches or even louder steeps and stones; the tall cliffs that stand up to the surge and re-echo the fierce come and go of a swirl over uncovering rocks, or (rare but best remembered) the tremendous booming of the rollers through half-drowned caverns swallowing the rising tide. But the sea, absolute in its unchallenged majesty, disdains to shout and clamour; it proclaims its advance, strength, and volume not by battle cries. A comber in deep water not far from land is awful in the might of its advance; it rears into the sky and fills it, overhanging the hollow like a doom; but it does not threaten audibly. The sweeping crest charges over as might a line of cavalry, but without thunder; it resolves into a seething which barely hisses over the slope it had threatened and it dies in long streaks of almost silent foam. . . .

Now if even in storm the sea makes less of cry or hail than any other creature in activity, in all other moods it gives out no voice at all. We may imagine its breathing but we hear none; though the large heave of it is the heave of a living breast. The sea contemplates itself and is content with that endless self-neighbourhood. On which account, I suppose, it is that you will hardly find any man bound to a seafaring life but has something profound about him, more than landsmen have. He is clasped all round about by an immeasurable companion from whose communion he can neither escape nor would do so, for the sea conditions him, and makes him, and is with him all his hours—even on land, if he have known the sea long enough for the sea to have formed him.

Hilaire Belloc, "The Silence of the Sea," *The Silence of the Sea and Other Essays* (London: Cassell, 1941), pp. 9–12.

━━━━◆━━━━

When he was a young man in Capri, Pacciale, a fisherman friend of his, lay dying. He was one of the truest and most pure-hearted of men. His wife and children had never known him to say an unfair word. The old priest had administered the Last Sacrament and now stood by the far side of the bed. Members of his family huddled silently in the shadows of the little room. Pacciale had fallen into a deep slumber and seemed to have left this world, when, slowly and for the last time, he opened his eyes. He gently stroked the hand of his doctor friend and whispered "Siete buono come il mare"—"You are good like the sea."

To many people the sea is hardly the personification of goodness. The sea is ungovernable, rough, and often cruel. But to the old fisherman who had lived all his time by the sea and on the rocks which came out of the sea, the great element had become all that the waving cornfield is to the countryman. It was his horizon, it had afforded him his living, it had given him his need of adventure, hopes, fears, dreams.

Gustaf Munthe and Gudrun Uexküll, *The Story of Axel Munthe* (London: Murray, 1953), p. 192.

———◆———

At cold predawn, while the mist still clung eerily to all the earth and waters, we hurried to the surf to seek our friend, the Brittany fisherman.

We found him, a small and wizened man, his face massed with wrinkles, his expression astringent from numberless seasons of salting. The web of wrinkles that covered his face showed him to be in latter years and yet his wiriness belied his age, so that looking at him one felt that the true secret of youth must somehow be bound up with battling the sea.

Doffing his grimy cap to the Boss and chuckling (for he knew a good fisherman when he saw one), he would bend toward the ropes that bound his little skiff. And, in a little while all of us, with the dogs centered nervously in the bow, would be drifting out toward dawn and deep water. . . .

Sometimes . . . my father could be seen watching the old man who tended the rudder with a strange look of envy and admiration. He loved the fisherman for his strength, which defied all weather and all hardship and was certainly composed of something deeper and more enduring than the mere physical power of his scrawny body. His envy of the old man and all the old men of Brittany arose, I think, from the thought of their peace of mind. For by their daily contact with the sea, which is older than life itself, they had come to know a great many truths which others, searching over the earth for a lifetime, might never discover. And if they could not express what they knew in their coarse, spare language, it mattered little, for it was written in their faces, as deeply grained as old wood, which showed simplicity, pride and humility and a strange but credible combination of fatalism and self-reliance. They were content with things as they were. And, although it was not in my father's nature to endure contentment for long, I believe he would happily, for a day or two, have exchanged his soul for that of a Brittany fisherman in order to experience its total peace.

Ellen Bromfield Geld, *The Heritage. A Daughter's Memories of Louis Bromfield* (New York: Harper, 1962), pp. 47–49.

———◆———

[George Bernard] Shaw is a very strong swimmer. I am not. Many times he would give me lessons. When he is teaching some exercises or art, away from the theatre, he is both patient and kind. He would tell me to put one hand upon his shoulder and just swim, on and on. We would find ourselves well out to sea. Then a change would come over Shaw, a sea change. He is vigorous on land but when he is swimming in the sea, he becomes for once tranquil. He would say to me as we swam: "We are in another world." If I were afraid when I saw the land slipping farther and farther away, he would say: "Have no fear, Lillah, gently and slowly does it."

Lillah McCarthy (Lady Keeble), *Myself and My Friends* (London: Thornton Butterworth, 1933), p. 88.

———◆———

The little isle of Earraid lies close in to the south-west corner of the Ross of Mull: the sound of Iona on one side, across which you may see the isle and church of Columba; the open sea to the other, where you shall be able to mark, on a clear, surfy day, the breakers running white on many sunken rocks. I first saw it, or first remember seeing it, framed in the round bull's-eye of a cabin port, the sea lying smooth along its shores like the waters of a lake, the colourless, clear light of the early morning making plain its heathery and rocky hummocks. . . .

But it was in Earraid itself that I delighted chiefly. The lighthouse settlement scarce encroached beyond its fences; over the top of the first brae the ground was all virgin, the world all shut out, the face of things unchanged by any of man's doings. Here was no living presence, save for the limpets on the rocks, for some old, gray, rain-beaten ram that I might rouse out of a ferny den betwixt two boulders, or for the haunting and the piping of the gulls. It was older than man; it was found so by incoming Celts, and seafaring Norsemen, and Columba's priests. The earthy savour of the bog plants, the rude disorder of the boulders, the inimitable seaside brightness of the air, the brine and the iodine, the lap of the billows among the weedy reefs, the sudden springing up of a great run of dashing surf along the sea-front of the isle, all that I saw and felt my predecessors must have seen and felt with scarce a difference. I steeped myself in open air and in past ages.

Robert Louis Stevenson, "Memoirs of an Islet," *Memories and Portraits*, 1887 (New York: Scribner, 1909), chap. VIII, pp. 251–52, 255.

Where the two carpets, the green and the blue, meet, men's houses become comelier. Brighter for the salt in the winds, more weathered with the weather, the homes of New England grow finer as they come nearer the ocean. This is especially so in Maine. The architecture takes shapeliness from the boats, both the vast sailing vessels of a century ago and from the fishing boats now. . . . But it is more than a matter of houses putting on the best appearances in the face of infinity. Something of that vastness at their front doors comes into the houses themselves; rooms grow larger without growing, for having the surf of white daisies and the meadows of whitecaps at all their small panes; a twelve-foot room grows in the sea-light into a large place where old people sit with eyes accustomed to far-seeing and the coming of good news or sad news from the sea.

Men's Sunday houses grew in loveliness, too. There are no churches on the world quite so good-looking as the white ones that serve as lighthouses to fishing men returning by day from trouble, chance, and hard work. Not only is there the carpet of green fields through the windows but the ocean's green pastures as well. And maybe sweet water will come past the windows to join the salt. Religion keeps young in such a house opening its windows upon two eternities.

Robert P. Tristram Coffin, *On the Green Carpet* (Indianapolis: Bobbs, 1951), pp. 180–81.

FLOWING WATERS

Some men crave islands, some crave mountain tops: it is water that calls to me. Fresh or salt, tranquil in a pool or thunderous on a shore, lapping at bent grasses or leaping from a prow, the insistence is the same. Psychologists may know the reason—I am content with the appetite.

Not long ago, when I was coming home by train from London, a stranger sitting in the opposite seat of the compartment spoke to me as we neared our destination.

'I think you must be the author of *Sweet Thames Run Softly*,' he said.

'How did you know?' I asked.

'Because every time we crossed the river or passed near it, you leaned forward to look out,' he answered. . . .

But it isn't only the Thames and its attendant brooks that bring my nose to the carriage window. Wherever I may be travelling, I rarely read lest by so doing I miss a glimpse of river, duck pond, or canal. Even if I buy papers, serious and light, before taking my seat, they serve only to pass the time until the train starts. At the first whistle from the guard, leading ladies find themselves face to face with leading editorials on the rack above my head.

There is nothing unusual in this love of water. Poets throughout the ages have sung of the peace of gently running streams. In the sacred writings a river is used constantly as a symbol of peace: 'Then had thy peace been as a river,' 'He leadeth me beside the still waters.' Throughout our own literature flows the timeless tranquillity of rivers. Spenser's *Prothalamion* is borne on the waters of Sweete Themmes. The tortured mind of Swift longed for a river at his garden's end. The gentler Stevenson wished to all 'a living river by the door.' I think it is the unbroken sequences of flowing water, the unchanging destinies of streams, that seem to knit a man's soul with the eternities. The rhythms of eddying pools, the rhymes of lapping wavelets, bring peace through eye and ear, emphasizing by their unceasing flow the unimportance of our passing lives. On and on they glide, not merely for the brief moments of our attention but through every hour of night and day, varying yet constant. The dancing of a mountain stream may be as entrancing as a ballet, but the quiet of an age-old river is like the slow turning of pages in a well-loved book. . . .

Robert Gibbings, *Till I End My Song* (London: Dent, 1957), pp. 232–34.

———◆———

Until I pass out I shall always long for the river and the warblers' song going on and on, and now and then the wind through the willows turning the surface blue and purple.—Then comes the first breath of autumn, and the willows still whiten, and the lines of the wooded horizons are dark and lowering, and the glory of the river-herbs is dying, and the long, decaying stalks of river-parsley lie yellow, straggling along the current, caught up by some standing rushy clump, sending the stream in wrinkles, and leaving eddies on either side. . . . And the wind comes in gusts, and the blown water is steely and puffed this way and that by unseen spirits, and swallows are gathering, and course and twist at speed on the surface.

Sir Alfred Munnings, *The Finish* (London: Museum Press, 1952), p. 297.

———◆———

I dare not publicly name the rare joys, the infinite delights, that intoxicate me on some sweet June morning, when the river and bay are smooth as a sheet of beryl-green silk, and I run along ripping it up with my knife-edged shell of a boat, the rent closing after me like those wounds of angels which Milton tells of, but the seam still shining for many a long rood behind me. To lie still over the Flats, where the waters are shallow, and see the crabs crawling and the sculpins gliding busily and silently beneath the boat,—to rustle in through the long harsh grass that leads up some tranquil creek,—to take shelter from the sunbeams under one of the thousand-footed bridges, and look down its interminable colonnades, crusted with green and oozy growths, studded with minute barnacles, and belted with rings of dark mussels, while overhead streams and thunders that other river whose every wave is a human soul flowing to eternity as the river below flows to the ocean,— lying there moored unseen, in loneliness so profound that the columns of Tadmor in the Desert could not seem more remote from life—the cool breeze on one's forehead, the stream whispering against the half-sunken pillars,—why should I tell of these things, that I should live to see my beloved haunts invaded and the waves blackened with boats as with a swarm of water-beetles?

Oliver Wendell Holmes, *The Autocrat of the Breakfast-Table* (Boston: Phillips, 1858), p. 196.

The pool-basins below the falls and cascades hereabouts, formed by the heavy down-plunging currents, are kept nicely clean and clear of detritus. . . . Sudden changes, however, are effected during the spring floods, when the snow is melting and the upper tributaries are roaring loud from "bank to brae." Then boulders that have fallen into channels, and which the ordinary summer and winter currents were unable to move, are suddenly swept forward as by a mighty besom, hurled over the falls into these pools . . .

One of these ancient flood boulders stands firm in the middle of the stream channel, just below the lower edge of the pool dam at the foot of the fall nearest our camp. It is a nearly cubical mass of granite about eight feet high, plushed with mosses over the top and down the sides to ordinary high-water mark. When I climbed on top of it to-day and lay down to rest, it seemed the most romantic spot I had yet found—the one big stone with its mossy level top and smooth sides standing square and firm and solitary, like an altar, the fall in front of it bathing it lightly with the finest of spray, just enough to keep its moss cover fresh; the clear green pool beneath, with its foam-bells and its half circle of lilies leaning forward like a band of admirers, and flowering dogwood and alder trees leaning over all in sun-sifted arches. How soothingly, restfully cool it is beneath that leafy, translucent ceiling, and how delightful the water music—the deep bass tones of the fall, the clashing, ringing spray, and infinite variety of small low tones of the current gliding past the side of the boulder-island, and glinting against a thousand smaller stones down the ferny channel! All this shut in; every one of these influences acting at short range as if in a quiet room. . . .

After dark, when the camp was at rest, I groped my way back to the altar-boulder and passed the night on it—above the water, beneath the leaves and stars—everything still more impressive than by day, the fall seen dimly white . . .

John Muir, *My First Summer in the Sierra*, 1911, reprinted in *Yosemite and the Sierra Nevada*, ed. Charlotte E. Mauk (Boston: Houghton, 1948), pp. 44–45.

Of all experiences which quickened the imagination of [Stopford] Brooke, or enabled him to apprehend directly the life that is in nature, the sight or sound of running waters was always the chief. I do not profess to know why this rather than any other of Nature's forms had the power to awaken the deepest vein of his mysticism. But the fact is unquestionable that from boyhood to extreme old age the presence of running water had upon him the virtue of a spell. The cataract haunted him like a passion; and not the cataract only, but the stream, the spring, the fountain, even the falling rain. It is scarcely an exaggeration to say that he understood the language of the waters as Eastern magicians are said to understand the language of birds. He wanted no better companion than the running stream, and I doubt if he had any more intimate. "They talked to me very pleasantly," is a sentence that often occurs in his notes of these experiences. Whenever in letters or diaries he sighs for escape from the hateful gloom of London, and pictures the life he desires to live, he always places himself in imagination among fountains and springs; and when he fled to the country his first walk was invariably to the banks of the nearest stream where he would sit alone for hours, "doing nothing, thinking of nothing," but living his life to the very full. At these times he lost all consciousness of himself and became a pure elemental, sharing a common existence with elves, fairies, naiads, sprites, or whatever name may be given to the presence which moves upon the waters or within them. One of the last acts of his life was to build a fountain in his garden, which he would visit every day, leaning on his stick by the side of the basin, happiest of all when the sun shone through the glittering drops, but quite content if he could only listen to their splash.

Lawrence Pearsall Jacks, *Life and Letters of Stopford Brooke* (London: Murray, 1917), vol. II, pp. 551–52.

————◆————

I know not why fountains should have gone out of fashion. Perhaps because they are beautiful. They were the life of the great gardens from the Renaissance onwards. They were the glory of the XVIIth century. They had, about them, all that best nourishes the mind of man: the right sound, coolness in heat, pleasant and natural motion, innocent vitality. They were symbolic, too, full of reserve and of continuity, and they had about them just enough surprise, just enough artifice, to bear witness to the creative power of man. They were more than ornaments—far more—they were companions; and their movements corresponded to the movements of the air, majestic in calm, lively in a strong breeze. Once a man had got used to fountains playing near his house, he could no more do without them than without any other consonant companion. . . .

. . . if there is one thing about a fountain more divine than another, it is the way in which the sound of its benediction is married to nature all around. One shall come upon a fountain which some wise man designed in the days when Europe was Europe; a fountain rising from a marble round, situated in an open glade, overshadowed by great trees. Come on such a fountain and you have come upon something which is at once part of the nature about you and more than that nature, something which inspires and makes alive in a special way all the leaves and branches of the place, all the air.

Hilaire Belloc, "On Fountains," *The Silence of the Sea and Other Essays* (London: Cassell, 1941), pp. 174, 177–78.

◆

From Pisa we went to Rome, where we arrived very late at night. It was eleven o'clock and we carried our bags to the hotel intending to go to bed. But instead Gus [Augustus Saint-Gaudens] said to me, "Let's take a walk first. Then you will see Rome at night." So we walked as far as the Place d'Espagne, through streets where there was no one, but where there were magnificent fountains splashing in the night air.

Alfred Garnier, letter to Louis Saint-Gaudens, 1900, in Augustus Saint-Gaudens, *The Reminiscences of Augustus Saint-Gaudens*, ed. Homer Saint-Gaudens (New York: Century, 1913), vol. II, p. 148.

WIND

———◆———

Certain things affected him [John Keats] extremely, particularly when "a wave was billowing through a tree," as he described the uplifting surge of air among swaying masses of chestnut or oak foliage, or when, afar off, he heard the wind coming across woodlands. "The tide! the tide!" he would cry delightedly, and spring on to some stile, or upon the low bough of a wayside tree, and watch the passage of the wind upon the meadow-grasses or young corn, not stirring till the flow of air was all around him, while an expression of rapture made his eyes gleam and his face glow . . .

William Sharp, *The Life and Letters of Joseph Severn* (New York: Scribner, 1892), pp. 20–21.

———◆———

The axe of the wood-cutter, the measured thud of a single threshing-flail, the crowing of chanticleer in the barn-yard, (with invariable responses from other barn-yards,) and the lowing of cattle—but most of all, or far or near, the wind—through the high tree-tops, or though low bushes, laving one's face and hands so gently, this balmly-bright noon, the coolest for a long time, (Sept. 2)—I will not call it *sighing,* for to me it is always a firm, sane, cheery expression, though a monotone, giving many varieties, or swift or slow, or dense or delicate. The wind in the patch of pine woods off there—how sibilant. Or at sea, I can imagine it this moment, tossing the waves, with spirits of foam flying far, and the free whistle, and the scent of the salt—and that vast paradox somehow with all its action and restlessness conveying a sense of eternal rest.

Walt Whitman, *Specimen Days,* 1882, reprinted in Walt Whitman, *Prose Works* (Philadelphia: McKay, n.d.), p. 102.

———◆———

A stormy and rainy day. Walked from the Court through the rain. I don't dislike this. Egad, I rather like it; for no man that ever stepped on heather has less dread than I of catch-cold; and I seem to regain, in buffeting with the wind, a little of the high spirit with which, in younger days, I used to enjoy a Tam-o'-Shanter ride through darkness, wind, and rain,—the boughs groaning and cracking over my head, the good horse free to the road and impatient for home, and feeling the weather as little as I did.

Sir Walter Scott, Journal, December 10, 1825, *The Journal of Sir Walter Scott* (New York: Harper, 1891), vol. I, p. 42.

As we ascended the hills it grew very cold and slippery. Luckily, the wind was at our backs, and helped us on. A sharp hail-shower gathered at the head of Martindale, and the view upwards was very grand—the wild cottages, seen through the hurrying hail-shower. The wind drove and eddied about and about, and the hills looked large and swelling through the storm. . . . O! the bonny nooks and windings and curlings of the beck, down at the bottom of the steep green mossy banks. We dined at the publick-house on porridge, with a second course of Christmas pies.

Dorothy Wordsworth, Grasmere Journal, December 29, 1801, *Journals of Dorothy Wordsworth*, ed. E. de Selincourt (London: Macmillan, 1941), vol. I, p. 97.

The wind roared unwearyingly among the trees; I could hear the boughs tossing and the leaves churning through half a mile of forest; yet the scene of my encampment was not only as black as the pit, but admirably sheltered. . . .

Then I gathered what I should want within reach, took off my wet boots and gaiters, which I wrapped in my waterproof, arranged my knapsack for a pillow under the flap of my sleeping-bag, insinuated my limbs into the interior, and buckled myself in like a bambino. . . . But I was rare and hungry; ate well, and smoked one of the best cigarettes in my experience. Then I put a stone in my straw hat, pulled the flap of my fur cap over my neck and eyes, put my revolver ready to my hand, and snuggled well down among the sheepskins.

I questioned at first if I were sleepy, for I felt my heart beating faster than usual, as if with an agreeable excitement to which my mind remained a stranger. But as soon as my eyelids touched, that subtle glue leaped between them, and they would no more come separate.

The wind among the trees was my lullaby. Sometimes it sounded for minutes together with a steady even rush, not rising nor abating; and again it would swell and burst like a great crashing breaker, and the trees would patter me all over with big drops from the rain of the afternoon. Night after night, in my own bedroom in the country, I have given ear to this perturbing concert of the wind among the woods; but whether it was a difference in the trees, or the lie of the ground, or because I was myself outside and in the midst of it, the fact remains that the wind sang to a different tune among these woods of *Gévaudan*. I hearkened and hearkened; and meanwhile sleep took gradual possession of my body and subdued my thoughts and senses; but still my last waking effort was to listen and distinguish, and my last conscious state was one of wonder at the foreign clamour in my ears.

Twice in the course of the dark hours . . . I was recalled for a brief while to consciousness, and saw a star or two overhead, and the lace-like edge of the foliage against the sky. When I awoke for the third time (*Wednesday, September 25th*), the world was flooded with a blue light, the mother of the dawn. I saw the leaves labouring in the wind and the ribbon of the road . . . I closed my eyes again, and set to thinking over the experience of the night. I was surprised to find how easy and pleasant it had been, even in this tempestuous weather.

Robert Louis Stevenson, *Travels with a Donkey in the Cevennes,* 1879 (New York: Scribner, 1900), chap. IV, pp. 178–80.

One summer I spent some weeks in Persia among the mountains of Elburz, and rode or walked about the passes that separate the Caspian jungle from the plain of Qazvin. I still think of these landscapes as among the most beautiful in the world, and remember long days on stony paths, with the bells of the mules tinkling behind me as they found their steps in valleys yet unmapped, by rarely visited streams. . . .

The mountains are high, and uninhabited stretches separate the last and smallest village from the first one on the other watershead; the track to the pass climbs among rocks with glistening scales of mica in waterless ravines; the trees that follow some vein of moisture die away in stunted growths of thorn until there is only juniper flattened by wind among boulders; and this, too, gives way at last to the short grass in the pockets of the snow. Then one may taste the northern wind and know that the pass is near. . . .

Usually, as the afternoon declines, human voices cease; some shepherd will talk or pipe to his flock from a rock where pastures end; apart from him the eagles fly alone. With the coming of night the babble of the streams rises from all their valleys, not loud but clear because of the silence of the waterless places where the smooth winds are heard as they move from shoulder to shoulder.

Then the pass becomes a gateway to the stars.

Beyond a black saddle, between buttresses whose detail is lost or wanly shining perhaps with snow, the stars hang as if the edge of the world were there and one could reach them. They swing in the night-wind that makes them twinkle and never touches earth; and their shivering light, and their steadfast journeying and their repeated presence make them companions as one lies sheltered in some corrie, as part of the shadow of the hills.

It happened that in this Elburz summer the constellation of *Perseus* night after night spanned the gap of the pass with his scimitar. He danced in a wind whose earthly brother blew thin from the north and the Caspian Sea. I came to feel his stars as a friendliness and a bond in the gaiety of spaces and the cold of night.

Freya Stark, *Perseus in the Wind*, 1948 (London: Murray, 1963), Foreword, pp. ix–x.

TREES

◆

But no weather interfered fatally with my walks, or rather my going abroad, for I frequently tramped eight or ten miles through the deepest snow to keep an appointment with a beech tree, or a yellow birch, or an old acquaintance among the pines . . .

Henry David Thoreau, *Walden, or Life in the Woods*, 1854 (Boston: Houghton, 1929), chap. XIV, p. 292.

I have seen him [John Constable] admire a fine tree with an ecstasy of delight like that with which he would catch up a beautiful child in his arms. The ash was his favourite, and all who are acquainted with his pictures cannot fail to have observed how frequently it is introduced as a near object, and how beautifully its distinguishing peculiarities are marked. I remember his pointing out to me, in an avenue of Spanish chestnuts, the great elegance given to their trunks by the spiral direction of the lines of the bark.

C. R. Leslie, *Life and Letters of John Constable*, R.A., 1843 (London: Chapman, 1896), chap. XVII, p. 352.

A deep snow upon the ground. . . . Wm. returned, and we walked through the wood into the Coombe to fetch some eggs. The sun shone bright and clear. A deep stillness in the thickest part of the wood, undisturbed except by the occasional dropping of the snow from the holly boughs; no other sound but that of the water, and the slender notes of a redbreast, which sang at intervals on the outskirts of the southern side of the wood. There the bright green moss was bare at the roots of the trees, and the little birds were upon it. The whole appearance of the wood was enchanting; and each tree, taken singly, was beautiful. The branches of the hollies pendent with their white burden, but still showing their bright red berries, and their glossy green leaves. The bare branches of the oaks thickened by the snow.

Dorothy Wordsworth, [Alfoxden] Journal, February 17, 1798, *Journals of Dorothy Wordsworth*, ed. E. de Selincourt (London: Macmillan, 1941), vol. I, pp. 8–9.

A veritable passion for poplars is a most intelligible passion. The eyes do gather them, far and near, on a whole day's journey. Not one is unperceived, even though great timber should be passed, and hill-sides dense and deep with trees. The fancy makes a poplar day of it. Immediately the country looks alive with signals; for the poplars everywhere reply to the glance. The woods may be all various, but the poplars are separate.

All their many kinds (and aspens, their kin, must be counted with them) shake themselves perpetually free of the motionless forest. It is easy to gather them. Glances sent into the far distance pay them a flash of recognition of their gentle flashes; and as you journey you are suddenly aware of them close by. Light and the breezes are as quick as the eyes of a poplar-lover to find the willing tree that dances to be seen. . . .

It is difficult to realize a drought where there are many poplars. And yet their green is not rich; the coolest have a colour much mingled with a cloud-gray. It does but need fresh and simple eyes to recognize their unfaded life. When the other trees grow dark and keep still, the poplar and the aspen do not darken—or hardly—and the deepest summer will not find a day in which they do not keep awake. No waters are so vigilant, even where a lake is bare to the wind.

When Keats said of his Dian that she fastened up her hair "with fingers cool as aspen leaves," he knew the coolest thing in the world. It is a coolness of colour, as well as of a leaf which the breeze takes on both sides—the greenish and the grayish. The poplar green has no glows, no gold; it is an austere colour, as little rich as the colour of willows, and less silvery than theirs. The sun can hardly gild it; but he can shine between. Poplars and aspens let the sun through with the wind. You may have the sky sprinkled through them in high midsummer, when all the woods are close.

Sending your fancy poplar-gathering, then, you ensnare wild trees, flying with life. No fisher's net ever took such glancing fishes, nor did the net of a constellation's shape ever enclose more vibrating Pleiades.

Alice Meynell, "In July," *Essays* (London: Burns & Oates, 1937), pp. 182–83.

Ours is eminently a country of the orchard. Horace Greeley said he had seen no land in which the orchard formed such a prominent feature in the rural and agricultural districts. Nearly every farmhouse in the Eastern and Northern States has its setting or its backgound of apple-trees, which generally date back to the first settlement of the farm. Indeed, the orchard, more than almost any other thing, tends to soften and humanize the country, and give the place of which it is an adjunct a settled, domestic look. The apple-tree takes the rawness and wilderness off any scene. On the top of a mountain, or in remote pastures, it sheds the sentiment of home. It never loses its domestic air, or lapses into a wild state. And in planting a homestead, or in choosing a building site for the new house, what a help it is to have a few old, maternal apple-trees near by,—regular old grandmothers, who have seen trouble, who have been sad and glad through so many winters and summers, who have blossomed till the air about them is sweeter than elsewhere, and borne fruit till the grass beneath them has become thick and soft from human contact, and who have nourished robins and finches in their branches till they have a tender, brooding look! The ground, the turf, the atmosphere of an old orchard, seems several stages nearer to man than that of the adjoining field, as if the trees had given back to the soil more than they had taken from it; as if they had tempered the elements, and attracted all the genial and beneficent influences in the landscape around.

John Burroughs, "The Apple," *Winter Sunshine* (Boston: Houghton, 1917), pp. 124–25.

———◆———

Now there is a path along the edge of the small stream flowing near this house where there grows an enormous and very ancient Willow. To this aged tree I have given the mystic name of the "Saviour-Tree," and here and now I recommend to all harassed and worried people who can find in their neighbourhood such a tree—and it needn't necessarily be a willow—to use it as I do this one. For the peculiarity of this tree is that you can transfer by a touch to its earth-bound trunk *all* your most neurotic troubles! These troubles of yours the tree accepts, and absorbs them into its own magnetic life; so that henceforth they lose their devilish power of tormenting you. Of course we all of us only manage to live at all by means of our power of forgetting. This is Nature's supreme gift. To "live according to Nature" is to possess the power to forget. No "Saviour-Tree" can ever take the place of the previous Fountain of Lethe in ourselves; into which we can acquire the power of flinging our neurotic troubles; but, as I am hinting, a tree of this kind can at least serve as "an outward and visible sign of an inward and spiritual grace."

John Cowper Powys, *Autobiography* (New York: Simon & Schuster, 1934), p. 593.

———◆———

The flat cross-country between Chartres and Fontainebleau, with an oppressive sense of Paris to the north, fretted me wickedly; when we got to the Fountain of Fair Water I lay feverishly wakeful through the night, and was so heavy and ill in the morning that I could not safely travel, and fancied some bad sickness was coming on. However, towards twelve o'clock the inn people brought me a little basket of wild strawberries; and they refreshed me, and I put my sketch-book in pocket and tottered out, though still in an extremely languid and woe-begone condition; and getting into a cart-road among some young trees, where there was nothing to see but the blue sky through thin branches, lay down on the bank by the roadside to see if I could sleep. But I couldn't, and the branches against the blue sky began to interest me, motionless as the branches of a tree of Jesse on a painted window.

Feeling gradually somewhat livelier, and that I wasn't going to die this time, and be buried in the sand, though I couldn't for the present walk any farther, I took out my book, and began to draw a little aspen tree, on the other side of the cart-road, carefully. . . .

Languidly, but not idly, I began to draw it; and as I drew, the languor passed away: the beautiful lines insisted on being traced,—without weariness. More and more beautiful they became, as each rose out of the rest, and took its place in the air. With wonder increasing every instant, I saw that they 'composed' themselves, by finer laws than any known of men. . . . But that all the trees of the wood (for I saw surely that my little aspen was only one of their millions) should be beautiful—more than Gothic tracery, more than Greek vase-imagery, more than the daintiest embroiderers of the East could embroider, or the artfullest painters of the West could limn,—this was indeed an end to all former thoughts with me, an insight into a new silvan world.

Not silvan only. The woods, which I had only looked on as wilderness, fulfilled I then saw, in their beauty, the same laws which guided the clouds, divided the light, and balanced the wave.

John Ruskin, *Praeterita*, 2d ed. (New York: Merrill and Baker, n.d.), vol. II, pp. 132–33, 136–37.

———◆———

I had now visited the usual objects of a pilgrim's devotion, but I had a desire to see the old family seat of the Lucys, at Charlecot, and to ramble through the park where Shakspeare, in company with some of the roysters of Stratford, committed his youthful offence of deer-stealing. . . .

I now found myself among noble avenues of oaks and elms, whose vast size bespoke the growth of centuries. The wind sounded solemnly among their branches, and the rooks cawed from their hereditary nests in the tree tops. The eye ranged through a long lessening vista, with nothing to interrupt the view but a distant statue; and a vagrant deer stalking like a shadow across the opening.

There is something about these stately old avenues that has the effect of gothic architecture, not merely from the pretended similarity of form, but from their bearing the evidence of long duration, and of having had their origin in a period of time with which we associate ideas of romantic grandeur. They betoken also the long-settled dignity, and proudly-concentrated independence of an ancient family; and I have heard a worthy but aristocratic old friend observe, when speaking of the sumptuous palaces of modern gentry, that "money could do much with stone and mortar, but, thank Heaven, there was no such thing as suddenly building up an avenue of oaks."

It was from wandering in early life among this rich scenery, and about the romantic solitudes of the adjoining park of Fullbroke, which then formed a part of the Lucy estate, that some of Shakspeare's commentators have supposed he derived his noble forest meditations of Jaques, and the enchanting woodland pictures in "As you like it." It is in lonely wanderings through such scenes, that the mind drinks deep but quiet draughts of inspiration, and becomes intensely sensible of the beauty and majesty of nature. The imagination kindles into reverie and rapture; vague but exquisite images and ideas keep breaking upon it; and we revel in a mute and almost incommunicable luxury of thought. It was in some such mood, and perhaps under one of those very trees before me, which threw their broad shades over the grassy banks and quivering waters of the Avon, that the poet's fancy may have sallied forth into that little song which breathes the very soul of a rural voluptuary:

> Under the green wood tree,
> Who loves to lie with me,
> And tune his merry throat
> Unto the sweet bird's note,
> Come hither, come hither, come hither.
> Here shall he see
> No enemy,
> But winter and rough weather.

Washington Irving, "Stratford-on-Avon," *The Sketch Book*, author's rev. ed. (New York: George P. Putnam, 1849), pp. 333, 339–40.

SOUNDS

The trumpet-like lowing of a cow—what does that speak to in me? Not to my understanding. No. Yet somewhat in me hears and loves it well.

Ralph Waldo Emerson, Journal, August 1841, *The Heart of Emerson's Journals*, ed. Bliss Perry (Boston: Houghton, 1926), p. 163.

As I walked along the field path I stopped to listen to the rustle and solemn night whisper of the wheat, so different to its voice by day. The corn seemed to be praising God and whispering its evening prayer. Across the great level meads near Chippenham came the martial music of a drum and fife band, and laughing voices of unseen girls were wafted from farms and hayfields out of the wide dusk.

Francis Kilvert, Diary, July 16, 1873, *Kilvert's Diary*, ed. William Plomer (London: Cape, 1939), vol. II, p. 356.

My green-house is never so pleasant as when we are just upon the point of being turned out of it. The gentleness of the autumnal suns, and the calmness of this latter season, make it a much more agreeable retreat than we ever find it in the summer; when, the winds being generally brisk, we cannot cool it by admitting a sufficient quantity of air, without being at the same time incommoded by it. But now I sit with all the windows and the door wide open, and am regaled with the scent of every flower, in a garden as full of flowers as I have known how to make it. We keep no bees, but if I lived in a hive, I should hardly hear more of their music. All the bees in the neighbourhood resort to a bed of mignonette opposite to the window, and pay me for the honey they get out of it by a hum, which, though rather monotonous, is as agreeable to my ears as the whistling of my linnets. All the sounds that Nature utters are delightful, at least in this country. I should not perhaps find the roaring of lions in Africa or of bears in Russia very pleasing; but I know no beast in England, whose voice I do not account musical, save and except always the braying of an ass. The notes of all our birds and fowls please me, without one exception. I should not, indeed, think of keeping a goose in a cage, that I might hang him up in the parlour for the sake of his melody, but a goose upon a common, or in a farm yard, is no bad performer. And as to insects, if the black beetle, and beetles, indeed, of all hues, will keep out of my way, I have no objection to any of the rest; on the contrary, in whatever key they sing, from the gnat's fine treble to the bass of the humble bee, I admire them all. Seriously, however, it strikes me as a very observable instance of providential kindness to man, that such an exact accord has been contrived between his ear, and the sounds with which, at least in a rural situation, it is almost every moment visited. All the world is sensible of the uncomfortable effect that certain sounds have upon the nerves, and consequently upon the spirits: and if a sinful world had been filled with such as would have curdled the blood, and have made the sense of hearing a perpetual inconvenience, I do not know that we should have had a right to complain. But now the fields, the woods, the gardens, have each their concert, and the ear of man is for ever regaled by creatures who seem only to please themselves.

William Cowper, letter to Rev. John Newton, September 18, 1784, *The Works of William Cowper*, 2d ed., ed. John S. Memes (Edinburgh: Fraser, 1835), vol. II, pp. 64–65.

———◆———

"Look, Sshh, Listen!" he would whisper, and made us aware of the sounds and, in our silent attention, the smell of so many things that one would never have thought of as having either a sound or a smell.

He taught us to know sound and smell of morning, when everything is still fresh and glistening before the wind and dust and heat of the day give the earth a tired look. At just about dawn, the mourning dove gives a cry so gentle and melancholy that it would never be heard during the constant roaring of the day. It is a cry that belongs to morning and freshness, just as the shriek of the screech owl belongs to the awesome stillness before dawn.

The very quiet is a sound. Then add to it the sawing of the crickets, the throaty swallowings of a bullfrog, the sounds of water. We listened for the minute, exclamatory jumping of a fish, the silent ripple of a muskrat across the pond in the moonlight, the muffled ring of steel on stone, as a horse stumbled down into the stream. And in the night, "Sshh, listen!" a tap and then another. Was it really? And in answer, a steady pounding which said, "All is well, go to sleep now, for the rain is coming, and the roof is over our heads."

Ellen Bromfield Geld, *The Heritage. A Daughter's Memories of Louis Bromfield* (New York: Harper, 1962), pp. 120–21.

A sweet morning. We have put the finishing stroke to our bower, and here we are sitting in the orchard. It is one o'clock. We are sitting upon a seat under the wall, which I found my brother building up, when I came to him with his apple. He had intended that it should have been done before I came. It is a nice, cool, shady spot. The small birds are singing, lambs bleating, cuckow calling, the thrush sings by fits, Thomas Ashburner's axe is going quietly (without passion) in the orchard, hens are cackling, flies humming, the women talking together at their doors, plumb and pear trees are in blossom—apple trees greenish —the opposite woods green, the crows are cawing. We have heard ravens. The ash trees are in blossom, birds flying all about us.

Dorothy Wordsworth, Grasmere Journal, May 6, 1802, *Journals of Dorothy Wordsworth*, ed. E. de Selincourt (London: Macmillan, 1941), vol. I, pp. 143–44.

Besides the singing and calling, there is a peculiar sound which is only heard in summer. Waiting quietly to discover what birds are about, I become aware of a sound in the very air. It is not the midsummer hum which will soon be heard over the heated hay in the valley and over the cooler hills alike. It is not enough to be called a hum, and does but just tremble at the extreme edge of hearing. If the branches wave and rustle they overbear it; the buzz of a passing bee is so much louder it overcomes all of it that is in the whole field. I cannot define it, except by calling the hours of winter to mind—they are silent; you hear a branch crack or creak as it rubs another in the wood, you hear the hoar-frost crunch on the grass beneath your feet, but the air is without sound in itself. The sound of summer is everywhere—in the passing breeze, in the hedge, in the broad-branching trees, in the grass as it swings; all the myriad particles that together make the summer are in motion. The sap moves in the trees, the pollen is pushed out from grass and flower, and yet again these acres and acres of leaves and square miles of grass blades—for they would cover acres and square miles if reckoned edge to edge—are drawing their strength from the atmosphere. Exceedingly minute as these vibrations must be, their numbers perhaps may give them a volume almost reaching in the aggregate to the power of the ear. Besides the quivering leaf, the swinging grass, the fluttering bird's wing, and the thousand oval membranes which innumerable insects whirl about, a faint resonance seems to come from the very earth itself. The fervour of the sunbeams descending in a tidal flood rings on the strung harp of earth. It is this exquisite undertone, heard and yet unheard, which brings the mind into sweet accordance with the wonderful instrument of nature.

Richard Jefferies, "The Pageant of Summer," *The Life of the Fields* (London: Chatto, 1908), pp. 7–8.

———◆———

Sometimes, on Sundays, I heard the bells, the Lincoln, Acton, Bedford, or Concord bell, when the wind was favorable, a faint, sweet, and, as it were, natural melody, worth importing into the wilderness. At a sufficient distance over the woods this sound acquires a certain vibratory hum, as if the pine needles in the horizon were the strings of a harp which it swept. All sound heard at the greatest possible distance produces one and the same effect, a vibration of the universal lyre, just as the intervening atmosphere makes a distant ridge of earth interesting to our eyes by the azure tint it imparts to it. There came to me in this case a melody which the air had strained, and which had conversed with every leaf and needle of the wood, that portion of the sound which the elements had taken up and modulated and echoed from vale to vale. The echo is, to some extent, an original sound, and therein is the magic and charm of it. It is not merely a repetition of what was worth repeating in the bell, but partly the voice of the wood; the same trivial words and notes sung by a wood-nymph.

Henry David Thoreau, *Walden, or Life in the Woods,* 1854 (Boston: Houghton, 1929), chap. IV, pp. 136–37.

One of the similes used by St Francis de Sales, which I love to repeat, is: 'I am like a bird singing in a thicket of thorns'; this must be a continual inspiration to me.

Pope John XXIII, "Retreat, 1930, at Rustchuk, in the house of the Passionist Fathers. 28 April–4 May," *Journal of a Soul* (Montreal: Palm, 1965), p. 218.

———◆———

The rooks fly in a long black thread across the uplands to the stubble-fields, and the sense of tranquillity is deepened by their erratic cawing. Some of the harshest tones of nature bring the deepest rest. Few things are so unmusical as the voices of rooks, yet a home with a rookery is a very peaceful place. Perhaps the continual cawing, like the ticking of a clock in a quiet room, emphasizes the surrounding hush; perhaps it is the associations of childhood and calm days; or is it something deep and old as earth that lurks in the harsh voices and comes poignantly to our hearts? Hear them on a windless evening, winging homeward heavily through the rain, with desultory cawing! Listen as they settle clamorously for the night . . .

Mary Webb, *The Spring of Joy*, 1928 (London: Cape, 1937), chap. III, p. 150.

———◆———

Swifts are no songsters, and have only one harsh screaming note; yet there are ears to which it is not displeasing, from an agreeable association of ideas, since that note never occurs but in the most lovely summer weather.

Gilbert White, *The Natural History of Selborne*, 1789 (London: Scott, n.d.), letter XXI, pp. 178–79.

———◆———

Did you ever chance to hear the midnight flight of birds passing through the air and darkness overhead, in countless armies, changing their early or late summer habitat? It is something not to be forgotten. A friend called me up just after 12 last night to mark the peculiar noise of unusually immense flocks migrating north (rather late this year.) In the silence, shadow and delicious odor of the hour, (the natural perfume belonging to the night alone,) I thought it rare music. You could *hear* the characteristic motion—once or twice "the rush of mighty wings," but oftener a velvety rustle, long drawn out—sometimes quite near— with continual calls and chirps, and some song-notes. It all lasted from 12 till after 2. Once in a while the species was plainly distinguishable; I could make out the bobolink, tanager, Wilson's thrush, white-crown'd sparrow, and occasionally from high in the air came the notes of the plover.

Walt Whitman, *Specimen Days*, 1882, reprinted in Walt Whitman, *Prose Works* (Philadelphia: McKay, n.d.), p. 84.

What, then, did I want?—what did I ask to have? If the question had been put to me then, and if I had been capable of expressing what was in me, I should have replied: I want only to keep what I have; to rise each morning and look out on the sky and the grassy dew-wet earth from day to day, from year to year. . . . To listen in a trance of delight to the wild notes of the golden plover coming once more to the great plain, flying, flying south, flock succeeding flock the whole day long. Oh, those wild beautiful cries of the golden plover! I could exclaim with Hafiz, with but one word changed: "If after a thousand years that sound should float o'er my tomb, my bones uprising in their gladness would dance in the sepulchre!"

W. H. Hudson, *Far Away and Long Ago* (New York: Dutton, 1918), pp. 293–94.

CAMPING

About two o'clock we stopped in an opening in a pine wood and ate our lunch. We had the good fortune to hit upon a charming place. A wood-chopper had been there, and let in the sunlight full and strong; and the white chips, the newly-piled wood, and the mounds of green boughs, were welcome features, and helped also to keep off the wind that would creep through under the pines. The ground was soft and dry, with a carpet an inch thick of pine-needles, and with a fire, less for warmth than to make the picture complete, we ate our bread and beans with the keenest satisfaction, and with a relish that only the open air can give.

A fire, of course,—an encampment in the woods at this season without a fire would be like leaving Hamlet out of the play. A smoke is your standard, your flag; it defines and locates your camp at once; you are an interloper until you have made a fire; then you take possession; then the trees and rocks seem to look upon you more kindly, and you look more kindly upon them. As one opens his budget, so he opens his heart by a fire. Already something has gone out from you, and comes back as a faint reminiscence and home feeling in the air and place. One looks out upon the crow or the buzzard that sails by as from his own fireside. It is not I that am a wanderer and a stranger now; it is the crow and the buzzard. The chickadees were silent at first, but now they approach by little journeys, as if to make our acquaintance. The nuthatches, also, cry "Yank! yank!" in no inhospitable tones; and those purple finches there in the cedars,—are they not stealing our berries?

How one lingers about a fire under such circumstances, loath to leave it, poking up the sticks, throwing in the burnt ends, adding another branch and yet another.

John Burroughs, "Winter Sunshine," *Winter Sunshine* (Boston: Houghton, 1917), pp. 18–19.

———◆———

Pleasant, as the fiery heat of the desert daylight is done, is our homely evening fire. The sun gone down upon a highland steppe of Arabia, whose common altitude is above three thousand feet, the thin dry air is presently refreshed, the sand is soon cold; wherein yet at three fingers' depth is left a sunny warmth of the past day's heat until the new sunrise. After a half hour it is the blue night, and clear hoary starlight in which there shines the girdle of the milky way, with a marvellous clarity. As the sun is setting, the nomad housewife brings in a truss of sticks and dry bushes, which she has pulled or hoed with a mattock (a tool they have seldom) in the wilderness; she casts down this provision by our hearthside, for the sweet-smelling evening fire. . . .

The foster-camels lie couched, before the booth of hair: and these Beduins let them lie still an hour, before the milking. . . . When the Arabs have eaten their morsel and drunken léban of the flock, the few men of our menzil begin to assemble about the sheykh's hearth, where is some expectation of coffee. The younger or meanest of the company, who is sitting or leaning on his elbow or lies next the faggot, will in-dolently reach back his hand from time to time for more dry rimth, to cast on the fire, and other sweet resinous twigs, till the flaming light leaps up again in the vast uncheerful darkness.

Charles M. Doughty, *Travels in Arabia Deserta*, 1888 (London: Cape, 1926), vol. I, chap. IX, pp. 259–60.

———◆———

We had reached a very elevated point, and in the valley below, and among the hills, were a number of lakes at different levels; some, two or three hundred feet above others, with which they communicated by foaming torrents. Even to our great height, the roar of the cataracts came up, and we could see them leaping down in lines of snowy foam. From this scene of busy waters, we turned abruptly into the stillness of a forest, where we rode among the open bolls of the pines, over a lawn of verdant grass, having strikingly the air of cultivated grounds. This led us, after a time, among masses of rock which had no vegetable earth but in hollows and crevices, though still the pine forest continued. Toward evening, we reached a defile, or rather a hole in the mountains, entirely shut in by dark pine-covered rocks.

Our table service was rather scant; and we held the meat in our hands, and clean rocks made good plates, on which we spread our mac-aroni. Among all the strange places on which we had occasion to en-camp during our long journey, none have left so vivid an impression on my mind as the camp of this evening. The disorder of the masses which surrounded us; the little hole through which we saw the stars overhead; the dark pines where we slept; and the rocks lit up with the glow of our fires, made a night-picture of very wild beauty.

John Charles Frémont, Journal of explorations in the Rocky Mountains, August 12, 1842: Charles Wentworth Upham, *Life, Explorations and Public Services of John Charles Frémont* (Boston: Ticknor, 1856), pp. 76–77.

———◆———

Night was falling when I set out and it was pitch dark when I reached the top. The glad, rejoicing storm in glorious voice was singing through the woods, noble compensation for mere body discomfort. But I wanted a fire, a big one, to see as well as hear how the storm and trees were behaving. After long, patient groping I found a little dry punk in a hollow trunk and carefully stored it beside my matchbox and an inch or two of candle in an inside pocket that the rain had not yet reached; then, wiping some dead twigs and whittling them into thin shavings, stored them with the punk. I then made a little conical bark hut about a foot high, and, carefully leaning over it and sheltering it as much as possible from the driving rain, I wiped and stored a lot of dead twigs, lighted the candle, and set it in the hut, carefully added pinches of punk and shavings, and at length got a little blaze, by the light of which I gradually added larger shavings, then twigs all set on end astride the inner flame, making the little hut higher and wider. Soon I had light enough to enable me to select the best dead branches and large sections of bark, which were set on end, gradually increasing the height and corresponding light of the hut fire. A considerable area was thus well lighted, from which I gathered abundance of wood, and kept adding to the fire until it had a strong, hot heart and sent up a pillar of flame thirty or forty feet high, illuminating a wide circle in spite of the rain, and casting a red glare into the flying clouds. Of all the thousands of camp-fires I have elsewhere built none was just like this one, rejoicing in triumphant strength and beauty in the heart of the rain-laden gale. It was wonderful,—the illuminated rain and clouds mingled together and the trees glowing against the jet background, the colors of the mossy, lichened trunks with sparkling streams pouring down the furrows of the bark, and the gray-bearded old patriarchs bowing low and chanting in passionate worship!

My fire was in all its glory about midnight, and, having made a bark shed to shelter me from the rain and partially dry my clothing, I had nothing to do but look and listen and join the trees in their hymns and prayers. . . .

I have enjoyed thousands of camp-fires in all sorts of weather and places, warm-hearted, short-flamed, friendly little beauties glowing in the dark on open spots in high Sierra gardens, daisies and lilies circled about them, gazing like enchanted children; and large fires in silver fir forests, with spires of flame towering like the trees about them, and sending up multitudes of starry sparks to enrich the sky; and still greater fires on the mountains in winter, changing camp climate to summer, and making the frosty snow look like beds of white flowers, and often-times mingling their swarms of swift-flying sparks with falling snow-crystals when the clouds were in bloom. But this Wrangell camp-fire, my first in Alaska, I shall always remember for its triumphant storm-defying grandeur, and the wondrous beauty of the psalm-singing, lichen-painted trees which it brought to light.

John Muir, *Travels in Alaska* (Boston: Houghton, 1915), pp. 22–24.

At the foot of a high ridge whose summit still caught the glow from the low-set sun, while the river valley grew dark in the twilight, I turned the dogs towards the south shore, and looked about for a camping-place. The lower bank sloped down to the ice abruptly, but dogs going to camp will drag a load up, over, or through anything, and the prospect of rest above is even a greater incentive to exertion than the fluent imprecations of the half-breed below. So by dint of hauling we reached the top, and then I made my camp in a pine-clump on the brink. When the dogs had been unharnessed, and the snow dug away, the pine brush laid upon the ground, and the wood cut, when the fire was made, the kettle filled with snow and boiled, the dogs fed with a good hearty meal of dry moose meat, and my own hunger satisfied; then it was time to think, while the fire lit up the pine stems, and the last glint of daylight gleamed in the western sky. A jagged pine-top laid its black cone against what had been the sunset. An owl from the opposite shore sounded at intervals his lonely call; now and again a passing breeze bent the fir-trees until they whispered forth that mournful song which seems to echo from the abyss of the past.

The fir-tree is the oldest of the trees of the earth, and its look and its voice tell the story of its age. . . .

I felt at last at home. The great silent river, the lofty ridge darkening against the twilight, yon star burning like a beacon above the precipice —all *these* were friends, and midst them one could rest in peace.

And now, as I run back in thought along that winter journey, and see again the many camp-fires glimmering throught the waste of wilderness there comes not to my memory a calmer scene than that which closed around my lonely fire by the distant Unchagah. I was there almost in the centre of the vast wilderness of North America, around, stretched in silence, that mystery we term Nature, that thing which we see in pictures, in landscapes, in memory; which we hear in the voice of wind-swept forests and the long sob of seas against ocean rocks. This mother, ever present, ever mysterious, sometimes terrible, often tender—always beautiful—stood there with nought to come between us save loneliness and twilight.

Sir William Francis Butler, *The Wild Northland*, 1873 (Toronto: Courier Press, 1911), chap. XVI, pp. 177–79.

PART SIX

The End of the Day

SUNSET

◆

Sunset in the city [Boston], as at Newport, he [William Ellery Channing] keeps as a holy hour, looking from upper windows, which command wide prospects, over the broad basin of Charles river and the undulating range of Brighton and Milton hills. During the winter twilight he likes to be silent and alone.

William Henry Channing, *Memoir of William Ellery Channing* (London: Routledge, n.d.), vol. II, p. 518.

◆

. . . I was a city clerk and toiled year after year in a basement office in London Wall, where the only daylight filtered down through a row of little glass cubes along one side of the ceiling for ever vocal to the hurrying feet of the passers-by in the street above. But sometimes, when twilight fell, eluding the eye of vigilant authority, I would steal upstairs and out into the street, where the lights glittered like diamonds against the crimson sunset, and gaze for a space on a certain graceful little cupola which, at that twilight hour, seemed to be afloat upon ethereal tides of azure, amethyst and purple. It helped to keep my soul alive.

J. Lewis May, *Thorn and Flower* (London: Bles, 1935), pp. 131–32.

◆

. . . I am sitting in the window of my studio. It is no ordinary window, for it is ten feet across and eight feet high, and it looks out upon water and birds and the green fields of Gloucestershire. From my armchair the window frames a picture of endless beauty, activity and diversity—a picture which gives me a peculiarly intense pleasure, because its composition is my own creation. A pool with islands reflects the flash of the setting sun in the ripples made by the ducks and geese that are swimming on it. . . .

This window is a dream come true, a dream born of other windows and of many ideas evolved and crystallised over the years. Neither it, nor the slightly curved room it enriches, nor the pool in front of it, existed at all four years ago. All were created from a bunch of rough drawings which I had handed to a dragline operator and an architect with the instruction to "get on with it". The window is also a magic window, for as well as the picture I see through it, there is a picture of the room itself which I can see reflected in it, and the reflection grows stronger as the sunset fades and the warm red-shaded lamps become the dominant part of this curious double image. I see myself, my wife, my children, my books lining the walls at one end, my easel and painting cabinet at the other, and the shelves of half-finished pictures, and below them the gramophone and the shelf of records.

The light has gone, but still very dimly I can see the black birds moving about on the dark blue water and the black shapes of them as they fly against the dark blue sky; the whole background of the picture beyond the window is ultramarine in contrast to the red light of the room, which lies across it in reflection.

A pair of ducks circles round over the pond, out over the pollard willows until the two black specks are lost against the loom of the elm trees beyond and in the red reflection of the lamp shade behind me.

Peter Scott, *The Eye of the Wind* (London: Hodder, 1961), pp. 3–5.

———◆———

The daylight has lingered on longer than expected, but now the gloom of the short January evening is settling down fast in the wood. The silent and motionless trees rise out of a mysterious shadow, which fills up the spaces between their trunks. Only above, where their delicate outer branches are shown against the dark sky, is there any separation between them. Somewhere in the deep shadow of the underwood a blackbird calls "ching, ching" before he finally settles himself to roost. In the yew the lesser birds are already quiet, sheltered by the evergreen spray; they have also sought the ivy-grown trunks. "Twit, twit," sounds high overhead as one or two belated little creatures, scarcely visible, pass quickly for the cover of the furze on the hill. The short January evening is of but a few minutes' duration; just now it was only dusky, and already the interior of the wood is impenetrable to the glance. There rises a loud though distant clamour of rooks and daws, who have restlessly moved in their roost-trees. Darkness is almost on them, yet they cannot quite settle. The cawing and dawing rises to a pitch, and then declines; the wood is silent, and it is suddenly night.

Richard Jefferies, "January in the Sussex Woods," *The Life of the Fields* (London: Chatto, 1908), p. 97.

———◆———

October 29. . . . The walk across the Park was very pleasant. I love these late autumnal evenings in Kensington Gardens, when the faint blue mist lies low on the water, and the birds cry in it like ghosts. A thin sickle of a moon hung over the church spire, ruddy gold in the purple sky, and an evening out of the long past seemed to flood into me and fill my being full. These slow, quiet, decaying evenings—what a power they have! They belong to the spirit, and move it like music.

Stopford Brooke, Diary, October 29, 1908, in Lawrence Pearsall Jacks, *Life and Letters of Stopford Brooke* (London: Murray, 1917), vol. II, p. 606.

———◆———

. . . took coach, it being about seven at night, and passed and saw the people walking with their wives and children to take the ayre, and we set out for home, the sun by and by going down, and we in the cool of the evening all the way with much pleasure home, talking and pleasing ourselves with the pleasure of this day's work . . . Anon it grew dark, and as it grew dark we had the pleasure to see several glow-wormes, which was mighty pretty . . .

Samuel Pepys, Diary, July 14, 1667, *The Diary of Samuel Pepys*, ed. Henry B. Wheatley (London: Bell, 1924), vol. VII, pp. 23–24.

———◆———

In the evening I had another long talk with Whitman—an unexpected treat. At 7 P.M. he was wheeled by Warry right past my hotel, according to his custom, down to the wharf, close to the river. I was waiting about with my camera in the hope of meeting him, when he accosted me, and invited me to accompany them down to the river's edge. As we approached the wharf he exclaimed: "How delicious the air is!"

On the wharf he allowed me to photograph himself and Warry (it was almost dusk and the light unfavourable), after which I sat down on a log of wood beside him, and he talked in the most free and friendly manner for a full hour, facing the golden sunset, in the cool evening breeze, with the summer lightning playing around us, and the ferry-boats crossing and re-crossing the Delaware.

J. Johnston, reminiscences of Walt Whitman in J. Johnson and J. W. Wallace, *Visits to Walt Whitman in 1890–1891* (London: Allen & Unwin, 1917), pp. 42–43.

———◆———

We had a remarkable sunset one day last November. I was walking in a meadow, the source of a small brook, when the sun at last, just before setting, after a cold gray day, reached a clear stratum in the horizon, and the softest, brightest morning sunlight fell on the dry grass and on the stems of the trees in the opposite horizon and on the leaves of the shrub-oaks on the hillside, while our shadows stretched long over the meadow eastward, as if we were the only motes in its beams. It was such a light as we could not have imagined a moment before, and the air also was so warm and serene that nothing was wanting to make a paradise of that meadow. When we reflected that this was not a solitary phenomenon, never to happen again, but that it would happen forever and ever an infinite number of evenings, and cheer and reassure the latest child that walked there, it was more glorious still.

The sun sets on some retired meadow, where no house is visible, with all the glory and splendor that it lavishes on cities, and perchance as it has never set before,—where there is but a solitary marsh-hawk to have his wings gilded by it, or only a musquash looks out from his cabin, and there is some little black-veined brook in the midst of the marsh, just beginning to meander, winding slowly round a decaying stump. We walked in so pure and bright a light, gilding the withered grass and leaves, so softly and serenely bright, I thought I had never bathed in such a golden flood, without a ripple or a murmur to it. The west side of every wood and rising ground gleamed like the boundary of Elysium, and the sun on our backs seemed like a gentle herdsman driving us home at evening.

Henry David Thoreau, "Walking," *Excursions*, 1863 (Boston: Houghton, 1899), chap. VI, pp. 302–3.

NIGHT

———◆———

When I came out the night was superb. The sky was cloudless, the moon rode high and full in the deep blue vault and the evening star blazed in the west. The air was filled with the tolling and chiming of bells from St. Paul's and Chippenham old Church. The night was soft and still and I walked up and down the drive several times before I could make up my mind to leave the wonderful beauty of the night and go indoors. To be alone out of doors on a still soft clear moonlit night is to me one of the greatest pleasures that this world can give.

Francis Kilvert, Diary, January 12, 1873, *Kilvert's Diary*, ed. William Plomer (London: Cape, 1939), vol. II, pp. 308–9.

———◆———

I came by the last train on Friday night the 27th, and walked out from Winchester, at midnight. It was warm and soft: I heard a nightingale, and one sedge warbler was singing within hearing of the road just where a piece of the river could be seen, light at the end of a little dark path. I walked with my hat off and once a little soft rain fell amongst my hair: there were great forms of leafy trees and a smell and spirit everywhere and I felt the soft country dust about my feet.

Edward Grey (Viscount Grey of Falloden), Notebook, April 1894, in Sir George Macaulay Trevelyan, *Grey of Falloden* (London: Longmans, 1937), p. 375.

———◆———

I think of nights on the Piazza Michelangelo, one of the most charming places to dine in midsummer, in the open, perched high over twilit Florence, with the wide Piazza spread before you, and a bronze cast of Michelangelo's *David* in the middle of its vacancy. Below, the city lies spread to the Cascine gardens in the west; in front the heights of Fiesole are already twinkling; the crumpled range of hills behind Vallambrosa are slowly fading into the dusk. It is one of life's unforgettable experiences to sit here of evenings with a pleasant friend, over excellent wine and food, watching the lights come up, the statue slowly becoming silhouetted against the green of the northern sky, and charm yielding place to awe. The Duomo and the campanile grow dim. A bat squeaks. The pines breathe. All the treasure-houses where you have been drinking beauty and energy through the days fall dark, and sleep. It is an immortal sleep and your heart so flows and fills again that the stars might be the eyes of the dead and the silence becomes a prayer. It is nights like these that make life worth living.

Sean O'Faolain, A *Summer in Italy* (London: Eyre, 1949), pp. 96–97.

. . . the lantern . . . lighted dimly the great barn, casting long shadows on rafters and walls. I have never forgotten those shadows there, or the smell of hay and of warm breaths penetrating the cold, or the stirring about of the horses in their stalls, their snortings and snufflings, or the way they turned their heads to fix solemn eyes upon us, or the white mist coming from their nostrils and just visible in the dim light. Sometimes, as I waited in the half-darkness, I put my hand on the nose of Lady, who, because she was a Morgan mare and much prized by my father, had a box stall to herself; and I always felt a sense of wonder at the warmth of her soft skin on the coldest of nights.

The barn in lantern light was never a frightening place to me. With its tightly closed doors against the cold and its loft crammed with hay, it seemed instead safe and secure in spite of its shadowy corners and its great gulfs of blackness which the rays of the lantern could not pierce; and I felt an odd kinship with the creatures there who, I imagined, returned my feeling and welcomed our brief entrance into their long, dark night.

Mary Ellen Chase, *The White Gate* (New York: Norton, 1954), pp. 90–91.

Night in this enchanting season is not night, but a miscellany of lights. The journeying twilight, the half-moon, the kindling Venus, the beaming Jove,—Saturn and Mars something less bright, and, fainter still, 'the common people of the sky,' as Crashaw said: then, below, the meadows and thickets flashing with the fireflies, and all around the farms the steadier lamps of men compose the softest, warmest illumination.

Ralph Waldo Emerson, Journal, July 20, 1839, *The Heart of Emerson's Journals*, ed. Bliss Perry (Boston: Houghton, 1926), p. 144.

◆

May 21 [1877].—Back in Camden. Again commencing one of those unusually transparent, full-starr'd, blue-black nights, as if to show that however lush and pompous the day may be, there is something left in the not-day that can outvie it. The rarest, finest sample of long-drawn-out clear-obscure, from sundown to 9 o'clock. I went down to the Delaware, and cross'd. Venus like blazing silver well up in the west. The large pale thin crescent of the new moon, half an hour high, sinking languidly under a bar-sinister of cloud, and then emerging. Arcturus right overhead. A faint fragrant sea-odor wafted up from the south. The gloaming, the temper'd coolness, with every feature of the scene, indescribably soothing and tonic—one of those hours that give hints to the soul, impossible to put in a statement. (Ah, where would be any food for spirituality without night and the stars?) The vacant spaciousness of the air, and the veil'd blue of the heavens, seem'd miracles enough.

As the night advanc'd it changed its spirit and garments to ampler stateliness. I was almost conscious of a definite presence, Nature silently near. The great constellation of the Water-Serpent stretch'd its coils over more than half the heavens. The Swan with outspread wings was flying down the Milky Way. The northern Crown, the Eagle, Lyra, all up there in their places. From the whole dome shot down points of light, rapport with me, through the clear blue-black. All the usual sense of motion, all animal life, seem'd discarded, seem'd a fiction; a curious power, like the placid rest of Egyptian gods, took possession, none the less potent for being impalpable. Earlier I had seen many bats, balancing in the luminous twilight, darting their black forms hither and yon over the river; but now they altogether disappear'd. The evening star and the moon had gone. Alertness and peace lay calmly couching together through the fluid universal shadows.

Walt Whitman, *Specimen Days*, 1882, reprinted in Walt Whitman, *Prose Works* (Philadelphia: McKay, n.d.), p. 101.

It was nearly dark when I parted from the Lloyds, that is night was come on, and the moon was overcast. But, as I climbed Moss, the moon came out from behind a mountain mass of black clouds. O, the unutterable darkness of the sky, and the earth below the moon! and the glorious brightness of the moon itself! There was a vivid sparkling streak of light at this end of Rydale water, but the rest was very dark, and Loughrigg Fell and Silver How were white and bright, as if they were covered with hoar frost. The moon retired again, and appeared and disappeared several times before I reached home. Once there was no moonlight to be seen but upon the island-house and the promontory of the island where it stands. "That needs must be a holy place", etc. etc. I had many very exquisite feelings, and when I saw this lowly Building in the waters, among the dark and lofty hills, with that bright, soft light upon it, it made me more than half a poet.

Dorothy Wordsworth, Grasmere Journal, March 18, 1802, *Journals of Dorothy Wordsworth*, ed. E. de Selincourt (London: Macmillan, 1941), vol. I, pp. 126–27.

————◆————

The day was dying, the night being born—but with great peace. Here were the imponderable processes and forces of the cosmos, harmonious and soundless. Harmony, that was it! That was what came out of the silence—a gentle rhythm, the strain of a perfect chord, the music of the spheres, perhaps.

It was enough to catch that rhythm, momentarily to be myself a part of it. In that instant I could feel no doubt of man's oneness with the universe. The conviction came that that rhythm was too orderly, too harmonious, too perfect to be a product of blind chance—that, therefore, there must be purpose in the whole and that man was part of that whole and not an accidental offshoot. It was a feeling that transcended reason; that went to the heart of man's despair and found it groundless. The universe was a cosmos, not a chaos; man was as rightfully a part of that cosmos as were the day and night.

Richard E. Byrd, *Alone* (New York: Putnam, 1938), p. 85.

————◆————

I knew a man once in the Tourdenoise, a gloomy man, but very rich, who cared little for the things he knew. This man took no pleasure in his fruitful orchards and his carefully ploughed fields and his harvests. He took pleasure in pine trees; he was a man of groves and of the dark. For him that things should come to an end was but part of an universal rhythm; a part pleasing to the general harmony, and making in the music of the world about him a solemn and, oh, a conclusive chord. This man would study the sky at night and take from it a larger and a larger draught of infinitude, finding in this exercise not a mere satisfaction, but an object and goal for the mind; when he had so wandered for a while under the night he seemed, for the moment, to have reached the object of his being.

Hilaire Belloc, "On Coming to an End," *On Nothing & Kindred Subjects*, 2d ed. (New York: Dutton, 1909), p. 259.

———————◆———————

. . . I am glad when I pass down Fleet Street to be able to say to myself, 'I too once lived in Arcadia' and knew the pleasant side of the life. There is something peculiarly delightful, when one's leader is finished, in lighting a pipe or a cigar and stretching out one's legs and feeling entirely at leisure. There is real leisure in the middle of the night, that is, between one and five. There are no appointments, no meals, no duties, no plans, no dependence on other people's arrangements. One is as completely isolated as a Trappist monk. If you see a friend in Fleet Street or Shoe Lane during those hours, he will be as free as you are yourself.

John St. Loe Strachey, *The Adventure of Living* (London: Hodder, 1922), p. 188.

———————◆———————

When the play was over and the last visitors had left his dressing-room, [Sir Henry] Irving changed and, if he did not go to one or other of his clubs, returned to Grafton Street, where he found a frugal supper waiting for him on the hearth. If he could persuade a friend to return with him to share it—so much the better. 'A little supper—eh?' he would grunt hospitably as he rummaged by the fire. 'Some soup—eh? and a kipper—very good, ye know—kipper!' The dishes were shared over a bottle of champagne, cigars were lit, and he settled down to beguile his companion into keeping him company until the early hours of the morning. For Irving, these were the best hours of the day . . .

Laurence Irving, *Henry Irving* (London: Faber, 1951), p. 324.

AGE

◆

We can't deny it any longer; it is autumn. You will recognize it in the flowering of the autumnal chrysanthemums—these autumnal flowers bloom with special vigour and fullness; they don't make much fuss, one flower is like the other, but how many they are! I tell you that this flowering of mature age is more vigorous and passionate than those restless and passing tossings of the young spring. In it there is the sense and consistency of a grown-up man; if you flower, do it thoroughly; and have plenty of honey so that the bees will come. What is a falling leaf to this rich autumnal display?

Karel Capek, *The Gardener's Year* (London: Allen & Unwin, 1931), p. 119.

◆

The primitive, physical, functional pattern of the morning of life, the active years before forty or fifty, is outlived. But there is still the afternoon opening up . . .

For is it not possible that middle age can be looked upon as a period of second flowering, second growth, even a kind of second adolescence? It is true that society in general does not help one accept this interpretation of the second half of life. And therefore this period of expanding is often tragically misunderstood. Many people never climb above the plateau of forty-to-fifty. The signs that presage growth, so similar, it seems to me, to those in early adolescence: discontent, restlessness, doubt, despair, longing, are interpreted falsely as signs of decay. In youth one does not as often misinterpret the signs; one accepts them, quite rightly, as growing pains. One takes them seriously, listens to them, follows where they lead. One is afraid. Naturally. Who is not afraid of pure space—that breath-taking empty space of an open door? But despite fear, one goes through to the room beyond.

But in middle age, because of the false assumption that it is a period of decline, one interprets these life-signs, paradoxically, as signs of approaching death. Instead of facing them, one runs away; one escapes—into depressions, nervous breakdowns, drink, love affairs, or frantic, thoughtless, fruitless overwork. Anything, rather than face them. Anything, rather than stand still and learn from them. One tries to cure the signs of growth, to exorcise them, as if they were devils, when really they might be angels of annunciation.

Angels of annunciation of what? Of a new stage in living when, having shed many of the physical struggles, the worldly ambitions, the material encumbrances of active life, one might be free to fulfill the neglected side of one's self. One might be free for growth of mind, heart, and talent; free at last for spiritual growth. . . .

Anne Morrow Lindbergh, *Gift From the Sea* (New York: Pantheon Bks., 1955), pp. 86–88.

. . . I find life a gift increasing in value. I have not found it a cup foaming and sparkling at the top, and growing vapid as I have drunk. In truth, I dislike altogether this old-fashioned simile. Life is not a little cup dipped from the stream of time. It is itself a *stream*; and though at its birth it may dance and send forth cheerful murmurs as it does not afterwards, still it is intended to flow, as it advances, through more beautiful regions, and to adorn its shores with richer verdure and more abundant harvests. Do not say that this end is frustrated. I do believe there are multitudes who have not found infancy and youth as happy as later years.

William Ellery Channing, letter, March 5, 1826, in William Henry Channing, *Memoir of William Ellery Channing* (London: Routledge, n.d.), vol. II, p. 477.

To say that youth is happier than maturity is like saying that the view from the bottom of a tower is better than the view from the top. As we ascend the spiral staircase, and glance from time to time through the narrow slits in the stone, the range of our view widens immensely; the horizon is pushed farther away. Finally as we reach the summit it is as if we had the world at our feet.

William Lyon Phelps, *Autobiography with Letters* (New York: Oxford, 1939), p. 965.

There is great doubt as to what may be the most enviable time of life with a man. I am inclined to think that it is at that period when his children have all been born, but have not yet begun to go astray or to vex him with disappointment; when his own pecuniary prospects are settled, and he knows pretty well what his tether will allow him; when the appetite is still good and the digestive organs at their full power; when he has ceased to care as to the length of his girdle, and before the doctor warns him against solid breakfasts and port wine after dinner; when his affectations are over and his infirmities have not yet come upon him; while he can still walk his ten miles, and feel some little pride in being able to do so; while he has still nerve to ride his horse to hounds, and can look with some scorn on the ignorance of younger men who have hardly yet learned that noble art. As regards men, this, I think, is the happiest time of life . . .

Anthony Trollope, *Orley Farm*, 1862 (London: Lane, 1906), vol. II, chap. XIX, p. 261.

◆

Some satirists have complained of life, inasmuch as all the pleasures belong to the fore part of it and we must see them dwindle till we are left, it may be, with the miseries of a decrepit old age.

To me it seems that youth is like spring, an overpraised season—delightful if it happen to be a favoured one, but in practice very rarely favoured and more remarkable, as a general rule, for biting east winds than genial breezes. Autumn is the mellower season, and what we lose in flowers we more than gain in fruits. . . . True, in old age we live under the shadow of Death, which, like a sword of Damocles, may descend at any moment, but we have so long found life to be an affair of being rather frightened than hurt that we have become like the people who live under Vesuvius, and chance it without much misgiving.

Samuel Butler, *The Way of All Flesh*, 1903 (New York: Dodd, 1957), chap. VI, p. 27.

◆

Under the general assertion of the well-being of age, we can easily count particular benefits of that condition. It has weathered the perilous capes and shoals in the sea whereon we sail, and the chief evil of life is taken away in removing the grounds of fear. The insurance of a ship expires as she enters the harbour at home. It were strange, if a man should turn his sixtieth year without a feeling of immense relief from the number of dangers he has escaped. . . . Meantime, at every stage we lose a foe. At fifty years, 'tis said, afflicted citizens lose their sick-headaches. I hope this *hegira* is not as movable a feast as that one I annually look for, when the horticulturists assure me that the rose-bugs in our garden disappear on the tenth of July; they stay a fortnight later in mine. But be it as it may with the sick-headache, 'tis certain that graver headaches and heart-aches are lulled once for all, as we come up with certain goals of time. The passions have answered their purpose; that slight but dread overweight, with which, in each instance, Nature secures the execution of her aim, drops off. To keep man in the planet, she impresses the terror of death. To perfect the commissariat, she implants in each a certain rapacity to get the supply, and a little over-supply, of his wants. To insure the existence of the race, she reinforces the sexual instinct, at the risk of disorder, grief, and pain. To secure strength, she plants cruel hunger and thirst, which so easily overdo their office, and invite disease. But these temporary stays and shifts, for the protection of the young animal, are shed as fast as they can be replaced by nobler resources. We live in youth amidst this rabble of passion, quite too tender, quite too hungry and irritable. Later, the interiors of mind and heart open, and supply grander motives. We learn the fatal compensations that wait on every act. Then—one after another—this riotous time-destroying crew disappear.

Ralph Waldo Emerson, "Old Age," *Society and Solitude* (Boston: Houghton, 1904), pp. 323–25.

❖

It is one of the consolations of healthy age that, although it cannot do anything to excess without having to pay a penalty afterwards, it can still do most things in moderation, and derive almost as much satisfaction from the limited and reasonable exercise of diminished powers as it once derived from excessive and often unnecessary exertions.

Philip Gilbert Hamerton, *The Quest of Happiness* (Boston: Roberts Brothers, 1897), p. 135.

❖

A friend of mine, just sixty, announced recently in his newspaper column that he was on the downward slope of life. And what inspired this melancholy reflection? The discovery of his inability to climb up some mountain with the zest of once upon a time. I hesitate to profane with my irreverence the sacred topic of athletic exercise, but I am old enough—yes, I really am old enough—to express a firm opinion that whatever disillusionment may accompany the old age of some men is nearly always due to what I consider their insensate devotion to physical activity after the body has begun to be weary of it. Far from condoling with my sexagenarian climber upon his intimations of debility, I congratulate him upon what I hope will henceforth be his freedom from the tyranny of exercise when he ought to be sitting in a chair, reading or writing or talking.

The exceptional man can still ride to hounds at eighty, but I doubt if such a man has taxed his mind overmuch in the course of a physically active life, and when the feebleness of the body at last asserts itself such a man will inevitably feel that life has lost its savour. But why a man with a rich intellectual and emotional life and a well-stored memory should feel old because he can no longer climb a mountain without puffing, or outplay Colonel Bogey on his local golf-links, passes my comprehension.

Sir Compton Mackenzie, "A Week on the Way to Seventy," *Echoes* (London: Chatto, 1954), p. 183.

———◆———

One of the delights known to age and beyond the grasp of youth is that of *Not Going*. When we are young it is almost agony not to go. We feel we are being left out of life, that the whole wonderful procession is sweeping by, probably for ever, while we are weeping or sulking behind bars. Not to have an invitation—for the dance, the party, the match, the picnic, the excursion, the gang on holiday—is to be diminished, perhaps kept at midget's height for years. To have an invitation and then not to be able to go—oh cursed spite! Thus we torment ourselves in the April of our time. Now in my early November not only do I not care the rottenest fig whether I receive an invitation or not, but after having carelessly accepted the invitation I can find delight in knowing that I am *Not Going*. I arrived at this by two stages. At the first, after years of illusion, I finally decided I was missing nothing by not going. Now, at the second and, I hope, final stage, I stay away and no longer care whether I am missing anything or not. But don't I like to enjoy myself? On the contrary, by Not Going, that is just what I am trying to do.

J. B. Priestley, *Delight* (London: Heinemann, 1949), pp. 152–53.

McKenna [Rt. Hon. Reginald McKenna] said one of the chief pleasures of advancing age is a sense of detachment which enables one to watch the drama as played by other people—one of the most interesting things in life.

Lord Riddell, Diary, January 19, 1913, in Lord Riddell, *More Pages from My Diary* (London: Country Life, Ltd., 1934), p. 118.

JOHNSON. 'Why, Sir, a man grows better humoured as he grows older. He improves by experience. When young, he thinks himself of great consequence, and every thing of importance. As he advances in life, he learns to think himself of no consequence, and little things of little importance; and so he becomes more patient, and better pleased. . . .'

James Boswell, *The Journal of a Tour to the Hebrides with Samuel Johnson, LL.D.*, 1786, ed. George Birkbeck Hill (New York: Harper, n.d.), p. 240.

—Some of the softening effects of advancing age have struck me very much in what I have heard or seen here and elsewhere. I just now spoke of the sweetening process that authors undergo. Do you know that in the gradual passage from maturity to helplessness the harshest characters sometimes have a period in which they are gentle and placid as young children? . . . One who saw the Duke of Wellington in his last years describes him as very gentle in his aspect and demeanor. I remember a person of singularly stern and lofty bearing who became remarkably gracious and easy in all his ways in the later period of his life.

And that leads me to say that men often remind me of pears in their way of coming to maturity. Some are ripe at twenty, like human Jargonelles, and must be made the most of, for their day is soon over. Some come into their perfect condition late, like the autumn kinds, and they last better than the summer fruit. And some, that, like the Winter-Nelis, have been hard and uninviting until all the rest have had their season, get their glow and perfume long after the frost and snow have done their worst with the orchards. Beware of rash criticisms; the rough and astringent fruit you condemn may be an autumn or a winter pear, and that which you picked up beneath the same bough in August may have been only its worm-eaten windfalls.

Oliver Wendell Holmes, *The Autocrat of the Breakfast-Table* (Boston: Phillips, 1858), pp. 91–92.

———◆———

I called on the dear old doctor [Oliver Wendell Holmes] this afternoon to say good-bye. I shall probably not find him here when I come back from the long voyage which I have in front of me. He is very fragile, and looks as though a puff of wind would blow him away. He said himself, with his old-time cheerfulness, that he was attached to this earth by only a little piece of twine. He has perceptibly failed since I saw him a month ago; but he was full of the wise and radiant talk to which all the world has listened, and will miss. I found him absorbed in a newly made card-catalogue of his library. "It was absurd of me to have it done," he remarked. "What I really require is a little bookcase holding only two volumes; then I could go from one to the other in alternation and always find each book as fresh as if I never had read it." This arraignment of his memory was in pure jest, for the doctor's mind was to the end like an unclouded crystal. It was interesting to note how he studied himself, taking his own pulse, as it were, and diagnosing his own case in a sort of scientific, impersonal way, as if it were somebody else's case and he were the consulting specialist. I intended to spend a quarter of an hour with him, and he kept me three hours. I went there rather depressed, but I returned home leavened with his good spirits, which, I think, will never desert him, here or hereafter. To keep the heart unwrinkled, to be hopeful, kindly, cheerful, reverent—that is to triumph over old age.

Thomas Bailey Aldrich, *Ponkapog Papers* (Boston: Houghton, 1903), pp. 45–46.

———◆———

Often, indeed, old age, when it is free from grave infirmities, and from great trials and privations, is the most honoured, the most tranquil, and perhaps on the whole the happiest period of life. The struggles, passions, and ambitions of other days have passed. The mellowing touch of time has allayed animosities, subdued old asperities of character, given a larger and more tolerant judgment, cured the morbid sensitiveness that most embitters life. The old man's mind is stored with the memories of a well-filled and honourable life. In the long leisures that now fall to his lot he is often enabled to resume projects which, in a crowded professional life, he had been obliged to adjourn; he finds (as Adam Smith has said) that one of the greatest pleasures in life is reverting in old age to the studies of youth, and he himself often feels something of the thrill of a second youth in his sympathy with the children who are around him. It is the St. Martin's summer, lighting with a pale but beautiful gleam the brief November day.

William Edward Hartpole Lecky, *The Map of Life* (London: Longmans, 1899), pp. 316–17.

———◆———

One hears of the disillusionment of age. It is true, one has learned how difficult it is for men to rise above the horizon line of daily life; we know the shallows as we do the depths, and cease to expect more from men than they are able and ready to give. We become more indulgent towards common frailties, complain less since we expect less, and we are grateful for the exchange of decencies and kindnesses. . . .

There comes, too, a St Martin's summer of the affections, bringing an ecstasy no less—perhaps because unexpected—than that of the high summer of life. A graciousness is extended by women to older men. To men, in their later years, comes a more disinterested understanding of the qualities peculiar to women, an affection which is not subject to the violent reactions, the intermittent hatred, which accompany closer relations between the sexes. 'When I was young my mind was a grub, my body a butterfly; now, in my old age, my body is a grub, my mind a butterfly,' said Yeats, as I drove back with him from Penns in the Rocks to London.

William Rothenstein, *Since Fifty: Men and Memories, 1922–1938* (London: Faber, 1939), pp. 328–29.

MEMORY

———◆———

I have often experienced, that scenes through which a man has passed, improve by lying in the memory: they grow mellow. *Acti labores sunt jucundi.* This may be owing to comparing them with present listless ease. Even harsh scenes acquire a softness by length of time; and some are like very loud sounds, which do not please, or at least do not please so much, till you are removed to a certain distance. They may be compared to strong coarse pictures, which will not bear to be viewed near. Even pleasing scenes improve by time, and seem more exquisite in recollection, than when they were present; if they have not faded to dimness in the memory. Perhaps, there is so much evil in every human enjoyment, when present,—so much dross mixed with it, that it requires to be refined by time; and yet I do not see why time should not melt away the good and the evil in equal proportions;—why the shade should decay, and the light remain in preservation.

James Boswell, *The Journal of a Tour to the Hebrides with Samuel Johnson, LL.D.,* 1786, ed. George Birkbeck Hill (New York: Harper, n.d.), pp. 379–80.

———◆———

Most of us have certain childish memories which we can never repeat, since they represent moments when life was in utter harmony and sense and spirit perfectly attuned. Such memories for me are all of Tweedside, and I have welcomed with delight any maturer experience which had a hint of their magic. Three I have always cherished. One was the waking on a hot July morning with a day of moorland wandering before me. Around me were the subtle odours of an old house, somewhere far off the fragrance of coffee, and the smell of new-mown hay drifting through the open window. Through the same window came a multitude of sounds—the clank of the neighbouring smithy, the clucking of hens, sheep fording the burn. From my bed I could see the sky blue as deep-sea water, and against it the bare green top of a hill. Even to-day a fine morning gives me something of the thrill of those summer awakenings.

Another memory is of a long tramp on a drove-road in the teeth of the wind, with the rain in my face and mist swirling down the glens. I felt that I was contending joyfully with something kindly at heart, something to stir the blood and at the same time instinct with a delicate comfort—the homely smell of sheep, the scent of peat-reek, the glimpse of firelight from a wayside cottage.

The third was family prayers of a Sabbath evening. It was the custom to return from church through the fields, which lay yellow in the sunset. While our elders cast a half-ashamed sabbatical eye over the crops of meadow hay and the kyloes in the pastures, we children, feeling the bonds of the Sabbath ritual slackening, were hard at work planning enterprises for the morrow. Then in the dusky parlour, with its comforting secular aroma of tobacco, my grandfather read chapters of both Testaments and a lengthy prayer from some forgotten *Family Altar*. I did not follow one word, for my thoughts were busy with other things. He read in a high liturgical manner, his voice rising and falling in reverent cadences. It seemed to us children a benediction on the enforced leisure of the day and a promise of a new and glorious week of wind and sun.

All my life I have been haunted—and cheered—by these recollections: the green summit against the unclouded blue above a populous friendly world, the buffets of rain on the moorland road, the drone of my grandfather's voice in the Sabbath twilight. Each was a summons to action. But there was a fourth which spoke only of peace. This was the coming down from the hills, very hungry and foot-sore, to a white-washed farm on the brink of the heather, where, in a parlour looking out on a garden of gooseberries and phloxes, with a glimpse beyond of running water, I was stayed with tea and new-baked scones and apple-and-rowan-berry jelly. Then I demanded nothing more of life except to be allowed to go on living in that quiet world of pastoral. The dying shepherd asked not for the conventional Heaven, but for "Bourhope at a reasonable rent," and, if Paradise be a renewal of what was happy and innocent in our earthly days, mine will be some such golden afternoon within sight and sound of Tweed.

John Buchan, *Memory Hold-the-Door* (Toronto: Musson, 1940), pp. 26–28.

◆

It is easy to fall into the delusion that the few things thus . . . distinctly remembered and visualized are precisely those which were most important in our life, and on that account were saved by memory while all the rest has been permanently blotted out. That is indeed how our memory serves and fools us; for at some period of a man's life—at all events of some lives—in some rare state of the mind, it is all at once revealed to him as by a miracle that nothing is ever blotted out. . . .

I was feeling weak and depressed when I came down from London one November evening to the south coast: the sea, the clear sky, the bright colours of the afterglow kept me too long on the front in an east wind in that low condition, with the result that I was laid up for six weeks with a very serious illness. Yet when it was over I looked back on those six weeks as a happy time! Never had I thought so little of physical pain. Never had I felt confinement less—I who feel, when I am out of sight of living, growing grass, and out of sound of birds' voices and all rural sounds, that I am not properly alive!

On the second day of my illness, during an interval of comparative ease, I fell into recollections of my childhood, and at once I had that far, that forgotten past with me again as I had never previously had it. It was not like that mental condition, known to most persons, when some sight or sound or, more frequently, the perfume of some flower, associated with our early life, restores the past suddenly and so vividly that it is almost an illusion. That is an intensely emotional condition and vanishes as quickly as it comes. This was different. To return to the simile and metaphor . . . it was as if the cloud shadows and haze had passed away and the entire wide prospect beneath me made clearly visible. Over it all my eyes could range at will, choosing this or that point to dwell on, to examine it in all its details; or in the case of some person known to me as a child, to follow his life till it ended or passed from sight; then to return to the same point again to repeat the process with other lives and resume my rambles in the old familiar haunts.

What a happiness it would be, I thought, in spite of discomfort and pain and danger, if this vision would continue! It was not to be expected: nevertheless it did not vanish . . .

It was to me a marvellous experience; to be here, propped up with pillows in a dimly-lighted room, the night-nurse idly dozing by the fire; the sound of the everlasting wind in my ears, howling outside and dashing the rain like hailstones against the window-panes; to be awake to all this, feverish and ill and sore, conscious of my danger too, and at the same time to be thousands of miles away, out in the sun and wind, rejoicing in other sights and sounds, happy again with that ancient long-lost and now recovered happiness!

W. H. Hudson, *Far Away and Long Ago* (New York: Dutton, 1918), pp. 2–4.

———◆———

. . . I spent some part of every year at the farm [in Missouri] until I was twelve or thirteen years old. The life which I led there with my cousins was full of charm, and so is the memory of it yet. I can call back the solemn twilight and mystery of the deep woods, the earthy smells, the faint odors of the wild flowers, the sheen of rain-washed foliage, the rattling clatter of drops when the wind shook the trees, the far-off hammering of woodpeckers and the muffled drumming of wood pheasants in the remoteness of the forest, the snapshot glimpses of disturbed wild creatures scurrying through the grass—I can call it all back and make it as real as it ever was, and as blessed. I can call back the prairie, and its loneliness and peace, and a vast hawk hanging motionless in the sky, with his wings spread wide and the blue of the vault showing through the fringe of their end feathers. I can see the woods in their autumn dress, the oaks purple, the hickories washed with gold, the maples and the sumachs luminous with crimson fires, and I can hear the rustle made by the fallen leaves as we plowed through them. . . . I know the look of Uncle Dan'l's kitchen as it was on the privileged nights, when I was a child, and I can see the white and black children grouped on the hearth, with the firelight playing on their faces and the shadows flickering upon the walls, clear back toward the cavernous gloom of the rear, and I can hear Uncle Dan'l telling the immortal tales which Uncle Remus Harris was to gather into his book and charm the world with, by and by; and I can feel again the creepy joy which quivered through me when the time for the ghost story was reached—and the sense of regret, too, which came over me, for it was always the last story of the evening and there was nothing between it and the unwelcome bed.

I can remember the bare wooden stairway in my uncle's house, and the turn to the left above the landing, and the rafters and the slanting roof over my bed, and the squares of moonlight on the floor, and the white cold world of snow outside, seen through the curtainless window. I can remember the howling of the wind and the quaking of the house on stormy nights, and how snug and cozy one felt, under the blankets, listening; and how the powdery snow used to sift in, around the sashes, and lie in little ridges on the floor and make the place look chilly in the morning and curb the wild desire to get up—in case there was any. I can remember how very dark that room was, in the dark of the moon, and how packed it was with ghostly stillness when one woke up by accident away in the night . . .

I remember the raging of the rain on that roof, summer nights, and how pleasant it was to lie and listen to it, and enjoy the white splendor of the lightning and the majestic booming and crashing of the thunder. It was a very satisfactory room . . .

Mark Twain, *Mark Twain's Autobiography* (New York: Harper, 1924), vol. I, pp. 109–10, 112–13.

◆

There is one kind of morning in early summer that is for me very special, the most delightful of all mornings. The sun is up and blazing somewhere but not visible yet down here, where there is a lot of gold mist about and the birds are singing from lost thickets. The warmth has not yet broken through, and the air has a cool sparkle: it is as if we were on mountains, high mountains but far south. Distances are hidden but everything close is sharply defined, very clear and gay, like new celestial toys. The hour has immense promise; perhaps Doomsday has come and gone. But what makes this kind of morning very special, the most delightful of all, is that it has a unique trick of lifting me out of time: I seem to be moving along a fifth dimension and to have a four-dimensional outlook. Or put it more sensibly like this. These mornings link up directly and vividly with similar mornings in my past, so that I am aware of myself as I was then. Practising with the tug-of-war team at school. Coming out of that moorland hut—when was it?—about 1912. Camps and billets and trenches in the First World War. Walking early up the Backs at Cambridge. All these selves on similar mornings down the years. And freed from the brutal hurry of time, I see this life of mine as if it were a play by Tchekhov, whose searching yet tender glance we seem to borrow at such moments. Everything matters, yet nothing matters. We have escaped from balance sheets, reports of progress. There are no itineraries, no goals. Success and failure are equally meaningless. Every detail is memorable, exquisite, catching at the heart; yet the totality is itself nothing but a long clear dream. Such is the timeless view; and it is on these mornings in early summer that I obtain a glimpse of it, and am shaken by delight.

J. B. Priestley, *Delight* (London: Heinemann, 1949), pp. 257-58.

———◆———

Few if any moments more rapturous than those no matter how fleeting that call up sensations of earliest childhood, babyhood almost. Yesterday looking at a runnel of pure mountain water I suddenly was flooded as it were by the memory of a trough near my home through which flowed water impregnated with iron and sulphur. The memory was as vividly poignant for a second as an actuality, and it made me vibrate with the fullness of the so distant past.

Bernard Berenson, Diary, August 21, 1949, in Bernard Berenson, *Sunset and Twilight*, ed. Nicky Mariano (New York: Harcourt, 1963), p. 138.

———◆———

One day as I sat here I heard the song of the olive-backed thrush down in the currant-bushes below me. Instantly I was transported to the deep woods and the trout brooks of my native Catskills. I heard the murmuring water and felt the woodsy coolness of those retreats—such magic hath associative memories!

John Burroughs, "The Pleasures of a Naturalist," *Under the Maples* (Boston: Houghton, 1921), p. 30.

———◆———

When I was quite a boy, my father used to take me to the Montpelier Tea-gardens at Walworth. Do I go there now? No; the place is deserted, and its borders and its beds o'erturned. Is there, then, nothing that can

"Bring back the hour
Of splendour in the grass, of glory in the flower?"

Oh! yes. I unlock the casket of memory, and draw back the warders of the brain; and there this scene of my infant wanderings still lives unfaded, or with fresher dyes. A new sense comes upon me, as in a dream; a richer perfume, brighter colours start out; my eyes dazzle; my heart heaves with its new load of bliss, and I am a child again. My sensations are all glossy, spruce, voluptuous, and fine: they wear a candied coat, and are in holiday trim. I see the beds of larkspur with purple eyes; tall hollyhocks, red or yellow; the broad sunflowers, caked in gold, with bees buzzing round them; wildernesses of pinks, and hot glowing peonies; poppies run to seed; the sugared lily, and faint mignionette, all ranged in order, and as thick as they can grow; the box-tree borders; the gravel-walks, the painted alcove, the confectionery, the clotted cream:—I think I see them now with sparkling looks; or have they vanished while I have been writing this description of them? No matter; they will return again when I least think of them. All that I have observed since, of flowers and plants, and grass-plots, and of suburb delights, seems to me borrowed from "that first garden of my innocence"—to be slips and scions stolen from that bed of memory. In this manner the darlings of our childhood burnish out in the eye of after years, and derive their sweetest perfume from the first heartfelt sigh of pleasure breathed upon them . . .

William Hazlitt, *Table Talk*, 1821 (London: Bell, 1889), chap. XXIII, pp. 359–60.

———◆———

Never have I enjoyed youth so thoroughly as I have in my old age. In writing *Dialogues in Limbo, The Last Puritan*, and now all these descriptions of the friends of my youth and the young friends of my middle age, I have drunk the pleasure of life more pure, more joyful, than it ever was when mingled with all the hidden anxieties and little annoyances of actual living. Nothing is inherently and invincibly young except spirit. And spirit can enter a human being perhaps better in the quiet of old age and dwell there more undisturbed than in the turmoil of adventure. But it must be in solitude. I do not need or desire to hob-nob artificially with other old men in order to revisit them in their salad days, and to renew my own. In Rome, in the eternal city, I feel nearer to my own past, and to the whole past and future of the world, than I should in any cemetery or in any museum of relics. Old places and old persons in their turn, when spirit dwells in them, have an intrinsic vitality of which youth is incapable; precisely the balance and wisdom that comes from long perspectives and broad foundations. Everything shines then for the spirit by its own light in its own place and time; but not as it shone in its own restless eyes. For in its own eyes each person and each place was the centre of a universe full of threatening and tempting things; but old age, having less intensity at the centre has more clearness at the circumference. . . .

George Santayana, *My Host the World* (New York: Scribner, 1953), vol. III, pp. 131–32.

———◆———

When the act of reflection takes place in the mind, when we look at ourselves in the light of thought, we discover that our life is embosomed in beauty. Behind us, as we go, all things assume pleasing forms, as clouds do far off. Not only things familiar and stale, but even the tragic and terrible are comely as they take their place in the picture of memory. The river-bank, the weed at the water-side, the old house, the foolish person, however neglected in the passing, have a grace in the past. . . . For it is only the finite that has wrought and suffered; the infinite lies stretched in smiling repose.

Ralph Waldo Emerson, "Spiritual Laws," *Essays*, 1st series, 1841 (Boston: Houghton, 1898), chap. IV, pp. 125–26.

SLEEP

———◆———

All the Arabs reverence a man's sleeping; he is as it were in trance with God, and a truce of his waking solicitude: in their households they piously withdraw, nor will any lightly molest him, until he waken of himself.

Charles M. Doughty, *Travels in Arabia Deserta*, 1888 (London: Cape, 1926), vol. I, chap. IX, pp. 249–50.

. . . rode easily to Welling, where we supped well, and had two beds in the room and so lay single, and still remember it that of all the nights that ever I slept in my life I never did pass a night with more epicurism of sleep; there being now and then a noise of people stirring that waked me, and then it was a very rainy night, and then I was a little weary, that what between waking and then sleeping again, one after another, I never had so much content in all my life, and so my wife says it was with her.

Samuel Pepys, Diary, September 23, 1661, *The Diary of Samuel Pepys*, ed. Henry B. Wheatley (London: Bell, 1924), vol. II, p. 101.

◆

This is an article for the reader to think of when he or she is warm in bed, a little before he goes to sleep, the clothes at his ear, and the wind moaning in some distant crevice. "Blessings," exclaimed Sancho, "on him that first invented sleep! It wraps a man all round like a cloak." It is a delicious moment certainly that of being well nestled in bed, and feeling that you shall drop gently to sleep. The good is to come—not past: the limbs have been just tired enough to render the remaining in one posture delightful; the labour of the day is done. A gentle failure of the perceptions comes creeping over one: the spirit of consciousness disengages itself more and more, with slow and hushing degrees, like a mother detaching her hand from that of her sleeping child; the mind seems to have a balmy lid closing over it, like the eye. 'Tis closing—'tis more closing—'tis closed. The mysterious spirit has gone to take its airy rounds.

It is said that sleep is best before midnight; and Nature herself with her darkness and chilling dews, informs us so. There is another reason for going to bed betimes; for it is universally acknowledged that lying late in the morning is a great shortener of life—at least, it is never found in company with longevity. It also tends to make people corpulent. But these matters belong rather to the subject of early rising than of sleep.

Sleep at a late hour in the morning is not half so pleasant as the more timely one. It is sometimes, however, excusable, especially to a watchful or overworked head; neither can we deny the seducing merits of "t'other dose"—the pleasing wilfulness of nestling in a new posture, when you know you ought to be up, like the rest of the house. But then you cut up the day, and your sleep the next night. . . .

The most complete and healthy sleep that can be taken in the day is in summer-time, out in a field. There is perhaps no solitary sensation so exquisite as that of slumbering on the grass or hay, shaded from the hot sun by a tree, with the consciousness of a fresh but light air running through the wide atmosphere, and the sky stretching far overhead upon all sides. Earth and heaven, and a placid humanity, seem to have the creation to themselves. There is nothing between the slumberer and the naked and glad innocence of Nature.

Next to this, but at a long interval, the most relishing snatch of slumber out of bed is the one which a tired person takes before he retires for the night, while lingering in his sitting-room. The consciousness of being very sleepy, and of having the power to go to bed immediately, gives great zest to the unwillingness to move. Sometimes he sits nodding in his chair; but the sudden and leaden jerks of the head, to which a state of great sleepiness renders him liable, are generally too painful for so luxurious a moment; and he gets into a more legitimate posture, sitting sideways with his head on the chair-back, or throwing his legs up at once on another chair, and half reclining. It is curious, however, to find how long an inconvenient posture will be borne for the sake of this foretaste of repose.

Leigh Hunt, "A Few Thoughts on Sleep," *The Indicator*, January 12, 1820, reprinted in *Leigh Hunt as Poet and Essayist*, ed. Charles Kent (London: Warne, n.d.), pp. 139–41.

The time of falling asleep is a child's immemorial and incalculable hour. It is full of traditions, and beset by antique habits. The habit of prehistoric races has been cited as the only explanation of the fixity of some customs in mankind. But if the inquirers who appeal to that beginning remembered better their own infancy, they would seek no further. See the habits in falling to sleep which have children in their thralldom. Try to overcome them in any child, and his own conviction of their high antiquity weakens your hand.

Childhood is antiquity, and with the sense of time and the sense of mystery is connected for ever the hearing of a lullaby. The French sleep-song is the most romantic. There is in it such a sound of history as must inspire any imaginative child, falling to sleep, with a sense of the incalculable; and the songs themselves are old. "Le Bon Roi Dagobert" has been sung over French cradles since the legend was fresh. The nurse knows nothing more sleepy than the tune and the verse that she herself slept to when a child. The gaiety of the thirteenth century, in "Le Pont d'Avignon," is put mysteriously to sleep, away in the *tête à tête* of child and nurse, in a thousand little sequestered rooms at night. "Malbrook" would be comparatively modern, were not all things that are sung to a drowsing child as distant as the day of Abraham.

Alice Meynell, "Under the Early Stars," *Essays* (London: Burns, 1937), pp. 260–61.

———◆———

Night is a dead monotonous period under a roof; but in the open world it passes lightly, with its stars and dews and perfumes, and the hours are marked by changes in the face of Nature. What seems a kind of temporal death to people choked between walls and curtains, is only a light and living slumber to the man who sleeps afield. All night long he can hear Nature breathing deeply and freely; even as she takes her rest she turns and smiles; and there is one stirring hour unknown to those who dwell in houses, when a wakeful influence goes abroad over the sleeping hemisphere, and all the outdoor world are on their feet. It is then that the cock first crows, not this time to announce the dawn, but like a cheerful watchman speeding the course of night. Cattle awake on the meadows; sheep break their fast on dewy hillsides, and change to a new lair among the ferns; and houseless men, who have lain down with the fowls, open their dim eyes and behold the beauty of the night.

At what inaudible summons, at what gentle touch of Nature, are all these sleepers thus recalled in the same hour to life? Do the stars rain down an influence, or do we share some thrill of mother earth below our resting bodies? Even shepherds and old country-folk, who are the deepest read in these arcana, have not a guess as to the means or purpose of this nightly resurrection. Towards two in the morning they declare the thing takes place; and neither know nor inquire further. And at least it is a pleasant incident. . . . We have a moment to look upon the stars, and there is a special pleasure for some minds in the reflection that we share the impulse with all out-door creatures in our neighborhood, that we have escaped out of the *Bastille* of civilisation, and are become, for the time being, a mere kindly animal and a sheep of Nature's flock. . . .

A faint wind, more like a moving coolness than a stream of air, passed down the glade from time to time; so that even in my great chamber the air was being renewed all night long. I thought with horror of the inn at *Chasseradès* and the congregated nightcaps; with horror of the nocturnal prowesses of clerks and students, of hot theatres and pass-keys and close rooms. I have not often enjoyed a more serene possession of myself, nor felt more independent of material aids. The outer world, from which we cower into our houses, seemed after all a gentle habitable place; and night after night a man's bed, it seemed, was laid and waiting for him in the fields, where God keeps an open house.

Robert Louis Stevenson, *Travels with a Donkey in the Cevennes*, 1879 (New York: Scribner, 1900), chap. X, pp. 219–22.

━━━◆━━━

My companions slept rolled up in their blankets, and the Indians lay in the grass near the fire; but my sleeping-place generally had an air of more pretension. Our rifles were tied together near the muzzle, the butts resting on the ground, and a knife laid on the rope, to cut away in case of an alarm. Over this, which made a kind of frame, was thrown a large India rubber cloth, which we used to cover our packs. This made a tent sufficiently large to receive about half of my bed, and was a place of shelter for my instruments; and as I was careful always to put this part against the wind, I could lie here with a sensation of satisfied enjoyment, and hear the wind blow, and the rain patter close to my head, and know that I should be at least half dry. Certainly, I never slept more soundly.

John Charles Frémont, Journal of a journey over the prairies to the Rocky Mountains, July 6, 1842: Charles Wentworth Upham, *Life, Explorations and Public Services of John Charles Frémont* (Boston: Ticknor, 1856), p. 43.

━━━◆━━━

. . . when at fourteen years of age I was promoted from "bundle boy" to be one of the five hands to bind after the reaper, I went to my corner with joy and confidence. For two years I had been serving as binder on the corners, (to keep the grain out of the way of the horses) and I knew my job.

I was short and broad-shouldered with large strong hands admirably adapted for this work, and for the first two hours, easily held my own with the rest of the crew, but as the morning wore on and the sun grew hotter, my enthusiasm waned. A painful void developed in my chest. My breakfast had been ample, but no mere stomachful of food could carry a growing boy through five hours of desperate toil. Along about a quarter to ten, I began to scan the field with anxious eye, longing to see Harriet and the promised luncheon basket.

Just when it seemed that I could endure the strain no longer she came bearing a jug of cool milk, some cheese and some deliciously fresh fried-cakes. With keen joy I set a couple of tall sheaves together like a tent and flung myself down flat on my back in their shadow to devour my lunch.

Tired as I was, my dim eyes apprehended something of the splendor of the shining clouds which rolled like storms of snow through the deep-blue spaces of sky and so, resting silently as a clod I could hear the chirp of the crickets, the buzzing wings of flies and the faint, fairy-like tread of smaller unseen insects hurrying their way just beneath my ear in the stubble. Strange green worms, grasshoppers and shining beetles crept over me as I dozed.

This delicious, dreamful respite was broken by the far-off approaching purr of the sickle . . .

Hamlin Garland, *A Son of the Middle Border* (New York: Macmillan, 1917), pp. 149–50.

———◆———

Sleep, deep untroubled sleep. Isn't it odd how we love oblivion? I often think that, when tossing and turning in bed, the best inducement to unconsciousness is to think of all the most comfortless places in which at one time or another we have beeen compelled to spend a night: wedged upright in a smoke-filled railway carriage, clinging to one's bunk during a Channel storm, herded in an air-raid shelter. Then we appreciate the uncramped luxury of a bed, and soon we are asleep. Perhaps, equally, it is good to dwell on the happiest of our drowsy moments—on a mountainside with no roof overhead but heaven and no sound in one's ears but of the wind in the grasses; or on an islet in a lake, with heaped-up rushes as a bed and hearing only the bleat of a snipe; or beside a river, under a canopy of lime-trees whose branches hum with the drone of bees.

Robert Gibbings, *Coming Down the Seine* (London: Dent, 1953), p. 54.

———◆———

Over [Charles] Lamb, at this period of his life, there passed regularly, after taking wine, a brief eclipse of sleep. It descended upon him as softly as a shadow. In a gross person, laden with superfluous flesh, and sleeping heavily, this would have been disagreeable; but in Lamb, thin even to meagreness, spare and wiry as an Arab of the desert, or as

Thomas Aquinas, wasted by scholastic vigils, the affection of sleep seemed rather a network of aerial gossamer than of earthly cobweb— more like a golden haze falling upon him gently from the heavens than a cloud exhaling upwards from the flesh. Motionless in his chair as a bust, breathing so gently as scarcely to seem certainly alive, he presented the image of repose midway between life and death, like the repose of sculpture; and, to one who knew his history, a repose affectingly contrasting with the calamities and internal storms of his life. I have heard more persons than I can now distinctly recall, observe of Lamb when sleeping, that his countenance in that state assumed an expression almost seraphic, from its intellectual beauty of outline, its child-like simplicity, and its benignity.

Thomas De Quincey, *Leaders in Literature* (Edinburgh: Adam & Charles Black, 1863), p. 152.

———◆———

Sleep . . . is in general so usual and so easy a refuge that its strangeness and mystery are apt to be as little heeded as are its incalculable value and its gifts of grace. We rely on it as carelessly as we accept the air we breathe, and that shallow skin of soil which alone ensures us the living company, the verdure and the beauty of the earth. Without sleep, would life be endurable? A dismal night or two of fever will be answer enough to the enquiry; or even the mere misgiving that, by reason of some folly or frailty or stealing incapacity or misuse of the mind, the old faithful habit is deserting us. Is there any ill in life which sleep cannot solace awhile; is there any 'remand' comparable to it? From hope deferred, from corrodine expectation, from pain, pining, anxiety, grief, anger, and passion, it is our only certain and swift release. What the will and reason are powerless to remove, sleep melts like snow in water. Even an obsession . . . comes to a halt at the edge of that narrow abyss.

Walter de la Mare, *Behold, This Dreamer* (London: Faber, 1939), p. 45.

Index

ALCOTT, BRONSON
  The Journals of Bronson Alcott, 51–52
ALDRICH, THOMAS BAILEY
  Ponkapog Papers, 200
AMIEL, HENRI-FRÉDÉRIC
  The Journal Intime of Henri-Frédéric Amiel, 130, 151
ANDERSON, ERICA
  Albert Schweitzer's Gift of Friendship, 29
AUSTEN, JANE
  Emma, 95

BACON, SIR FRANCIS
  Essays, 65
BARBELLION, W. N. P.
  The Journal of a Disappointed Man, 41, 58
BARING, MAURICE
  Lost Lectures, 64–65
BELLOC, HILAIRE
  On Nothing & Kindred Subjects, 110, 192–93
  The Silence of the Sea and Other Essays, 154–55, 162–63
BENNETT, ARNOLD
  The Journals of Arnold Bennett 1911–1921, 29
BERENSON, BERNARD
  Rumour and Reflection, 107, 143–44
  Sunset and Twilight, 14, 35, 63, 138, 207
BORROW, GEORGE
  Lavengro, 121–22
BOSWELL, JAMES
  The Journal of a Tour to the Hebrides with Samuel Johnson, LL.D. 199, 202

  The Life of Samuel Johnson, 35–36, 48, 54, 94, 97
BROMFIELD, LOUIS
  The Wild Country, 139–40
BROWNE, SIR THOMAS
  Religio Medici, 63
BRYANT, SIR ARTHUR
  Historian's Holiday, 109–10
BUCHAN, JOHN
  Memory Hold-the-Door, 133–34, 202–4
BURROUGHS, JOHN
  Essays in Naturalism, 127–28
  Under the Maples, 142–43, 207
  Winter Sunshine, 147, 169–70, 178–79
BUTLER, SAMUEL
  The Way of All flesh, 196
BUTLER, SIR WILLIAM FRANCIS
  The Wild Northland, 182
BYRD, RICHARD E.
  Alone, 15–16, 192

CAMPBELL, MRS. PATRICK
  My Life and Some Letters, 87
CAPEK, KAREL
  The Gardener's Year, 142, 194
CARDUS, SIR NEVILLE
  Autobiography, 123–24
CARSON, RACHEL L.
  The Sea Around Us, 154
CHALMERS, PATRICK R.
  Kenneth Grahame, 105
CHAMBERLAIN, SIR AUSTEN
  Down the Years, 66
CHANNING, WILLIAM HENRY
  Memoir of William Ellery Channing, 30, 64, 185, 195
Charles Dickens. A Bookman Extra Number 1914, 153

CHASE, MARY ELLEN
  The White Gate, 190
CHURCH, RICHARD
  Calm October, 131–32
CHURCHILL, SIR WINSTON
  Thoughts and Adventures, 9, 17
COBBETT, WILLIAM
  Advice to Young Men and (Incidentally) to Young Women, 26–27
COFFIN, ROBERT P. TRISTRAM
  On the Green Carpet, 125, 158
COLE, G. D. H.
  The Life of William Cobbett, 52
COLLIS, MAURICE
  Stanley Spencer, 19, 111
COWPER, WILLIAM
  The Works of William Cowper, 59, 173–74
CURIE, MARIE
  Pierre Curie, 33
CUSHING, HARVEY
  The Life of Sir William Osler, 55

DAUDET, LÉON
  Alphonse Daudet, 61–62
DARWIN, FRANCIS
  The Life and Letters of Charles Darwin, 34, 66–67
DE LA MARE, WALTER
  Behold, This Dreamer, 215
DE QUINCY, THOMAS
  Leaders in Literature, 214–15
DICK, CHARLES
  John Buchan, by His Wife and Friends, 70
DICKENS, CHARLES
  The Letters of Charles Dickens, 115
  The Personal History of David Copperfield, 51
  The Posthumous Papers of the Pickwick Club, 72
  Sketches by Boz, 67–68
DOUGHTY, CHARLES M.
  Travels in Arabia Deserta, 179–80, 209

EADE, CHARLES (ed.)
  Churchill by his Contemporaries, 89
EDMAN, IRWIN
  Under Whatever Sky, 9–10
ELIOT, CHARLES W.
  A Late Harvest, 6
ELIOT, GEORGE
  Adam Bede, 41
ELLIS, HAVELOCK
  Impressions and Comments, 16, 92
EMERSON, RALPH WALDO
  Essays, 8, 209
  The Heart of Emerson's Journals, 17, 65, 111, 126, 144, 173, 190–91
  Nature, Addresses and Lectures, 129, 140–41
  Society and Solitude, 196–97

FARRELL, JAMES T.
  Reflections at Fifty and Other Essays, 122
FIELDS, JAMES T.
  Yesterdays with Authors, 141
FITZGERALD, EDWARD
  Letters of Edward Fitzgerald, 60
FRANCK, FREDERICK
  Days with Albert Schweitzer, 14–15
FRÉMONT, JOHN CHARLES
  Journals, 180, 213

GARLAND, HAMLIN
  A Son of the Middle Border, 213–14
GELD, ELLEN BROMFIELD
  The Heritage: A Daughter's Memories of Louis Bromfield, 156–57, 174–75
GIBBINGS, ROBERT
  Coming Down the Seine, 214
  Till I End My Song, 69–70, 144–45, 159–60
GIMPEL, RENÉ
  Diary of an Art Dealer, 41
GISSING, GEORGE
  The Private Papers of Henry Ryecroft, 43–44, 55–56, 61, 116–17, 147–48
GLASGOW, ELLEN
  The Woman Within, 132–33

GORDON, MARY WILSON
A Memoir of John Wilson, 105
GOSSE, PHILIP
Traveller's Rest, 80
GREY, EDWARD
Fly Fishing, 42, 80–81

HAIG-BROWN, RODERICK
Fisherman's Summer, 81–82
HAMERTON, PHILIP GILBERT
The Quest of Happiness, 3, 122,
140, 197
HAWKINS, SIR JOHN
The Works of Samuel Johnson,
LL. D. Together with His Life, 99
HAZLITT, WILLIAM
Essays of William Hazlitt, 56–57
Table Talk, 74, 207–8
HOCKING, WILLIAM ERNEST
The Self: Its Body and Freedom, 34–
35
HOLMES, OLIVER WENDELL
The Autocrat of the Breakfast-Table,
160–61, 199–200
HONE, JOSEPH
The Life of George Moore, 76
HOOVER, HERBERT
Fishing For Fun—And To Wash
Your Soul, 78
HUDSON, W. H.
Far Away and Long Ago, 139, 178,
204–5
Nature in Downland, 146–47
HUNT, LEIGH
The Indicator, 210–11
The Reflector, 71–72
HUXLEY, ALDOUS
The Perennial Philosophy, 134

IRVING, LAURENCE
Henry Irving, 193
IRVING, WASHINGTON
The Sketch Book, 82–83, 124, 171–
72

JACKS, LAWRENCE PEARSALL
Life and Letters of Stopford Brooke,
162, 187

JACKSON, HOLBROOK
Occasions, 57
JAMES, ALICE
Alice James: Her Brothers—Her Jour-
nal, 138
JAMES, WILLIAM
Talks to Teachers, 22–23
JEFFERIES, RICHARD
The Hills and the Vale, 137–38
The Life of the Fields, 148–49, 175–
76, 186–87
The Open Air, 29–30
JOAD, C. E. M.
A Year More or Less, 11
John Buchan by his Wife and
Friends, 70
JOHN XXIII, POPE
Journal of a Soul, 87, 127, 177
JOHNSON, ROBERT UNDER-
WOOD
Remembered Yesterdays, 10, 18–19
JOHNSTON, J., AND WALLACE,
J. W.
Visits to Walt Whitman in 1890–
1891, 119, 187–88

KIERAN, JOHN
Footnotes on Nature, 4–5, 18
KILVERT, FRANCIS
Kilvert's Diary, 123, 152, 173, 189
KRUTCH, JOSEPH WOOD
More Lives Than One, 3

LAMB, CHARLES
Elia—Essays, 104
The Last Essays of Elia, 115–16
Letters of Charles Lamb, 15, 97
LAVER, JAMES
Museum Piece, 130–31
LECKY, WILLIAM EDWARD
HARTPOLE
The Map of Life, 4, 37, 200–1
LESLIE, C. R.
Life and Letters of John Constable,
R.A., 168
LEWES, G. H.
The Life and Works of Goethe, 94–
95, 99–100

LEWIS, C. DAY
The Buried Day, 91
LINDBERGH, ANNE MORROW
Gift From the Sea, 6–7, 13–14, 106–
7, 194–95
LLOYD GEORGE, DAVID
War Memoirs of David Lloyd
George, 24
LOCKHART, JOHN GIBSON
Memoirs of Sir Walter Scott, 28
LOWELL, JAMES RUSSELL
Letters of James Eliot Norton, 141

McCARTHY, LILLAH
Myself and My Friends, 103, 157
MACHEN, ARTHUR
Dog and Duck, 72–73
MACKAIL, J. W.
The Life of William Morris, 20
MACKENZIE, SIR COMPTON
Echoes, 119, 197–98
MAY, J. LEWIS
Thorn and Flower, 185
MERTON, THOMAS
Conjectures of a Guilty Bystander,
88, 128, 143
MEYNELL, ALICE
Essays, 168–69, 211–12
MORGAN, CHARLES
Reflections in a Mirror, 30–31
MORGAN, EDWARD P. (ed.)
This I Believe, 66, 90–91
MUIR, JOHN
My First Summer in the Sierra, 161
Travels in Alaska, 152–53, 180–81
MÜLLER, F. MAX
Auld Lang Syne, 101
MUNNINGS, SIR ALFRED
The Finish, 50, 160
MUNTHE, GUSTAF, AND UEX-
KÜLL, GUDRUN
The Story of Axel Munthe, 155–56

NICOLL, SIR WILLIAM ROBERT-
SON
The Day Book of Claudius Clear,
32

NEILSON, WILLIAM ALLAN (ed.)
Charles W. Eliot: The Man and His
Beliefs, 10, 47
NEWMAN, JOHN HENRY CAR-
DINAL
The Idea of a University, 90
NIGHTINGALE, FLORENCE
Notes on Nursing, 149–50

O'DONNELL, JOSEPHINE
Among the Covent Garden Stars,
31–32
O'FAOLAIN, SEAN
A Summer in Italy, 19, 189–90
OGILVIE, SIR HENEAGE
No Miracles Among Friends, 27
OSLER, SIR WILLIAM
Aequanimitas, With other Addresses,
6, 87

PEACOCK, THOMAS LOVE
Memoirs of Percy Bysshe Shelley,
125
PEARSON, HESKETH
Thinking It Over, 123
PEMBERTON, T. EDGAR
The Life of Bret Harte, 43
PENFIELD, WILDER
The Second Career, with Other Es-
says and Addresses, 36–37
PEPYS, SAMUEL
The Diary of Samuel Pepys, 45–46,
60, 93, 187, 210
PERRY, BLISS
Pools and Ripples, 79
PHELPS, WILLIAM LYON
Autobiography with Letters, 195
POWYS, JOHN COWPER
Autobiography, 170
PRICE, LUCIEN
Dialogues of Alfred North White-
head, 49
PRIESTLEY, J. B.
Delight, 25–26, 58, 198, 206–7

REID, STUART J.
A Sketch of the Life and Times of
the Rev. Sydney Smith, 50, 98

RENARD, JULES
  The Journal of Jules Renard, 107
RENOIR, JEAN
  Renoir, My Father, 121
RIDDELL, LORD
  More Pages from My Diary, 199
ROBERTS, CECIL
  Gone Rambling, 68–69, 70–71
ROTHENSTEIN, WILLIAM
  *Since Fifty: Men and Memories,
  1922–1938,* 67, 201
ROWSE, A. L.
  West-Country Stories, 25
RUSKIN, JOHN
  Praeterita, 17, 42–43, 45, 170–71
RUTHERFORD, MARK
  More Pages From a Journal, 88, 102

SAINT-EXUPÉRY, ANTOINE DE
  Flight to Arras, 8, 31
SAINT-GAUDENS, HOMER (ed.)
  *The Reminiscences of Augustus
  Saint-Gaudens,* 12, 163
SANTAYANA, GEORGE
  My Host the World, 12–13, 208–9
SCOTT, PETER
  The Eye of the Wind, 4, 185–86
SCOTT, SIR WALTER
  Guy Mannering, 53–54
  The Journal of Sir Walter Scott, 111,
  164–65
SCUDDER, HORACE ELISHA
  James Russell Lowell, 53
SEELIG, CARL
  Albert Einstein, 11
SHARP, WILLIAM
  *The Life and Letters of Joseph Sev-
  ern,* 164
SHEEAN, VINCENT
  First and Last Love, 62–63
SITWELL, SIR OSBERT
  The Scarlet Tree, 117–18
SMITH, ALEXANDER
  Dreamthorp, 126
SMITH, LOGAN PEARSALL
  All Trivia, 49, 94, 128, 129

SPENCER, HERBERT
  *Essays: Scientific, Political & Specu-
  lative,* 21–22
STANLEY, DOROTHY (ed.)
  *The Autobiography of Sir Henry
  Morton Stanley,* 20
STARK, FREYA
  Perseus in the Wind, 120, 126–27,
  129–30, 166–67
STEVENSON, ROBERT LOUIS
  An Inland Voyage, 60–61
  Memories and Portraits, 98, 157–58
  *Travels with a Donkey in the Ce-
  vennes,* 165–66, 212–13
  *Virginibus Puerisque and Other Pa-
  pers,* 77
STRACHEY, JOHN ST. LOE
  The Adventure of Living, 193
SWINNERTON, FRANK
  Tokefield Papers, 24–25, 89, 92–93

TAYLOR, JEREMY
  *The Rule and Exercises of Holy
  Living,* 5
THOMAS, EDWARD
  The South Country, 75, 150
THOREAU, HENRY DAVID
  Excursions, 7, 76–77, 188
  Walden, or Life in the Woods, 44–
  45, 83–84, 102, 108–9, 137, 145–
  46, 151–52, 167, 176
TREVELYAN, G. OTTO
  *The Life and Letters of Lord
  Macaulay,* 55
TREVELYAN, SIR GEORGE
  MACAULAY
  Clio, a Muse and Other Essays, 75–
  76, 119–20
  Grey of Falloden, 153–54, 189
TROLLOPE, ANTHONY
  Orley Farm, 101, 196
TWAIN, MARK
  Mark Twain's Autobiography, 205–6

VAN DOREN, MARK
  *The Autobiography of Mark Van
  Doren,* 100

WALTON, IZAAK
  The Compleat Angler, 78
WATTS-DUNTON, THEODORE
  Old Familiar Faces, 18
WEBB, MARY
  The Spring of Joy, 117, 177
WHIPPLE, EDWIN PERCY
  Recollections of Eminent Men, 32–33, 96
WHITE, GILBERT
  The Natural History of Selborne, 177

WHITMAN, WALT
  Prose Works, 59, 103, 108, 142, 164, 177–78, 191
WILSON, DAVID ALEC
  Carlyle to "The French Revolution" (1826–1837), 23
WOOLF, VIRGINIA
  A Room of One's Own, 46–47
WORDSWORTH, DOROTHY
  Journals of Dorothy Wordsworth, 73, 165, 168, 175, 192